Exploring Shakespeare

The Dynamics of Playmaking

S Viswanathan

Orient Longman

ORIENT LONGMAN PRIVATE LIMITED

Registered Office
3-6-752 Himayatnagar, Hyderabad 500 029 (A.P.), India
Email: hyd2_orlongco@sancharnet.in

Other Offices
Bangalore, Bhopal, Chennai, Ernakulam,
Guwahati, Hyderabad, Jaipur, Kolkata,
Lucknow, Mumbai, New Delhi, Patna

ISBN 81 250 2663 0

Typeset in Aldine 401 of 10.5/12.5 by
OSDATA
Hyderabad 500 029

Printed in India at:
Sai Printopack Pvt. Ltd.
New Delhi

Published by
Orient Longman Private Limited
1/24 Asaf Ali Road
New Delhi 110 002
Email: olldel@del6.vsnl.net.in

To
the memory
of
my wife
Nirmala
'. . . . oh,/ the difference to me.'

Contents

Sources

The essays in this volume were first published as follows:
'"Illeism with a difference" in certain middle plays of Shakespeare', *Shakespeare Quarterly*, 20 (Autumn1969), 407–15.

'A Shakespearian device: The scene within the scene', *Anglia*, 90 (1972), 458–69.

'Sleep and death: The twins in Shakespeare', *Comparative Drama*, 13 (1979), 49–65.

'Shakespeare's metamorphoses of Actaeon', *Essays on Shakespeare in Honour of A.A. Ansari,* ed. T.R. Sharma (Meerut: Shalabh Book House, 1986), 46–57.

'Shakespeare's books at play', *CIEFL Bulletin,* 12 (Dec. 2002), 13–27.

'Stage movement as stage moment: Some Shakespeare instances', *The Aligarh Critical Miscellany,* 12 (1999), 10–21.

'What happened to Reynaldo: Vanishing characters in Shakespeare', *The Aligarh Critical Miscellany*, 13 (2000), 115–30.

'Shakespeare's "single-speech Hamiltons" and "shadows"', *Points of View,* 9 (2001), 1–14.

'The Shakespeare inset and its poetic of illusion', *The Aligarh Critical Miscellany*, 12 (1999), 101–18.

'The profession of playhouse and player in the Shakespeare inset', *Points of View*, 9 (2001), 101–19.

'The impugnable as inexpugnable: Censorship and English Renaissance drama', *Points of View*, 5 (1997), 37–49.

'*Hamlet*: The curious perspective of "visuality" ', *Critical Essays in Honour of V.S. Seturaman,* ed. S. Viswanathan, C.T. Indra and T. Sriraman (Madras: Macmillan, 1987), 115–30.

'*Hamlet*: A necessary "question" of the play', *Aligarh Critical Miscellany*, 13 (2000), 150–63.

'Some uses of *Topoi* in Shakespeare's *Coriolanus*: An approach to the play', *Renaissance Essays for Kitty Scoular Datta,* ed. Sukanta Chaudhuri (Calcutta: Oxford University Press, 1995), 132–41.

'*Antony and Cleopatra*: The functions of theatricalism', *Shakespeare: Varied Perspectives,* ed. Vikram Chopra (New Delhi: D.K. Publishers, 1996), 427–39.

'Theatricality and mimesis in *The Winter's Tale*: The instance of "taking one by the hand" ', *Shakespeare in India* (New Delhi: Oxford University Press, 1987), 42–52.

'*Mucedorus* and Shakespeare—and his company', *Points of View*, 2 (1995), 1–11.

'Some Sanskrit dramaturgical principles: Possible applications to English drama', *A Carnival for the Grammarian: Essays for N. Krishnaswamy*, ed. Amruthavalli et.al. (Madras: Macmillan, 1991).

'The application of *dhwani* to Shakespeare's *Macbeth*', *Points of View*, 10 (2003), 3–19.

'Dramatic illusion as dream: The "dream plays" of Shakespeare and Bhasa', *Points of View,* 3 (1996), 1–10.

'Effects of *trompe l'oeil*: Some Shakespeare, Bhasa and Kalidasa instances', *Points of View,* 4 (1997), 1–13.

Preface

The book presents a bunch of studies of different devices or certain generally less noticed processes of Shakespeare's playmaking. The essays seek to consider what the techniques and methods involved in these may contribute to our response to the plays and how. It is a selection from among my papers that have appeared in journals and collections over the years. Most of the twenty-one essays brought together in this volume have appeared in recent years as part of my ongoing work. I have, however, ventured to include also a few which appeared around the seventies of the last century. I have made a few minor revisions in some of the essays and titles of the essays. In the Acknowledgments, I furnish details of original publication in each case. I now record my gratitude to the editors and publishers of the journals and collections concerned. I thank the Oxford University Press, New Delhi, for copyright permission to reprint two of the essays, which figured in books of their publication.

I thank Orient Longman Ltd., for publishing the book, especially Mrs Usha Aroor and Dr Madhavi Menon, the in-house editor, for the care they have bestowed on it. My grateful thanks go to many scholars and critics in the field and a host of colleagues and students in India and abroad, such as Professors R.A. Foakes, M.M. Mahood, the late Kenneth Muir and V.S. Seturaman, S. Nagarajan, S. Ramaswami and S. Jagadisan, among others. They have, over the decades, been an unfailing source of support, encouragement and inspiration. I alone am responsible for whatever inadequacies and faults the studies may have. I owe my thanks in particular to M. Satyanarayana Murthy and L. Rajendra Goud of the University of

Hyderabad for their ready and unstinting cooperation all along in working these and other writings of mine into soft copy on systems. My deepest debt is recorded in the Dedication.

S. Viswanathan

Acknowledgements

The author and the publishers acknowledge with grateful thanks the permission accorded by Pentagram Design Ltd., UK and Oxford University Press, New Delhi for the use of the following:

Pentagram Design Ltd. UK for the picture of the Globe theatre in use (1996) reproduced on the cover of the book

and

Oxford University Press, New Delhi for the reproduction of the following articles from books published by them:

'Theatricality and Mimesis in *The Winter's Tale*' from *Shakespeare in India,* ed. S Nagarajan and S Viswanathan

'Some Uses of *Topoi* in Shakespeare's *Coriolanus*: An approach to the play' from *Renaissance Essays for Kitty Scoular Datta,* ed. Sukanta Chaudhuri

Introduction

The studies that follow are in the nature of explorations of certain particular processes, not generally much attended to but none the less significant, of Shakespearian playmaking and dramatico-theatrical communication. These processes, often participating as they do both in the formation and structural movement of the plays and in their actual theatrical dynamics, are no mere devices, no mere cogs in the machine. We may call them devices, as they are usually styled, so long as we keep in mind their role in the life of the drama. They supply part of the driving energy behind the dynamics of the plays. Perhaps we may also keep in a corner of our mind that the word 'device' was often used in the theatrical parlance of Shakespeare's day to refer to an imaginative invention by way of an entertainment, interlude or playlet for visual presentation. The devices considered in the studies are of several different kinds—rhetorical, topological, poetic, visual, theatrical and those of professional stage practice. Some of these may appear rather fine-grained. Yet they may be found to make a contribution to the play as a whole, to set up interesting interaction with many of its aspects and also to carry larger implications.

A study of Shakespeare's handling of these devices may serve to reaccentuate our sense of the total theatrical language which Shakespearian drama has, and help to attune us to it. The essays together, one hopes, will give us an idea of both Shakespeare's versatility and virtuosity, his easy and masterly command and sureness of touch with a range and variety of devices and conventions. More important is the concert or rather consort in which the playwright orchestrates the play of these devices in the structure and movement of drama. Also, such play processes as are considered in the book should ultimately make themselves felt in and through the difference their effect subtly makes to our response to the plays; they serve as clues, if sometimes somewhat hidden. Some of the internal processes discussed, by their very nature, function and work their effect in a sort of subterranean or 'back-room' manner, themselves often unnoticed. Hence spectators or for that matter, readers many not find these apparent straightaway.

It may be worth noting (at this point) a couple of general features of Shakespeare's use of these devices, which I hope emerge in the studies taken together. One is what may be called his exploratory–creative address to these resources. Critics have often emphasised that Shakespeare makes an exploratory–creative use of the medium of verbal language, of poetry in the sense of his imaginative creation taking place in and through the very process of exploration of words and language and their possibilities. Such an exploratory–creative use in which the very medium he engages with as he works along itself suggests new possibilities extends as much to Shakespeare's way with the verbal and the visual devices and conventions of the kind considered here. Whether these be rhetorical modes or topoi or commonplaces of expression (which in Shakespeare's day had, in a way, become habits of thought and ideation) or whether they are rhetorical devices or stage conventions or professional practices and exigencies, Shakespeare may be seen to engage in a mutually interactive, heuristic encounter with these. And that leads to creative exploitation of the possibilities of these devices to the optimum. Thus these devices may be said to be with Shakespeare not merely modes of expression but very much part of the modes of conception and perception behind the process of imaginative creation and embodiment in drama and theatre.

Secondly, Shakespeare's introduction and development of these dramatico-poetic means may be found to carry several sociocultural or cultural–political implications, even as these are part of the artistic design of drama. However, we may have to be on our guard not to press the cultural–political suggestions too hard, at the expense of their dramatico-theatrical orientation, purpose, function and effect. Looking at it in another perspective, cultural–political commentators often insist that we talk of the plays in terms of the historical–material contexts in which they were written, produced and flourished. But the irony is that they hardly advert to or take sufficiently into account the immediate context of the material circumstance of the stage and theatrical practices, the actual tradition where the resources and conventions of staged drama actively operated. We need to pursue the cultural–political significances of the plays in general and of the operativeness of devices and conventions in particular with adequate recognition and alert awareness of the role of these as both artistic loci and sociocultural signifiers, perhaps the one in terms of the other or at least in relation to the other.

The twenty-one essays in this collection are presented in three sections. Section 1 consists of essays each of which deals with a particular convention as it operates in a cross-section of plays in the canon. Section 2 considers yet other conventions or manners of procedure; each essay takes up the operativeness of a particular process or phenomenon in a particular play. Section 3 brings together studies in which I explore some ways of bringing to bear a crossover or comparative perspective that of the Sanskrit and Indian dramatic tradition on some of Shakespeare's play practices.

SECTION 1

Across the Canon

1

'Illeism with a Difference' in Certain Middle Plays

Ever since E. E. Kellett,[1] George Rylands,[2] and, most extensively and deliberatively of all, G. Wilson Knight[3] and Caroline F. E. Spurgeon,[4] if not that strange, late eighteenth-century anticipator of all these and others, Walter Whiter,[5] that single swallow which did not make a summer, drew attention to significant iterativeness in Shakespeare's use of imagery, a good deal of commentary on patterns of iterativeness in images and image-clusters has been available. Shakespeare's repeated use of certain dramatic and stage devices and conventions,[6] as also his repeated use of certain rhetorical and stylistic devices,[7] not to mention recurrences of rhetorical 'commonplaces', themes and moods, character-types, and types of dramatic situations, has also

1. E. E. Kellett, 'Some notes on a feature of Shakespeare's style', *Suggestions* (1923).
2. G. H. W. Rylands, *Words and Poetry* (1928).
3. G. Wilson Knight, *The Wheel of Fire* (1930); *The Imperial Theme* (1931); and *The Shakespearean Tempest* (1932).
4. Caroline F. E. Spurgeon, *Leading Motives in the Imagery of Shakespeare's Tragedies* (1930); *Shakespeare's Iterative Imagery* (1931); *Shakespeare's Imagery and What it Tells Us* (1935).
5. Walter Whiter, *Specimen of a Commentary* (1794).
6. P. V. Kreider, *Repetition in Shakespeare's Plays* (1941).
7. Sister Miriam Joseph, *Shakespeare's Use of the Arts of Language* (1947); F. C. Kolbe, *Shakespeare's Way* (1930); William Empson, *The Structure of Complex Words* (1951).

been amply dealt with. Perhaps in this late age of criticism, a close and patient look at the playwright's frequent employment of certain minor, less obvious and so hitherto generally unnoticed devices which are at once stylistic, and dramatic and theatrical too, will provide us with some sidelights on Shakespearian drama. One such instance, a strikingly persistent recurrence of an at once stylistic and dramatic habit on the part of the dramatist in some of the middle plays, alone is to be noticed now. The phenomenon is all the more curious because of its frequency only in certain plays which are linked by chronological concurrence or proximity. More intriguing is its absence from other plays, usually assigned to the same period.

For want of a more suitable term, the device has to be designated as 'illeism with a difference'. It is one by which the dramatist makes a character, speaking in the first person, refer to himself in the third person, not simply as 'he', which would be illeism proper, a traditional grammatical mode, but by name. A fairly extensive and reiterated use of this device occurs in *Julius Caesar* and *Troilus and Cressida*, and an occasional but none the less significant use in *Hamlet* and *Othello*. To quote some examples,

Caesar — *Caesar* shall forth; the things that threatened me
Ne'er looked but on my back. When they shall see
The face of *Caesar*, they are vanished.
(*Julius Caesar*, II.ii.10–12)

Hector — . . . *Hector's* opinion
Is this, in way of truth. Yet ne'er the less,
My spritely brethren, I propend to you
In resolution to keep Helen still.
(*Troilus and Cressida*, II.ii.188–91)

Hamlet — And what so poor a man as *Hamlet* is
May do t'express his love and friending to you,
God willing, shall not lack.
(*Hamlet*, I.v.185–7)

Othello — Farewell! *Othello's* occupation's gone
(*Othello*, III.iii.361)

Apart from several minor characters in these plays using it, Caesar, Brutus, Cassius, Troilus, Hector, Cressida, Hamlet, and Othello employ it: they switch to the third person and refer to themselves by name while speaking in the first person. Should the count and the proportion interest anybody, there are thirty such uses in *Julius Caesar*,[8] fifteen uses in *Troilus and Cressida*,[9] eight in *Hamlet*,[10] and four in *Othello*[11] (30:15:8:4). Instances of it in the other plays are sparse and there dictated mostly by immediate theatrical necessity.

In itself the device is essentially a simple, traditional one, handed down to Shakespeare from the medieval theatre, by which a character has perforce to announce himself and reveal his identity tritely enough as an elementary trick of the stage. It is part of the primitive stage convention of self-revelation, of 'direct self-explanation', which is born of an inevitable theatrical exigency, going back farther still than the Herod of the medieval Miracle cycle but extending even into the latest drama.The survival of this larger convention in the Elizabethan soliloquy has been underlined by E. E. Stoll[12] and L. L. Schucking.[13] But, just as Shakespeare has naturally made a very delicate and subtle use of this legacy of the older theatrical tradition,[14] so also the use of the 'illeism with a difference' in discussion

---

8. Instances in *Julius Caesar* are found in I.iii.90 (2); II.i.58, 286; II.ii.10, 12, 29, 30, 42, 44, 45, 48, 65, 68, 129; III.i.40, 47; III.ii.21, 23; IV.iii.93, 94, 106, 112; V.i.72, 111; V.iii.90; V.iv.7(2), 8(2). References are throughout to Peter Alexander's edition of *The Complete Works*. The numbers in parentheses indicate the number of uses in the same line.

9. Examples in *Troilus and Cressida* are to be seen in I.i.5; I.iii.32, 239, 254, 291; II.ii.14, 188; II.iii.1; III.ii.170, 178, 192, 198; IV.i.16; IV.ii.17, 99.

10. The *Hamlet* instances are in I. v. 185; V. ii. 225, 226, 228 (2), 230, 231.

11. The *Othello* examples are in III.iii.361; V.ii.269, 270, 287.

12. E. E. Stoll, *Shakespeare Studies* (1927). In origin, the device of 'illeism' is a joint legacy to Elizabethan drama of the native English medieval stage tradition and of the Senecan translations, and one already used before Shakespeare by Kyd, Peele, and Marlowe. Also, this 'illeism' was a mannerism of the historical Julius Caesar as in evidence in his *Commentaries*; Shakespeare knew the work and has a character (Lord Say) cite and quote from it (*King Henry VI*, Pt. 2 [IV.viii.55–60]).

13. L. L. Schucking, *Character Problems in Shakespeare's Plays* (1922).

14. Wolfgang Clemen, *Shakespeare's Soliloquies and Other Studies* (1964).

by Shakespeare is not determined by mere theatrical exigency, but turns out to be a master-stroke of dramatic artistry in the plays mentioned, though elsewhere it is no more than a basic, essential stage device. No wonder greater and subtler purposes than that of a rudimentary professional skill are served by certain Shakespearian uses of it.

Neither Abbott's *Shakespearian Grammar* nor the *Shakespeare Grammatik* by Franz records Shakespeare's use of this device, for the simple reason that it is not classifiable under any conventional grammatical category. Cognisance seems to have been taken at all of this particular stylistic and dramatic habit of the dramatist and its recurrence only once, by R. A. Foakes in his article, 'An Approach to *Julius Caesar*',[15] where he makes acknowledgement to Allardyce Nicoll for bringing the existence of this phenomenon to his notice.

An examination of some of the contexts of the use of this device, in fact, of this 'address to the world'[16] (literally as well as metaphorically) of a character, reveals sure, if rather subtle, hints about the way a particular character and situation are to be taken. Above all, it throws light on Shakespeare's keen and never-failing awareness of the actor's actual performance and execution of the role and the speech assigned to him, the actor's point of view on it, in short. We can see that the device, trivial and insignificant as it may seem at first sight, becomes in the hands of Shakespeare a suggestive, if oblique, means of conveying rich dramatic meaning, a great deal more than a mere rhetorical and theatrical variation and prop, though, in part, that too. First of all, it comes in handy to the dramatist for purposes of spotlighting, as it were, in a flash, the relationship between the character using it, especially the central character or the tragic hero, and his inner self.

Brutus That every like is not the same, O Caesar,
The heart of *Brutus* earns to think upon.
(*Julius Caesar*, II.ii.128–9)

Hamlet Was't *Hamlet* wrong'd Laertes? Never *Hamlet*
If *Hamlet* from himself be ta'ken away,

15. R. A. Foakes, 'An approach to *Julius Caesar*', *SQ*, V (1954), pp. 259–70.
16. Arthur Sewell, *Character and Society in Shakespeare* (1951).

And when he's not himself does wrong Laertes,
Then *Hamlet* does it not, *Hamlet* denies it.
(*Hamlet*, V.ii.125–8)

The device turns out to be an effective way of underlining and bringing to focus this relationship, a way of making the character momentarily detach himself from himself, achieve a measure of dramatic (and philosophical) depersonalisation, and create a kind of aesthetic distance from which he can contemplate himself. Paradoxically enough, it is a seeming objectification which brings deeper, hidden subjective realities to the fore, a dramatic monologue in miniature. Secondly, it suggests the importance, in the contexts in which it occurs, of the difference as well as the tension between the public and the private selves of the characters. The difference and the tension are dramatically exploited, and would have come home to Elizabethan audiences, accustomed to the old dichotomy between public and private virtues and vices, with greater force than to us today.

Caesar Shall *Caesar* send a lie?
Have I in conquest stretch'd mine arm so far,
To be afeard to tell greybeards the truth?
Decius, go tell them *Caesar* will not come.
(*Julius Caesar*, II.ii.65–8)

Brutus And I am *Brutus*, Marcus *Brutus*, I!
Brutus, my country's friend! Know me for *Brutus*.
(*Julius Caesar*, V.iv.7–8)

Thirdly, it raises the question of the way in which the character is seen to behave and to order his very modes of feeling and thought in accordance with a rightly or wrongly conceived image or idea of himself. At times, the whole conception of one's self which governs the character may result in the harbouring of illusions and obsessions about himself, as in the case of Brutus and Troilus.

Troilus True swains in love shall in the world to come
Approve their truth by *Troilus*, when their rhymes
Full of protest, of oath, and big compare
Want similes, truth tir'd with iteration.
(*Troilus and Cressida*, III.ii.170–2)

Brutus O Rome, I make thee promise,
If the redress will follow, thou receivest
Thy full petition at the hand of *Brutus*
(*Julius Caesar*, II.i.56–8)

It is an indication of the hiatus between the reality that the character is and the legendary image of himself conceived by him and by others, and of his desperate attempts to make approximations and to close the gap. These questions, to avoid the expression 'themes' for the nonce, are 'necessary questions of the plays' involved. The humble device has its own function in the dramatic communication of these questions. Fourthly, to indulge in a short-winded, hedge-hopping metaphysical flight, this seemingly pointless device, in the context of the total meanings of the plays in question, is a pointer towards the general philosophical problem of the search for identity of the human self. This, of course, will not readily be granted to be 'a necessary question of the plays'. But, to take a firm foothold on the stage, on the Elizabethan stage, the implications of the use of this device from the point of view of the actor's craft, especially our knowledge of the Elizabethan style of acting and the attitude of the Elizabethan actor to the role played by him, are interesting. Aside from, and more than, being a stock theatrical convention of identity-revelation by the character, it is made to lend, by the weight of the context, the scene and the situation an additional dramatic dimension and depth. What is involved on such occasions is a complex intertexture of identity-in-difference and difference-in-identity between three selves, the actor with his bodily presence and his own personality, the character in his inner self, and the character in his outer self or the public image into which he has to project himself. We are fairly certain today that the Elizabethan actor was not expected to forget his own identity completely and to identify himself with, or lose himself in, the role, which he represented rather than impersonated. Though B. L. Joseph's[17] and A. Harbage's[18] views on Elizabethan acting emphasising its extremely conventionalised mode have been

17. Bertram L. Joseph. *Elizabethan Acting* (1951); *The Tragic Actor* (1958); *Acting Shakespeare* (1960).
18. Alfred Harbage, 'Elizabethan acting', *PMLA*, LIV (1939).

revised by themselves in their later writings, and have been challenged by some[19] who champion the view that the acting of those days tended more in the direction of the naturalistic, the general consensus is that the acting was mainly formalised with a judicious, occasional admixture of naturalism. An actor in such a situation would certainly do well to remind himself that he is Caesar, and yet not Caesar, but yet Caesar still; he is Hector, and yet not Hector, but yet Hector still; and so on. The device is a means of ensuring and exhibiting such multiple layers of awareness on the actor's part.

A look at some of the actual uses of the device will bear out these general considerations. In *Julius Caesar* occur the largest number of uses. R. A. Foakes, in the article mentioned above, has commented on Caesar's and Brutus's habit of repeatedly alluding to themselves as Caesar and Brutus, and has shown how 'this rhetorical device' serves to make their utterances sound impersonal, distanced, and dignified, and also to underline their consciousness of their worth and grandeur. More than this, the device, which is at once rhetorical and dramatic, points to their constant tendency to think and to act in terms of their *ideas* of themselves, which are actually based on public and historical and legendary images (partly anachronistic, maybe, but dramatically impressive), whatever the gap between the idea and the actual reality about themselves.

The widest, most significant variety of the uses of the device is to be found in *Troilus and Cressida*. At the beginning of the play, Troilus and Nestor use it as a simple device of introducing themselves.

Troilus Each Troyan that is master of his heart,
Let him to field; *Troilus*, alas, hath none!

(I.iii.5–6)

Nestor With due observance of thy godlike seat,
Great Agamemnon, *Nestor* shall apply
Thy latest words.

(I.iii.31–3)

19. Marvin Rosenberg, 'Elizabethan actors: men or marionettes?', *PMLA*, LXIX (1954); R. A. Foakes, 'The player's passion: Some notes on Elizabethan psychology and acting', *Essays and Studies*, New Series, VII (1954); W. A. Armstrong, 'Actors and theatres', in *Shakespeare in his Own Age, Shakespeare Survey* 17 (1964) , pp. 191–205.

But when Hector uses it twice in II.ii, it is not for revelation of identity, for his identity has already been revealed.

Hector Though no man lesser fears the Greeks than I,
As far as toucheth my particular,
Yet, dread Priam,
There is no lady of more softer bowels,
More spongy to suck in the sense of fear,
More ready to cry out 'who knows what follows?'
Than *Hector* is.

(II.ii.8–14)

Hector *Hector's* opinion
Is this, in way of truth. Yet, ne'er the less,
My spritely brethren, I propend to you
In resolution to keep Helen still.

(II.ii.188–91)

It is meant to put us in mind of the difference between Hector as in himself he really is and would like to be, and the public image he has to live and act up to. This inner confrontation is exemplified in the shifting of his standpoint over the return of Helen. The public image of Hector fairly fills the play, and we are made aware by this device how Hector himself conceives it and has to bear it in mind all the time. When, immediately after, Thersites is made to use the device though primarily as self-announcement:

Thersites How now, *Thersites*! What lost in the labyrinth of thy fury?

(II.iii.1–2)

there results an illuminating dramatic juxtaposition, the underlying contrast and parallelism being between Hector and Thersites, in addition to the one between Achilles and Thersites, quite in keeping with the ironical conception and technique of the play. We find Troilus, Cressida, and Pandarus, all three, using this mode of address in III.ii, and Diomedes too (IV.i.16).

Troilus True swains in love shall in the world to come
Approve their truth by *Troilus*, when their rhymes
Full of protest, of oath, and big compare,
Want similes, truth tir'd with iteration—
....

'As true as Troilus' shall crown up the verse
(III.ii.170–4, 178)

Cressida Yea, let them say, to stick of the heart of falsehood,
'As false as *Cressid*'.
(III.ii.191–2)

Pandarus . . . call them all *Pandars*; let all constant men be
Troiluses, all false women Cressids, and all brokers
between Pandars.
(III.ii.197–200)

Diomedes The one and other *Diomed* embraces.
(IV.i.16)

The enhancement of the dimensions of the dramatic situation is considerable, and we marvel at 'the multiconsciousness' (S. L. Bethell's useful phrase) on the part of the audience *and the actors* alike. Here is a living encounter between the legendary selves of these storied figures of Troy and Greece, their actual selves as the dramatist conceives them, and the actors with their own personalities playing their roles. An aspect of this quality of the play has been noted and commented upon by L. C. Knights.[20]

Perhaps it may not be illegitimate to surmise that the idea of a complex use of this device was hit upon by Shakespeare when in *Julius Caesar* and *Troilus and Cressida* he came to deal with the history of Caesar and his assassination and the legends of Troy and Greece, both long celebrated and familiar in popular as well as learned traditions.[21] No wonder that, dealing with such well-known celebrities of history and of legend (the distinction between the two was hardly present to the average Elizabethan mind),[22] the dramatist wanted to highlight the contrast as well as the relations between the grand historical and legendary images of these and the real,

---

20. L. C. Knights, *Some Shakespearean Themes*, pp. 78–9.
21. T. J. B. Spencer, 'Shakespeare and the Elizabethan Romans', *Shakespeare Survey* 10 (1957); Ernest Schanzer, *The Problem Plays of Shakespeare* (1963); R. K. Presson, *Shakespeare's 'Troilus and Cressida' and the Legends of Troy* (1953).
22. Hardin Craig, *The Enchanted Glass* (1936).

'unaccommodated men', the bare truth behind the images, a Montaigne-like perception available to the mind of the turn of the century, whether Shakespeare himself had by then, or even at all, read Montaigne or no.[23] 'His story requires Romans or Kings, but he thinks only on men.' For this purpose, the device we consider came in handy, and he seems to have exploited it on a fairly large scale in these two plays. Subsequently, in writing *Hamlet* and *Othello*, he seems to have remembered enough of it to use it occasionally.

At this point a caveat had better be entered. Our awareness of Shakespeare's preoccupation with the contrast between the real man and the public image, of his depiction of the attempts of these figures to live up to the public image, need not, and as a matter of fact, should not, when we bear in mind 'the ceremony of innocence' of the Elizabethans, lead us to associate with Shakespeare anything like a modern tendency to 'debunk' these gods of history and legend or to push them from their pedestals or to show these demigods to have but feet of clay. No doubt, the inner-outer, public-private polarity and tension within the personality of the character as well as the character's attempt either to work up or work himself up to a public image of himself are of the essence of these plays. It is the truth of these plays to the experience of these tensions within the characters, of which the device in question is a means and an expression, that has led quite a few modern commentators to attribute to Shakespeare almost an anticipation of the modern Stracheyan attitude to his heroes. As a result of this assumption, what bids fair to become a campaign for the 'debunking' of the Shakespearian tragic hero, especially Hamlet and Othello, has been afoot for some time now. The mischief started when Eliot advanced the notion of the Shakespearian tragic hero trying 'to cheer himself up'[24] on the point of his death. An adequate remembrance of the fact that to a public figure in the situation of the old-world, Elizabethan culture and society, the public image of

---

23. Theodore Spencer, *Shakespeare and the Nature of Man* (1942); G. C. Taylor, *Shakespeare's Debt to Montaigne* (1925).
24. T. S. Eliot, 'Shakespeare and the stoicism of Seneca', in *Selected Essays* (1958), pp. 129–32.

himself mattered greatly even to the poor, erring, weak Adam in him, and that he was expected to see and order himself in the light of this public image, would put a new, revealing angle on the whole issue. Despite whatever falterings are exhibited by the tragic hero, his is a brave and honest attempt, and on the whole meant to be taken as successful, to live up to the grand public image of himself. To us, readers and spectators, from the Elizabethan and Shakespearian point of view, the public image is the permanent face, the public face which is to be kept in view, in spite of the glimpses of the private faces in public or private places vouchsafed by the dramatist who takes us into his confidence and reveals the inner truth of the struggle within the hero. The confidence, let us remember, is not meant to be betrayed. It is a pity that it tends to be betrayed and that the Shakespearian tragic hero has fallen now on evil days, though on *good* tongues which talk ill of him (the more is the pity). He has to be saved from dwindling into the anti-hero before it is too late.

It is interesting to note a variation between the use of the device under consideration in *Julius Caesar* and *Troilus and Cressida*, and its use in *Hamlet* and *Othello*. Hamlet and Othello resort to it in situations in which what impresses us is a curious, ambivalent co-presence of self-pity and a high sense of his worth as a public figure on the part of the speaker. The device becomes a subtle indication of this intriguing mixture. At the first blush, one may be inclined to take it as a sign of mere self-pity.

> Was 't *Hamlet* wrong'd Laertes? Never *Hamlet*.
> If *Hamlet* from himself be ta'ken away,
> And when he's not himself does wrong Laertes,
> Then *Hamlet* does it not, *Hamlet* denies it.
> Who does it, then? His madness. If't be so,
> *Hamlet* is of the faction that is wrong'd;
> His madness is poor *Hamlet's* enemy.
> (*Hamlet*, V.ii.225–31)

> 'Tis a lost fear;
> Man but a rush against *Othello's* breast,
> And he retires. Where should *Othello* go?
> (*Othello*, V.ii.268–70)

That's he that was Othello—here I am.
(*Othello*, V.ii.287)

But due attention to the force of the repeated use of this habit within a few lines will make us see that it embraces more than self-pity and suggests a paradoxical, simultaneous coexistence of feelings of self-contempt and a proper sense of one's public worth, not necessarily vanity, producing a dramatically profitable tension between the two attitudes to oneself. But the overall worth and dignity of Hamlet or Othello is never in question; it is, in fact, to the credit of the character that he can face, experience, and overcome the tension of the dilemma, and he is *shown* by the dramatist as doing exactly that. In short, there is more to it than mere egotism, than self-pity, self-flattery, and self-dramatisation.

A final question springs to mind. Why this concentration of the recurrence of this 'illeism with a difference' in a few plays, more or less belonging to 1599–1602? Why is the device used elsewhere (but for the exceptional case of *Timon of Athens*), generally only by strict dramatic necessity of disguise or announcement of identity, or very rarely for some dramatic or contemplative effect, as in *King Lear*[25] (V.iii.239), or in *Antony and Cleopatra*[26] (V.ii.219)? Could it be that Shakespeare thought of a subtle use of this device after coming across it in, and picking it up from, the plays of a contemporary playwright like Ben Jonson, Chapman, or Marston, from whom he seems to have learned and adopted a few dramatic modes in 1599 or thereabout?[27] Or from Montaigne? Could it be that Shakespeare had in mind a particular actor or a group of actors, and that he came to use the device for their benefit? Or could it be that the use of the device has something to do with Shakespeare's being probably struck by the Greek idea of every man having his guardian angel and his evil angel, which he must have encountered in Plutarch, and adopting it in his *Julius Caesar* and applying it in his

25. '*Edmund*: Yet *Edmund* was belov'd.'

26. '*Cleopatra*: . . . and I shall see Some squeaking Cleopatra boy my greatness.'

27. O. J. Campbell, *Comicall Satyre and Shakespeare's 'Troilus and Cressida'* (1938); *Shakespeare's Satire* (1943).

later tragedies?[28] Could it be, that is, that the impersonality of this mode of address of the character to himself is due to the character looking at himself from the point of view of his guardian or evil angel, as the case may be? Whatever the answer, the device as handled by Shakespeare is stylistic and dramatic alike. It will be too venturesome to hazard a conjecture that a very minor, though idiosyncratic, device may guide us in the matter of speculation about dates of composition of plays, especially after Moody E. Prior's warning about the use of the evidence of imagery in discussing problems of authorship.[29] The use of this device, which is dictated by dramatic situation, cannot be a valid criterion on which to base conclusions about dates of plays. Yet it is tempting to wonder whether the absence of this sort of 'illeism with a difference' in plays like *All's Well That Ends Well* and *Twelfth Night* could be one of the minor considerations in support of arguments advanced by some for later dates, or radical revisions at later dates, for these plays.[30]

---

28. J.A.K. Thomson, *Shakespeare and the Classics* (1952), pp. 195–203.
29. Moody E. Prior, 'Imagery as a test of authorship', *SQ*, VI (1955).
30. Cf. G. K. Hunter's account of John Livingstone Lowes's proposal of a later date for *All's Well*, in his New Arden edition of the play, p. xxii; Dover Wilson and Quiller-Couch in their New Shakespeare ed. of *All's Well* (1929), pp. vii–xi; G. Wilson Knight in *The Sovereign Flower* (1958); Dover Wilson in the New Shakespeare ed. of *Twelfth Night* (1959), pp. 91–101.

2

A Shakespearian Device: The Scene within the Scene

Shakespeare's use of some minor dramatic devices hitherto unattended to by commentators would seem to repay close attention. Most of these devices such as the soliloquy, the aside, the dramatic induction and the play within the play are part of the stock-in-trade of the Elizabethan dramatist; how subtly individual and uniquely dramatic Shakespeare's handling of a number of these and some other less obvious conventions is has been well enough brought out, especially by German scholars.[1] In this essay Shakespeare's use of one such dramatic formula, which seems to constitute a distinctive aspect of his stagecraft, will be examined in brief.

For convenience, the device may be referred to as that of 'the scene within the scene.' The principle behind the device is a skilful combination through individual modification of the methods of the play within the play, of the dramatic induction, and of the aside. There are scenes in the early as well as the later plays which exemplify this device, scenes which belong to a genus of the species of

---

1. See, for instance, Wolfgang Clemen, *Shakespeare's Soliloquies* (Cambridge, 1964); Francis Berry, *The Shakespeare Inset* (London, 1965); Robert J. Nelson, *The Play Within a Play* (New Haven, 1958); Dieter Mehl, *The Elizabethan Dumb Show* (London, 1965) and Arthur Brown, 'The Play Within the Play: An Elizabethan Dramatic Device', *Essays and Studies by the Members of the English Association* (1960). W. Habicht and H.W. Gabler, 'Shakespeare studies in German: 1959–68', *Shakespeare Survey*, 23 (Cambridge, 1970), pp. 115–17 list such recent German studies.

the 'framed scene'. Such a scene turns out to be a play within the play 'as with a difference' or in miniature. That is, in it there are one or, usually, more characters in the role of player-spectators who comment on the words and deeds of the other character or characters. By this device, the characters who enact a scene are, in effect, divided into two groups; one set, given the role of spectators and commentators, look on and pass remarks by way of asides or conversation among themselves while the other set constitute the centre of observation and engage in dramatic action and speech without being conscious of the presence of observers. Instances are to be found in *King Henry VI* Pt. III (II. v), *Love's Labour's Lost* (IV, iii), *As You Like It* (III, iii), *Troilus and Cressida* (V, ii), *All's Well that Ends Well* (IV, i), *Twelfth Night* (II, v), *Othello* (IV, i) and *Macbeth* (V, i). Such scenes may be distinguished from what are sometimes called 'discovery scenes' like the one in which Prospero and Alonso discover Miranda and Ferdinand playing at chess[2] and from scenes which are overlooked by a group of characters, like the 'nunnery' scene in Hamlet,[3] on the one hand, and from the play within the play or dumb shows or masques, on the other. The scenes in question exemplify one particularly interesting and well-developed mode of 'grouping' which in general has been commented on by J. L. Styan in his *Shakespeare's Stagecraft* (Cambridge, 1967), Ch. 4.

Basically the technique is a means by which Shakespeare on the strength of the conventional nature of Elizabethan drama effectively exploits the complexities of dramatic illusion. The 'multiconsciousness' of the Elizabethan audience and the part played by it in the interesting ambivalences of the process of dramatic illusion have been pointed out by S.L. Bethell.[4] More recently, Anne Righter[5] has called attention to other aspects of dramatic illusion and its multiple dimensions as conceived by Shakespeare and the Elizabethans. It is the 'multiconsciousness' on

2. *The Tempest* (V. i). But *The Tempest* (III. i) is an instance of the 'scene within the scene'.
3. *Hamlet* (III, i).
4. S.L. Bethell, *Shakespeare and the Popular Dramatic Tradition* (London, 1944).
5. Anne Righter, *Shakespeare and the Idea of the Play* (London, 1962).

the part not only of Elizabethan audiences but of actors as well and the bewilderingly various dimensions of dramatic illusion and irony which are involved in Shakespeare's use of this device. One may not readily go all the way along with Anne Righter or Philip Edwards when they see metaphysical implications such as 'All the world's a stage' or 'Men are puppets enjoying only an illusory freedom of action' in the technique as it is used in Kyd.[6] But it will be clear that, besides lending an additional depth and extra dimensions to dramatic illusion and investing it with a Chinese-box-like intricacy, the device comes in handy for focusing attention and for bringing about a built-in, choric mediation between play and audience. Most interesting of all, the scene which is enacted within the scene is, in terms of the 'reality' of the play world, no illusion but reality, and this is the striking difference between 'the scene within the scene and the more familiar play within the play. The comments of the player-spectators in 'the scene within the scene' serve as a running commentary on the main action of the scene. Their presence, no doubt, does more than provide a mere frame for the action as the dramatic induction does. Yet, even though it is a means of putting across dramatic meanings through the reaction of certain characters to certain events even as these take place, it does not have an impact on the action which goes on within the frame.

As a method of stage-business, the device, though it belongs with the mode of non-naturalistic conventions, exhibits touches of

---

6. Anne Righter op.cit. pp.77–81. Philip Edwards, *Thomas Kyd and Early Elizabethan Tragedy* (London, 1966), pp. 31–3. Kyd's use of the scene within the scene, as of many another theatrical formula is, no doubt, an illustrative, pioneer one. See *The Spanish Tragedy* (II, ii) in which Balthazar and Lorenzo watch the love-making of Horatio and Bel-Imperia. In Greene's *Friar Bracon and Friar Bungay*, in several scenes in which Bacon's 'glass prospective', his magic television apparatus, is brought into operation, the scene-within-the-scene technique is drawn upon. But it is the use of the magic glass which dictates this technique to Greene. It may be recalled in this connection that there are several Tudor plays which are enclosed within a frame of observation-cum-induction such as, for example, Henry Medwall's *Fulgens and Lucrece* (in which two characters A and B not only introduce the play rushing on to the stage from among the audience but serve as choric commentators on the action throughout), *Love and Fortune*, *The Spanish Tragedy* and *Soliman and Perseda*.

naturalism characteristic of the 'impure art' (as Eliot designated it, pointing to the intermixture of realism and convention) of the Elizabethan theatre. An attempt to relate the use of the device to the actual physical conditions of the Elizabethan stage is fraught with difficulties. What with the rival theories and controversies about 'the discovery-space' and 'the gallery' and about the location of acting levels and parts on the stage, which are attendant upon modern reconstructions of the Elizabethan stage, it is risky to speculate about the actual location of the actors on the stage in 'scenes within scenes'. Questions arise such as whether the posts or pillars on the stage served as props in such scenes for concealment as suggested by J.C. Adams,[7] whether the side-wing of the tiring-house facade served this purpose as proposed by J.W. Saunders,[8] whether there was a property tree on the stage which could be climbed up or the upper gallery was used for this purpose, or whether mansions or houses were in use, as in the medieval theatre at times or in the theatre of the Italian *commedia erudita*, as suggested by Leslie Hotson.[9] One need hardly venture beyond the safe conjecture that in such scenes, while characters who were the player-spectators stood in one acting area or level of the stage, the other group of characters stood in another. The central truth to be borne in mind is that manipulation of space and time on the Elizabethan stage was as free as on the medieval stage. The presence of the observing characters is, in terms of the conventions, assumed to be unnoticed by the other group of characters, even though on the stage they may be just standing by. Even so, the observing characters are supposed to go into hiding and to observe and to comment on what happens from the vantage of hiding either behind or in a tree or behind a hedge or on a hill. The comments are made mostly in the form of asides, whether marked in stage directions as such or not. These asides are not supposed to be heard by the other set of characters, and are addressed more or less directly to the audience.

The earliest which is naturally also the simplest and most direct use of this device by Shakespeare is to be found in *Henry VI Pt. III*

---

7. J.C. Adams, *The Globe Playhouse* (Cambridge, USA, 1942), pp. 165–6.
8. J.W. Saunders, 'Vaulting the rails', *Shakespeare Survey*, 7 (Cambridge, 1954), p. 75.
9. Leslie Hotson, *Shakespeare's Wooden O* (London, 1960).

(II, v). The meek, saintly King Henry VI in near-exile from the Towton battlefield feels so averse from the horrors of war and the uncertainty of its issue that he sits on a mole-hill, and, with pastoral nostalgia, longs for either his death or the ease and leisure, innocence and simplicity of a shepherd's life in contrast to the luxury and cares of kingship. Exactly then, in quick succession, two pictures present themselves, a son discovering that he has killed his father in battle and a father discovering that he has killed his son in battle. The king makes his comments on each of the lamentations of both. Through this device of an inset spectacle and a running commentary on it, the theme of the utter disorder, the total disruption of 'degree' brought about as a result of the 'jars', the Civil Wars, is impressed upon the reader and spectator. Not only is the man in the king, the essential man who gets the better of the king, brought to the fore, but the stark human realities behind kingship and war and the way in which war could involve the uninvolved and the innocent are illustrated.

> *King Henry* O piteous spectacle! O bloody times!
> Whilst lions war, and battle for their dens,
> Poor harmless lambs abide their enmity.—
> Weep, wretched man, I'll aid thee tear for tear;
> And let our hearts and eyes, like civil war,
> Be blind with tears, and break o'ercharg'd with grief.

Most of all, the sense of doomedness and the death-wish which are key aspects of the character of the king are underscored effectively at the same time.

> *King Henry* Sad-hearted men, much overgone with care,
> Here sits a king more woeful than you are.

The scene is telling in its effect, none the less so because the spectacles and the king's comments are patterned with as mechanical a symmetry as the neat rhetorical balance of the contemplative king's meditative soliloquy at the opening of the scene. Stylised, emblematic and tableau-like as the scene may be, it is anything but static; and it is, in fact, the formality of the device in discussion that enables the young dramatist to achieve a striking ease and skill of manipulation in what may well be his earliest-but-one play.

Just as the very first use of the device of 'the scene within the scene' is seen to bring out a key emphasis in *Henry VI Pt. III* at a central moment in the play, so also the second occurrence of this device is found situated at a turning point in *Love's Labour's Lost*, the breaking in of reality into the artificial world of Navarre and his companions. The formality of the device is seen to be much the same as in the first instance. Yet its dramatic uses are more various.

With the advent of the Princess of France and her companions, the 'academicians' Navarre and his lords Berowne, Longaville and Dumain, each individually, and unknown to the others, forget their resolve and get ensnared in love, in spite of themselves. In IV, iii, the device of 'the scene within the scene' is employed to portray the discovery by all the four that they are not each alone in giving their ideals the go-by. At the opening of the scene, Berowne the realist, who could shrewdly anticipate the inevitable disaster that would overtake the recluse-like ambitions of 'the little Academe' even at the outset, enters the park reading a love-sonnet of his and soliloquising about the predicament of falling in love. He sees the King of Navarre enter with a paper, gets up into a tree and watches. He discovers in a moment that in his love-smitten condition he has the company of the king. He keeps commenting with keen, double-edged irony on the stance of the king, which is that of the conventional Petrarchan sonneteering lover in a lovelorn state. It is then the king's turn, as he steps aside and watches, to know that his companion Longaville, like himself, is forsworn and in love. Berowne could watch and comment with self-critical cynicism on both Navarre and Longaville unobserved by both while Navarre sees and comments on Longaville only. Berowne's comment on the sonnet read out by Longaville is characteristic in its anti-Petrarchan and anti-romantic vein:

> This is the liver vein, which makes flesh a deity
> A green goose a goddess: pure, pure idolatry
> God amend us, God amend! we are much out o'the way.

With simultaneous involvement in and detachment from the predicament of the lover, Berowne becomes a means for Shakespeare of voicing an anti-romantic criticism of the conventional love-literature of the period. The inclusiveness with which romantic and anti-romantic attitudes could be brought together is characteristically Shakespearian. Dumain arrives on the scene and is noticed by the other three independently. Navarre notices

Longaville and Dumain no doubt; but Longaville notices Dumain only. The ironical self-consciousness of Berowne reaches its climax in his remarks on the arrival of Dumain.

Berowne (*aside*) All hid, all hid, an old infant play.
Like a demi-god here sit I in the sky,
And wretched fools' secrets heedfully o'er-eye.
More sacks to the mill! O heavens, I have my wish!
Dumain transform'd: four woodcocks in a dish!

A series of stichomythic comments follow before Dumain, quite unaware of the presence of others, reads out his love sonnet and wishes that he had fallen in love in the good company of his associates. It is after this that the others reveal themselves one after another. It is real revelation in more than one sense of the term, which is effectively, if a little mechanically, staged with the aid of the device of the 'scene within the scene'. It is a total self-discovery, a revelation of the truth about themselves and about their companions, the truth that they have been surprised alike by love.

The device, as it is pressed into service in *As you Like It, Twelfth Night* and *All's Well that Ends Well*, by then is rid of its earlier mechanical quality and turns out to be a powerful instrument of the comic imagination, and a subtle means to the end of comedy. It is employed in *As You Like It* but slightly when Jaques is in on the scene of the wooing of Audrey by Touchstone. The cynical Jaques's comic interest in the fool as a kindred spirit, and the ironical comedy of the cynical melancholic's attempts to help the anti-romantic's romantic venture serving only to hinder it are well brought out through this device in this wedding scene without the wedding. The comments of Jaques from his hidden post of observation are very few and it is Touchstone who steals the show with his display of wit.

The hilarious scene of the gulling of Malvolio in *Twelfth Night* (II. v) is cast in the form of 'the scene within the scene' and it is here that the device is handled in the maturest and most remarkable way for the purposes of comedy. It is a sort of drama within the drama in the drama of *Twelfth Night*. Maria, the brain behind the missive trap set for Malvolio, is the stage-manager of the show 'fitting' the actor-spectators. The hiding place behind the box-tree for the trio of Sir Toby, Sir Andrew and Fabian whetting their appetite as they look forward to the comedy is chosen by Maria. The stage is set for Malvolio's appearance on the scene. As Malvolio enters rapt in solemn contemplation of his self-importance and having already got it into his head that Olivia is in love with him, every one of his moves is watched and every one of his statements reviewed by the three observers, who ruthlessly underline the folly of the dupe, make no secret of their resentment against the officious steward, and gloat over the victim's plight. An effect of two-fold comedy, the comedy of Malvolio walking right into the trap, and the comedy of the response of Sir Toby and his crew is achieved through the use of the device. The half-naturalistic calls to silence and restraint made by one or the other of the three observers lest they should be heard by Malvolio lend a piquancy to the whole scene. Even before he comes by the letter dropped in his way[10] by way of bait, Malvolio, Alnaschar-like, stages a drama of absurd day-dreaming and wish-fulfilment, casting himself in the role of Count Malvolio in this drama within a drama within a drama in the drama of *Twelfth Night*. The way in which the three spectators who are the 'invisible' audience of this drama involve themselves in it is excellent audience participation indeed!

Malvolio	Besides, you waste the treasure of your time with a foolish knight.
Sir Andrew	That's me, I warrant you.
Malvolio	One Sir Andrew.
Sir Andrew	I knew 'twas I; for many do call me fool.

No wonder that, as Malvolio identifies the hand in which the letter is written as that of Olivia, Sir Andrew draws attention to the *double entendre* in the expression 'her c's, her u's and her t's' by repeating it. Thus by setting the three observers to watch and comment, Shakespeare at one stroke strikes two veins of comedy. Not only do the two comedies run abreast of each other but the device is a dramatic means of emphasis and of fixing attention on details. While the device no doubt retains the elements of non-naturalistic convention, it is made to appear quite natural; no longer do the bare bones of the stage trick show as in the early instances.

---

10. It may be noted in passing that Shakespeare uses the formula of the dropped letter as a recurrent stage device.

The ambush scene in *All's Well that Ends Well*, in which the braggart soldier Parolles is caught and blindfolded, though a scene of ambush when considered from the point of view of its action, is an instance of the device of 'the scene within the scene' when considered from the point of view of its structure. The first Lord with five or six soldiers is behind a hedge as Parolles enters, making a confession about his cowardice, and planning, in order to avoid disgrace, 'to give myself some hurts and say I got them in exploit.' The first Lord's remarks on these utterances of Parolles are in the nature of a choric comment and an expression of contempt for the coward. These raise questions not only about the character of Parolles but Shakespeare's mode of character portrayal, as, for example, the question

> Is it possible he should know what he is, and be that he is?

which is a comment on Parolles's

> What the devil should move me to undertake the recovery of this drum; being not ignorant of the impossibility, and knowing I had no such purpose? I must give myself some hurts, and say I got them in exploit: yet slight ones will not carry it: they will say, came you off with so little? and great ones I dare not give. Wherefore, what's the instance? Tongue I must put you into a butter-woman's mouth, and buy myself another of Bajazet's mule, if you prattle me into these perils.[11]

---

11. Incidentally, the following suggestion may be ventured about the reference to 'Bajazet's mule' of which no satisfactory explanation has been offered so far. In the passage Parolles, in a mood of self-criticism, blames it all on his braggart tongue and chides it for getting him into his present situation. Yet he knows that the only way left for him is to prattle himself out of these perils even as he prattled himself into them. His tongue has been wagging and rattling like that of a butter-woman whose volubility and vociferousness would be evident in her street-cries, a common sound of the streets of Elizabethan London. Cf. 'the right butter-women's rank (rant?) to market.' *As You Like It* (III, ii). This fairly simple topical reference is followed by another, multiple and indirect, through which Parolles expresses his wish that he had kept his mouth shut instead of letting it wag as it did. This idea is put across in terms of an allusion to the big theatrical scenes in Marlowe's *Tamburlaine* in which Bajazet's cage (and later Tamburlaine's chariot) is drawn across the stage by the captive kings serving

The answer to the first Lord's question is provided in Parolles's pronouncement later:

> Simply the thing I am shall make me live.

It may not be exceptional to say that the question of the first Lord is a striking instance of how Shakespeare's dramatic consciousness could at once include and transcend a convention, how unjust it would be to the characteristic Shakespearian inclusiveness to tie Shakespeare down to a convention of the soliloquy as the primitive device of mere self-exposition. In the light of the first Lord's question, the monologue of Parolles cannot be explained away merely as 'direct self-explanation'. The question complicates the dramatic situation, and imports a degree of naturalistic psychological probing into the formality and conventionality of the stage device.

How the device is used for securing the subtlest dramatic communication and impact in three instances at a tragic climax of action can be seen now.

In *Troilus and Cressida* it is Shakespeare's masterstroke of dramatic artistry to have structured the scene of the discovery by Troilus of the breach of faith by Cressida on this principle. The moral horror of Cressida's betrayal of faith is very effectively emphasised when the flirtations of Cressida with Diomedes in the Grecian camp take place as Troilus in the company of Ulysses looks on and experiences a profound shock to his moral sensibility and a consequent transvaluation of values. What is more, Thersites watches all the proceedings from a distance, so that two opposed points of view are simultaneously brought to bear on what happens between Cressida and Diomedes. The telling dramatic effect of ambivalence and of a precarious balance between cynicism and faith in values is achieved

---

for horses with their mouths bridled and bitted, the jocular transformation being that of 'horses' into 'mules', of 'the horse-men' into the 'the ass-mares'. Implicit in the reference to Bajazet's mule in this context is an oblique dig at the rant of the Marlovian hero and at the acting style in the 'big bow-wow strain' of Alleyn. For both Marlovian drama and acting in the ranting, Alleyn style (as contrasted with the Burbage style) had at the time of writing of *All's Well that Ends Well* come to be regarded as old-fashioned, though these had been the great hits of the recent past.

in the scene mainly through the use of the device. The situation combines devastating irony with poignant pathos. For it is Troilus who observes the goings-on between Cressida and Diomedes, points to every move and utterance of the two, and provides a running commentary on them as though he stage-managed the show, and the comments of Troilus are counterpointed by those of Thersites. The gains in perspective are due to the device of 'the scene within the scene' by means of which three areas of vision are made available. A piquant intermingling of conventionality and of some attempt at naturalism is present in the use of the device in this scene, as in the scene of the gulling of Malvolio. Let alone the stage-direction 'Enter Troilus and Ulysses, at a distance; after them Thersites', we have the warnings of Ulysses to Troilus.

> Stand where the torch may not discover us
> O, contain yourself;
> Your passion draws ears hither.

Towards the end of the scene, Aeneas brings news to Troilus about the war and about Hector getting ready for battle. As all three – Troilus, Ulysses and Aeneas – leave, we have Thersites staying on the stage to make his comment.

> Lechery, Lechery! Still wars and lechery! Nothing else holds
> fashion. A burning devil take them.

The juxtaposition of the themes of love and war in the present context is paradigmatic of Shakespeare's handling of the two themes in the play. What we find in the play as a whole is a subtle, ironical reversal of the themes of love and war as they figure together in conventional heroic poetry or tragedy. The obverse of love, which is lust as exemplified in Cressida's faithlessness, and of war, which is false stratagem as exemplified in the treacherous slaughter of Hector, is exhibited in the play. One could almost suggest 'All is fair in love and war' in an ironical sense as an epigraph of the play.

The stage utility and theatrical effectiveness of this dramatic practice of Shakespeare's are seen at their best in the sleepwalking scene in *Macbeth*. A significant heightening of the climactic tragic effect of the scene results when the somnambulistic movements, gestures and utterances of Lady Macbeth are pointed up by the waiting gentlewoman and the doctor of physic who stand by. Almost a preview of the sleepwalking actions of Lady Macbeth is provided at the beginning of the scene in the gentlewoman's account and the doctor's comment on it and his eagerness to know what the actual somnambulistic words are. In this and other respects, the use of the device in this scene is an illustration of the excellent sense of the theatre which enabled Shakespeare not only to prepare the audience but provide guidelines for a proper and full view of the main event of the scene, to ensure, in short, that effects were not missed. Eliot remarked about the adequacy of 'the objective correlative' found in this scene, and pointed out how the state of mind of Lady Macbeth as she walks in sleep is rendered by 'a skilful accumulation of imagined sense impressions'.[12] These 'imagined sense impressions' are vividly communicated through the close comments of the two observing characters. Between themselves the two provide a close-up of Lady Macbeth as she enters with a taper and walks about in sleep. Every detail such as the lighted taper, the eyes wide open in sleep, the obsessive 'washing' of her hand (a 'Freudian' symptom), every word of self-incriminating confession, and the deep sigh, is called attention to. Without raising the issue whether visibility was poor in the Elizabethan theatre or sightlines were not clear enough, one may say that the device served to rouse and rivet ocular as well as auricular attention. The doctor almost hangs on the lips of the sleepwalking Lady Macbeth and takes care to record her words on paper. The comments of 'the good doctor' at the close have the truth and objectivity of a choric observer. It is significant that, even though the doctor of physic disclaims any capacity to act as 'the mind-doctor', he indirectly makes available his diagnosis that what is involved is a question of sin and expiation rather than crime and punishment. 'Shakespeare', said Maurice Morgann, 'contrives to make secret impressions upon us', and the device of the scene within the scene as used in the sleepwalking scene is one of the means of producing such impressions. The device contributes in no small measure to the status of the scene as a theatrical masterpiece at once the pride and despair of Shakespearian actresses right from Mrs Siddons.

---

12. T.S. Eliot, 'Hamlet', *Selected Essays* (London, 1934), p. 145.

A remarkable variation of this dramatic formula is employed in IV.i of *Othello*, one more instance of the virtuosic handling of this device by Shakespeare. It is Iago who, here as elsewhere in the play, sets and stage-manages the scene as he stations Othello at just the right distance so that he might watch but not hear the exchange between Iago and Cassio, and between Cassio and Bianca over the handkerchief. A stroke of the deepest dramatic effectiveness and tragic irony is secured by making Othello witness every gesture and movement of Cassio's and express his reaction of forcibly suppressed anger and scorn in asides at every step, so that he is deluded into the belief that he has clinching evidence about Cassio's and Desdemona's crime as he looks on and misconstrues the pantomime with grim consequences.

Even as the reconstruction of the exact location of the scenes in which the device is used is difficult, so also determination of the mode of acting which was employed in such scenes is not easy. While the elements of stylisation and formal convention inherent in the nature and function of the device are indisputable, in his later, supple handling of the device, Shakespeare rids it of its stiffness and makes it a pliant, rich and sensitive instrument of dramatic communication. The rhythmic movement, the ritual disposition of the characters on the stage in two or more groups, and the accepted, conventional assumptions behind the use of the device — all these would have called for formalised acting. Yet the admixture of naturalism in the scenes, which has been already pointed out, perhaps necessitated half-naturalistic, half-formal acting. What J.L.Styan says about scenes in Shakespeare in which three-and-four-fold grouping is employed, 'the audience feels the pleasure of gaining an omniscient perspective through the grouping,[13] is all the more true in the case of the scene-within-the-scene. Perhaps the greatest advantage the device brings is the evocation on the part of the spectators of a fruitful tension between a sense of reality and a sense of illusion, and between alienation and participation.

---

13. J.L. Styan, *Shakespeare's Stagecraft* (Cambridge, 1967), p. 127.

3

Sleep and Death[1]: The Twins in Shakespeare

The similitude of death for sleep and sleep for death is one of the commonplaces of both classical and biblical lineage and one of considerable vogue in early medieval and Renaissance literature and iconography. It is one of the *topoi* which Shakespeare returns to and dramatically exploits time and again, and it is worthwhile considering to what fine uses he puts this received idea. The most extensive as well as the subtlest use of the

1. T.W. Baldwin, *Shakespeare's Small Latine and Lesse Greeke* (Urbana: Univ. of Illinois Press, 1944), pp. 591–3, 675–7, 705. On the great vogue of the idea during the Renaissance, see, for example, Samuel Chew, *The Pilgrimage of Life* (New Haven: Yale Univ. Press, 1962), pp. 250–2. It was current in early medieval literature, though, as Rosemary Woolf points out (*The English Religious Lyric in the Middle Ages* [Oxford, 1968], pp. 68–9), in the Middle English religious lyrics, in spite of death being a frequent theme, the sleep–death motif is conspicuous by its absence. Two examples from early medieval literature may be cited. In the Anglo-Saxon *Solomon and Saturn*, II, Saturn declares: 'Sleep is most like death' (1. 313). The Anglo-Saxon Latin writer Alcuin uses the identification in this passage: 'Q. What is sleep? A. The image of death' (Quoted by Helen Waddell, *The Wandering Scholars* [London, 1927], pp. 45–6). Naive as the identification of sleep and death with one another may appear, its 'mythical' force may be recognised if we note its currency in the Oriental tradition. In a context almost identical with the one in *Solomon and Saturn*, the idea occurs in a memorable passage in the Sanskrit epic, *The Mahabharata*. Surprisingly, E.R.Curtius, *European Literature and the Latin Middle Ages* (New York, 1953), does not mention this *topos*.

idea as dramatic image is to be found in *Macbeth*. But in a good many other plays the sleep–death coalescence is employed by Shakespeare not merely as an incidental stroke of dramatic rhetoric, but often to larger ends as well. What Shakespeare makes of this traditional motif is at once an illustration of what a genius does to an apparently minor convention or cliché and also further evidence that the links in the chain of the imagistic associations of Shakespeare are to be sought at least as much in traditional habits of thought and expression inherited by the artist as in the psychological make-up of the man in the way suggested by Caroline Spurgeon and Edward Armstrong.

Warburton and Malone traced the Duke's words to Claudio in *Measure for Measure*:

> Thy best of rest is sleep,
> And that thou oft provok'st; yet grossly fear'st
> Thy death, which is no more
>
> (III.i.17–19)

back to Cicero. But, as T.W. Baldwin has pointed out, despite the occurrence of the idea of death as sleep in three different instances in Cicero, this classical author had no monopoly over it. Shakespeare could have absorbed the idea from Cicero, or from the school-text, the *Sententiae Pueriles* (*somnus mortis imago*), or Palingenius's *Zodiacus* in the original or Barnabe Googe's translation,[2] or for the matter from the *Book of Job* (14.10–12), probably in the Geneva version where the marginal gloss insists that the idea does not involve anything like the mortalist heresy. The classical idea of sleep as the image of death chimed in well with the biblical one of death as sleep. The approximation of death to sleep was hence a commonplace in the traditions of the *consolatio* and the *ars moriendi*. Furthermore, there were certain established literary as well as iconographical associations of the two-in-one imagery of sleep as death (and death as sleep) with night, dream, and darkness. For instance, St Chrysostom's classic statements calling life a dream

2. J.E. Hankins believes that the Shakespearian uses of this similitude echo its occurrences in Barnabe Googe's translation of Palingenius. See *Shakespeare's Derived Imagery* (Lawrence: Univ. of Kansas Press, 1953), pp. 125–38.

or a drama and associating it with sleep and death commended themselves to the Elizabethan mind.[3] The conception of Sleep and Death as siblings—that is, as the two children of Night—goes back to Homer and Hesiod, and was revived in Renaissance mythography, as we see from the dictionaries, the iconological accounts of Pausanias and Cartari, and Renaissance iconographical practice.[4] More immediately, the sleep–death coalescence was often used by Sidney and Spenser. Some of these associations attached to the sleep–death imagery could well have suggested to Shakespeare dramatic possibilities which he turns to good imaginative account. Examples of Shakespeare's pursuit of the significances of the sleep–death imagery may now be surveyed.

The earliest instance occurs in the Induction to *The Taming of the Shrew*. The sportive lord chances upon the drunken tinker Sly; just before the idea flashes upon his mind of making the 'lorel into a lord' for that one night, he remarks as he takes a good look at the man who is fast asleep: 'Grim death, how foul and loathsome is thine image' (Induction, i.35). Spoken with reference to the figure of the besotted Sly lying supine on the stage with the contortions of face and of limbs suggesting death (and it takes some time for the lord and his men to decide whether the man lies dead or asleep), the traditional analogy in words is supported here by what is actually seen onstage. Sly fast asleep thus in effect turns out to be an emblem of the conceit of sleep and death. Of course, the tableau is not without a touch of the incidental moral about how ugly and repulsive the state of drunkenness is. The comedy of taming and 'supposes' is presented to Sly the lord as something like a dream dreamt by him; in the Epilogue of *A Shrew*, as against *The Shrew*, Sly on awaking indeed thinks it a dream. One might say that Shakespeare's forgetting or abandoning of the Induction frame (and of Sly himself after the last reference to him as the nodding but nevertheless prime spectator at the end of the first scene) has a

3. See Baldwin, p. 675.
4. Jean Seznec, *The Survival of the Pagan Gods* (1953; rpt. New York, 1961), pp. 255, 291; Edgar Wind, *Pagan Mysteries in the Renaissance* (London, 1958), p. 138. Henry Green, *Shakespeare and the Emblem Writers* (London, 1870), pp. 469–70, thought that Shakespeare probably picked up the ideas from the pictures in Holbein's *Simulachres de la Mort* (Lyons, 1538).

peculiar appropriateness. The Induction Sly is, after all, present throughout and remains at the last onstage; leaving the epilogue end of the frame unclosed strengthens the impression of the play within the play being like a dream. Despite indications that Sly is an experienced theatregoer contained in the 'play-scraps' from *The Spanish Tragedy*, the great hit of the times, of which his speeches at the beginning are full,[5] he asks, 'Is not a commonty a Christmas gambold or a tumbling trick?' (Induction, ii.140–41) and goes to sleep before the end of the first scene of the play, and the rest with him is silence.

In *The Rape of Lucrece* in the sensuous portrait of Lucrece fast asleep as Tarquin approaches her is employed the commonplace of sleep as death in keeping with the general technique of the poem which is one of the Ovid-like evocation of the attributes of tragedy such as night, darkness, and beasts of prey and birds of evil omen.

Her hair, like golden threads, play'd with her breath;
O modest wantons! wanton modesty!
Showing life's triumph in the map of death,
And death's dim look in life's morality:
Each in her sleep themselves so beautify,
As if between them twain there were no strife,
But that life liv'd in death, and death in life.

(II.400–6)

What is remarkable here is that sleep, though 'a map of death' anticipating thus with a sort of dramatic irony, the death by suicide of Lucrece, is at the same time a map of life as well so that the idea of sleep serves as a mediating factor in the antithesis of life and death: 'in the midst of life we are in death'. It is exactly this paradox implicit in the idea of sleep—its points of contact with both life and death—which is at once theatrically and rhetorically exploited in *Romeo and Juliet* and in *Macbeth*. The image of sleep as death's counterfeit is employed in *Romeo and Juliet* with thematic, presentational, and situational aptness; yet, compared with the imaginative stretch acquired by the idea as it figures in *Macbeth*, its use in this early play

5. Anne Righter believes that in contrast to the Sly of *A Shrew*, 'Shakespeare's Sly has never seen a play' (*Shakespeare and the Idea of the Play* [London, 1962], p. 95).

is predictably as much emblematic and rhetorical in an obvious way as it is dramatic. Nevertheless, in *Romeo and Juliet* the motif is a 'figure-in-words' which does turn out to be a 'figure-in-action', and thus it adds to and reinforces the ironical double significance of 'complementarity', which the 'death-marked love' of the star-cross'd lovers exhibits. It has been well recognised that the *Liebestod* theme of love as death and death as love—the idea so central to the play that the ultimate fulfilment of love can be only in death—is supported by the paradoxical significances which emerge in the light–darkness imagery in the play. The paradoxical impressions produced by the imagery of sleep on account of its double relations with death and life confirm the total imagistic and thematic structure. As part of her attempt to keep up her pretence and make-believe for her mother's benefit, Juliet makes her grief for the banished Romeo appear as though it were for the dead Tybalt and feigns eagerness to revenge his death in these terms:

> . . . Indeed, I never shall be satisfied
> With Romeo, till I behold him—dead
> Is my poor heart so for a kinsman vex'd:
> Madam, if you could find out but a man
> To bear a poison, I would temper it,
> That Romeo should, upon receipt thereof,
> Soon *sleep* in quiet.
>
> (III.v.94–100; *italics mine*)

These terms ironically prove too true indeed. The pattern of ominous anticipation and foreboding by way of dramatic irony and the pattern of grieving and lamenting for the dead (making the play akin to the tragedies of grief which were common around 1590) are key factors in this play as in the historical tragedies leading to and culminating in *Richard III*. Sleep as an euphemism or metaphor for death, and sleep as a game of make-believe for feigning death played for purposes of love and life by Juliet with the help of Friar Lawrence's sleeping potion thus fit well into this pattern of the play and contribute to its meaning. The sleeping potion would send Juliet into such a sleep as would be taken for no less than death. Her animation would be so thoroughly suspended by the working of the drug that

> No warmth, no breath, shall testify thou liv'st;

> The roses in thy lips and cheeks shall fade
> To paly ashes; thy eyes' windows fall,
> Like death, when he shuts up the day of life
>
> * * *
>
> And in this borrowed likeness to shrunk death
> Thou shalt continue two-and-forty hours,
> And then awake as from a pleasant sleep.
>
> (IV.i.98–106)

Taken to be her death, her sleep elicits lamentations from all around her—except, of course, the friar. No wonder that Juliet has foreboding about 'the horrible conceit of death and night' as she is about to drink the potion. Her death-like sleep as she lies in the tomb of the Capulets is most importantly taken for her death by Romeo. He had earlier received the doubly ironic news of Juliet's 'death' ('Her body sleeps in Capel's monument,' IV.i.18), and procured poison from the apothecary; drinking it, he 'sleeps in quiet' by the side of Juliet (to use Juliet's earlier words, III.v.100). Juliet awakes from her sleep only to find Romeo lying dead beside her and then stabs herself into the sleep of death with Romeo's dagger.

In *A Midsummer Night's Dream* the use of the idea is alike casual and traditional ('Till o'er their brows death-counterfeiting sleep/ With leaden legs and batty wings doth creep' (III.ii.364–5). King Henry IV's apostrophe to sleep by way of a futile attempt to woo her in *2 Henry IV* (III.i.4–32) and Oliver's story of lying asleep in the Forest of Arden with his rescue by Orlando from the lioness and the snake in *As You Like It* (V.iii.100–22) contain references to death in conjunction with sleep. Again, so does the passage in *2 Henry IV* (IV.v.35–7) in which Prince Hal takes his sleeping father for dead.

> This sleep is sound indeed; this is a sleep
> That from his golden rigol hath divorc'd
> So many English kings.

These references are demanded by the context and at the same time show that sleep and death are twinned in the dramatist's imagination so much so that to him sleep must bring death to mind. In *Hamlet* the sleep–death motif figures in the best-known speech in all Shakespeare, in the 'To be or not to be' soliloquy:

> To die: to sleep;
> No more; and, by a sleep to say we end
> The heart-ache and the thousand natural shocks
> That flesh is heir to, 'tis a consummation
> Devoutly to be wish'd. To die, to sleep;
> To sleep: perchance to dream: ay, there's the rub;
> For in that sleep of death what dreams may come
> When we have shuffled off this mortal coil
> Must give us pause
>
> (III.i.59–67)

It is neither necessary nor desirable for purposes of this essay to go into the still-vex'd problem of the meaning and orientation of this enigma of a soliloquy. But so far as the use of the sleep–death analogy and its implications go, Hamlet does consider the question of what the after-life may hold in store for him and for Everyman, of 'the dread of something after death'. The equation *to die=to sleep* is made more than once in the speech. The dreams which may assail the sleep of death are the experiences of one's after-life. The equivalence of sleep and death, and the near-equivalence of both with dreams in the sense of an existential after-life, are prompted by—and lead to—an equivalence between being and doing, between the existential and the active, and at the same time between the existential (both in the here and now, and in the hereafter) and the eschatological. It will not do to try to reduce the complexity—especially the bustling, action-packed quality of the whole play—to a series of scenes, situations, and discourses or meditations relating to the *ars moriendi* or the *memento mori* conventions. Nor would it be adequate to our total impression of the play to say that it is a dramatisation of Hamlet's coming to terms with the fact of death or that Hamlet is death-ridden from first to last. But one may chart the line of progression in the play as extending through the dread of something after death on Hamlet's part to his acquisition and consciousness of his readiness for 'felicity' and 'silence' at the close of the play.

In *Measure for Measure* the use of the sleep–death motif gives rise to some piquant effects of juxtaposition and cross-reference. The Duke in his guise as friar meets the condemned Claudio in his cell and delivers a standard piece of oration on death by way of teaching Claudio the art of dying well. The speech employs the habits of thought of the *contemptus mundi* and the *ars moriendi* traditions. After trying to take the sting out of death by saying,

> Thy best of rest is sleep,
> And that thou oft provok'st; yet grossly fear'st
> Thy death, which is no more.
>
> (III.i.17–19)

the Duke goes on to remind him of the many ills that flesh is heir to, of the revenges that the whirlgig of mutability will bring, especially those of middle age and old age. As he now puts it, life itself is a dull sleep. So why not exchange the sleep of life for the deeper, more restful sleep of death?

> Thou hast nor youth nor age;
> But, as it were, an after-dinner's sleep,
> Dreaming on both . . .
>
> (III.i.32–34)

Not that the latter end of his sermon forgets the first; if the distinction between life and death is levelled by the suggestion that both are a sleep and a dream, such a double sense of sleep is one exploited in the tradition. (There is a curious similarity between the argument of the Duke and the rhetoric of Despair in Spenser's *The Faerie Queene*, Book I, which all but persuades Red Cross to take his own life.) But the 'sentence' of the friar ultimately brings little 'solace' to Claudio; in the very next scene Claudio expresses a most vividly realised fear of what it is to resign this pleasing, anxious being which we call life.[6] The sleep–death motif is invested with yet another strikingly ironic dimension by the fact that it is Barnardine who seems to live up to the friar's counsel. It is all characteristic of the shifting duality of tone of this play, which is due to its balanced, contrived patterns of movement through what one may call the comedic frustrations and reversals and surprises. This duality of tone owes itself also to the fact that the Duke, puppet-master as he may be almost resembling Providence, is himself a puppet. His counsel

6. On Claudio's speech and its similarities with Hamlet's famous soliloquy, there is an interesting comment in Robert D. Eagleson, 'Eschatological speculations and the use of the infinitive,' *Shakespeare Quarterly*, 26 (1975), pp. 206–8.

almost stood on its head when we hear the Provost say of Barnardine:

> A man that apprehends death no more dreadfully but as a drunken sleep; careless, reckless, and fearless of what's past, present, or to come; insensible of mortality, and desperately mortal. . .
>
> (IV.ii.142–5)

Again, Pompey, of the same ilk as Barnardine, uses the similitude in his role as the hangman's lieutenant:

> *Barnardine* You rogue, I have been drinking all night; I am not fitted for't.
>
> *Pompey* O, the better, sir; for he that drinks all night, and is hang'd betimes in the morning, may sleep the sounder all the next day.
>
> (IV.iii.42–7)

The old piety of death as sleep drawn upon by the Duke would seem to be followed over-literally by Barnardine and understood better by Pompey than by Claudio who takes it to heart less well. This little irony of the play is paradigmatic of its general irony. The concrete presence on the stage of the figure of sleep is that of the recalcitrant Barnardine who refuses to be coaxed into death in spite of the joint efforts of Abhorson, Pompey, and the Duke, and who is a thing 'unfit either to live or to die.'

Of the highest interest are the workings of the sleep–death identity and its associations in *Macbeth*. 'This night's great business' of the murder of Duncan is planned and carried out by Macbeth and his Lady; it is reacted to by them and others in terms which have reference (among other things) to the sleep–death equation as well as to the associations of both sleep and death with night, darkness, and tragedy. The 'figure-in-words' of the sleep–death coalescence realises itself as a 'figure-in-action-and-situation,' but with the important difference that neither the sleeping figure of Duncan before, during, or after his murder, nor the sleeping figures of Duncan's guards are actually to be seen on the stage for all their being lurid 'absent presences'. It is a virtuoso master-stroke of theatrical art and economy that merely presentative or non-presentational means of evocation could produce effects no less vivid and immediate than visual significances. Perhaps Shakespeare had in mind certain requirements of decorum in order to please his royal patron before whom the play was probably presented. Perhaps on the first night in the hall at the Hampton Court Palace, the play was presented as a 'nocturnal' with the use of darkening effects. However that may be, the traditional equivalence between sleep and death and their affinity with night is exploited by Shakespeare in close correlation with darkness and also blood and hell as conventional attributes of tragedy.

Lady Macbeth, who wins over her wavering husband and confirms him in his decision to murder Duncan in his sleep, does so by rousing his 'manliness' and by emphasising the practicality that the chamberlains of Duncan could be plied with drink and drugs into a death-like sleep during which the act could be accomplished.

> When in swinish sleep
> Their drenched natures lie, as in death,
> What cannot you and I perform upon
> The unguarded Duncan?
>
> (I.vii.67–70)

This is the second in a whole series of images of sleep which crowd themselves into the play. As Professor Foakes has put it:

Of the many references to sleep, sleeplessness, and kindred ideas, eighteen occur in one scene (II.ii) and thirty-one in the whole of Act II. Macbeth has murdered Duncan in his sleep, and his punishment is

> Glamis hath murder'd sleep, and therefore Cawdor
> Shall sleep no more, Macbeth shall sleep no more.
>
> (II.ii.39–40)

It is also Lady Macbeth's punishment, as is seen in the sleep-walking scene (V. i.) There is a concentrated emphasis on sleep which is dramatically powerful in these two parts of the play.[7]

It is worth noting that in Act II many of the sleep references occur in the form of the sleep–death equation. In Lady Macbeth's view, killing King Duncan reduces to ensuring that the guardsmen

7. R.A. Foakes, 'Suggestions for a new approach to Shakespeare's imagery,' *Shakespeare Survey*, 5 (1952), p. 85.

are sent into a death-like sleep. There is, in her conception, no more to it than that:

> He is about it;
> The doors are open, and the surfeited grooms
> Do mock their charge with snores: I have drugged their
> possets,
> That death and nature do contend about them,
> Whether they live or die.
>
> ⋆⋆⋆
>
> Alack! I am afraid they have awak'd,
> And 'tis not done; the attempt and not the deed
> Confounds us.
>
> (II.ii.4–11)

Macbeth is subconsciously aware of the enormity of his deed, quite in contrast to Lady Macbeth. It is this awareness which expresses itself in the form of the weird and at the same time lyric utterance:

> Methought I heard a voice cry 'Sleep no more!
> Macbeth does murder sleep', the innocent sleep,
> Sleep that knits up the ravell'd sleave of care,
> The death of each day's life, sore labour's bath,
> Balm of hurt minds, great nature's second course,
> Chief nourisher in life's feast.
>
> (II.ii.32–7)

By now the double signification of 'sleep' as partaking as much of the qualities of life as death, emerges very clearly. Thus sleep becomes the meeting ground between what G. Wilson Knight has called the life themes in the play—that is, the forces of nature and the good life which rise against the death forces of evil and crime and their opposites. It is as though by the time the point is reached at which Macbeth frantically rehearses the uncanny voices he heard crying

> Sleep no more. . .
> 'Glamis hath murder'd sleep, and therefore Cawdor
> Shall sleep no more, Macbeth shall sleep no more!'
>
> (II.ii.38–40)

the sleep imagery has established itself as a middle ground between great creating nature and destructive death. So much so that when Lady Macbeth facilely repeats the old commonplace, 'The sleeping and the dead/ Are but as pictures,' she fails to be alive to its new meanings in the context. She in fact quite forgets what she herself had felt and said a few moments earlier: 'Had he not resembled/ My father as he slept I had done't' (II.ii.12–13). At the gate of Macbeth's castle the half-asleep and half-awake figure of the porter impersonates the porter at Hell-gate, as if he were giving an impromptu performance of a scene from a mystery cycle in his sleep and dream, and provides a meaningful enactment of sleep, which has reference to the murderers and their deed just done. The porter, equivocated into sleep by drink, finds himself doing his office at the gates of hell and behaves as though he were a creature of the after-world, thus providing an indirect value-judgement on the fact of the criminals and evoking a picture of hell and darkness consistent with the tragedy being enacted. The eschatological suggestion is sustained and deepened with Macduff's announcement of the horror of his discovery of Duncan murdered in sleep. Recent criticism[8] has noted the manner in which Macduff's announcement and a number of characters in their night-gowns rushing onto the stage from different directions to hear news of Duncan's death by murder immediately suggest the souls being called to parley at the last trump on Doomsday. Macduff raises an alarm through these words:

Awake, awake!
Ring the alarum bell. Murder and treason!
Banquo and Donalbain! Malcolm! Awake!
Shake off this downy sleep, death's counterfeit,
And look on death itself, up, up, and see
The great doom's image! Malcolm! Banquo!
As from your graves rise up, and walk like sprites,
To countenance this horror! Ring the bell.

(II.iii.74–80)

---

8. D.E. Jones, *The Plays of T.S. Eliot* (London, 1960), p. 17; William Armstrong, *Shakespeare's Typology: Miracle and Mystery Motifs in 'Macbeth'* (London, 1970).

When Macduff uses the phrase 'sleep, death's counterfeit' in conjunction with the 'great doom's image,' the idea of sleep and the cumulative effect of all that has gone on before at once suggest the notion of spirits asleep in their graves being called up for judgement; when Lady Macbeth enters with the innocent-seeming question,

> What's the business,
> That such a hideous trumpet calls to parley
> The sleepers of the house?
>
> (II.iii.81–3)

this forceful impression of the eschatological associations of sleep is complete.

The affinities in imaginative conception and technique between *The Rape of Lucrece* and *Macbeth* have been pointed out by M. C. Bradbrook.[9] Not only does Macbeth make telling use of the traditional suggestions of 'sleep' for a variety of tragic effects, but the slight impressions of life with which the idea is invested in the poem are given vivid dramatic embodiment in the play. No wonder that when Macbeth envies the peace enjoyed by the dead Duncan in words such as 'Duncan is in his grave; After life's fitful fever he sleeps well' (III.ii.22–3), it is Macbeth and his Lady who 'sleep no more' that are in the universe of death and not the dead Duncan. Amidst the almost inexhaustible significances of the great theatrical highlight of the sleepwalking scene is the way in which Lady Macbeth as well as re-enacting the actions of the past in her somnambulism has a proleptic glimpse of the hell to which she would be consigned. That would seem to be the point of her 'hell is murky!' which comes in the midst of her despairing attempt to wipe off her guilt consciousness as evidenced in her washing her hands with 'Out, damned spot! out, I say' and in her recollection of the crucial moment of the past—the moment before Duncan's murder—in 'One; two; . . . why, then, 'tis time to do it.' The sleeping figure of Lady Macbeth performs all the tell-tale actions while uttering the revealing words. The fact that her eyes are closed in sleep all the time along with the details of her gestures and actions

9. M.C. Bradbrook, 'The sources of *Macbeth*,' *Shakespeare Survey*, 4 (1951).

is pointed up for the benefit of the audience who on account of none-too-good sight-lines in the Elizabethan theatre may not be able to have a clear and close view by the running commentary of the waiting gentlewoman and the doctor. Lady Macbeth's movements across the stage, lighted candle in hand, may be for purposes of both lighting up and thus providing a close-up of her face and gestures on the one side, and of bringing to mind the emblematic figure of the penitent whose repentance is an impossibility.[10] In any case, the eschatological suggestions of sleep as well as its function of recalling the guilt-ridden past are delicately exploited in the scene.

After a full exploration of the possibilities of evoking tragic meaning with the sleep–death similitude in *Macbeth*, when Shakespeare resorts considerably later to the twinned imagery in *Cymbeline*, *The Winter's Tale*, and *The Tempest*, he employs it to quite other ends.[11] Especially the association of sleep with dreams together with the notion that life is a dream as well as a drama—a notion confirmed by dream-like happenings in these last plays—are brought to bear on *Cymbeline* and *The Tempest*. In *Cymbeline*, Iachimo in the bed-chamber of Imogen, looking on her fast asleep on her bed, proceeds to unclasp her bracelet, saying,

> O sleep! thou ape of death, lie dull upon her;
> And be her senses but as a monument
> Thus in a chapel lying.
>
> (II.ii.31–3)

Shakespeare uses a phrase very similar to the 'map of death', which he had used while describing Tarquin's approach to the sleeping Lucrece, just as he introduces an indirect reference to the outrage of Philomela (a myth which he uses in *Titus Andronicus*, the sonnets, and elsewhere) while portraying Iachimo's outrage to Imogen. Later in the play the gaoler as part of his routine trick of gallows-humour uses the death–sleep similitude in his banter with

10. Martha Hester Golden, 'Stage imagery in Shakespearean studies,' *SRO*, 1 (1965), 15, makes the suggestion about the curious relation of the scene to the emblematic figure of the penitent.

11. See 'but she looks like sleep. As she would catch another Antony/ In her strong toil of grace' (*Antony and Cleopatra*, V.ii.347–9; cf. V.ii.7, IV.xii.35 in the same play).

Posthumus while about to lead him to the scaffold: 'Indeed, sir, he that sleeps feels not the toothache; but a man that were to sleep your sleep, and a hangman to help him to bed, I think he would change places with his officer' (V.iv.172–6). Earlier Imogen in the guise of Fidele goes into a death-like sleep which is taken for death by Belarius, Guiderius, and Arviragus. Yet it is a sleep which brings her very near death. It stops short of death only through the care for human lives which Cornelius had when he prepared the poison at the command of the wicked Queen. But what a difference from the sleep which Juliet went into! Posthumus in prison goes into a sleep ardently wishing that the sleep should be his death: 'great powers/ If you will take this audit, take this life, /and cancel these cold bonds' (V.iv.26–8). But in his sleep he dreams and has a vision of his ancestors and Jupiter, and the prophecy about a happy resolution of his and others' embroglios is pinned to his bosom.

In the momentous statue scene in *The Winter's Tale*, Paulina, on the point of discovering to Leontes the 'statue' of Hermione (sculpted by the painter Giulio Romano), bids him 'Prepare/To see the life as lively mock'd as ever/ Still sleep mock'd death' (V.iii.18–20). In the paradox of miraculous resurrection by which the 'dead' Hermione comes to life, it is no surprise that 'sleep' paradoxically communicates with both death and life. But owing to Shakespeare's singular technique peculiar to this play—a technique similar to the manner of Fletcher—of withholding knowledge about the true fate of a main character, the sleep–death equation can be apprehended by the audience only in a straightforward way, as a faithful echo of the tag in the *Sententiae Pueriles*, 'somnus mortis imago,' not in its double signification.

In *The Tempest* the sleep–death equivalence is explicitly employed in the tableau-like scene of Alonso and Gonzalo lying asleep, and Antonio and Sebastian drawing to kill Alonso and Gonzalo at the instigation of Antonio. Antonio educates Sebastian in the virtues and ways of usurpation:

> Here lies your brother,
> No better than the earth, he lies upon,
> If he were that which now he's like, that's dead;
> Whom I, with this obedient steel, —three inches of it,—
> Can lay to bed for ever.
>
> (II.i.280–4)

The whole stage situation with Alonso and Gonzalo fast asleep and with Antonio pointing to them as he speaks to Sebastian, and also later with the standing aghast of Antonio and Sebastian with their swords drawn ready to smite as the sleeping are awakened from their sleep in the nick of time by Ariel,[12] produces a tableau-like effect. Such an effect together with the all-too-obvious theatricality of the lions-or-bulls story invented by Sebastian and with the theatrical self-consciousness which marks this and other final plays would bring to mind to the audience the fact that on the stage the sleeping and the dead are the same; *stage death* and *stage sleep* are alike counterfeit. The concept of the world as well as the theatre as an illusion and of life as a drama or a dream are perceptions which inform the whole play. This cluster of ideas is given the richest dramatic embodiment in *The Tempest*. Such a rich and strange sea-change is undergone by this cluster of hackneyed ideas in the play that one might say that through the dramatic reality they are invested with, the ideas authenticate themselves too well to be accepted as wholly true. In other words, the reality of the dramatic illusion is as much brought home to us as the illusory nature of reality. It is but natural that in the tragicomedies, which are 'myths of immortality' in Wilson Knight's phrase, 'sleep' in effect is an indication of 'the danger but not the death.'

In sum, the dramatic life which the rhetorical idea of sleep as death and of death as sleep takes on in Shakespeare is a good illustration of the interplay of visual and non-visual motifs in drama. The interplay, as has been seen especially with reference to the

---

12. The tableau-like figure of a man arrested and frozen in the stance of lifting his sword to strike curiously occurs also elsewhere in *The Tempest* (see Ferdinand at I.ii.467, and Alonso, Sebastian, and the others at III.iii.59) and in several plays of the period. The most famous example is that of Pyrrhus in *Hamlet* (II.ii) – a verbal, not a visual image: 'So, as a painted tyrant, Pyrrhus stood, /And like a neutral to his will and matter, /Did nothing.'

See also Ferdinand who draws but is charmed from moving in *The Tempest* (I..ii.462) and Sir Giles Overreach in Massinger's *A New Way to Pay Old Debts* (V.i.362), unable to draw his sword out of the scabbard. I wish to thank Professor R. A. Foakes for advice with regard to this article (chapter).

use of the idea in *Macbeth*, is not a matter of direct, one-to-one correspondence between what is said by the characters and what is seen on the stage. The relation between the two could be subtler than that. To put it simply, effects can at times be made palpable even without the visible lending direct support to the audible, that is to say, rendered palpable by an imaginative evocation through the compelling logic of situation and imagery which can make off-stage characters and events vividly present, as in the case of Duncan and his sleeping guardsmen. In the words of the Third Gentleman in *The Winter's Tale* (V.ii.31–2), 'that which you hear you'll swear you see, there is such unity in the proofs.' In any case, the sleep–death equivalence whether in early Shakespeare or late bears a specific, if at times intricate, relation to the particular stage situation or situations in the play; in short, it is embedded in a context of rich dramatic meanings, and serves as a mode of apprehension as well as expression. A hackneyed motif thus comes to life through its embodiment in actual dramatic situations. The variations which Shakespeare makes on this conventional theme can be said to exhibit a pattern of change besides continuity in Shakespeare's developing dramatic techniques. Only a master such as Shakespeare could realise the imaginative truth and possibilities of a cliché—precisely the elements which, unfortunately, make it a cliché.

4
Shakespeare's Metamorphoses of Actaeon

Easily one of the most fascinating of the classical legends to cast its spell on the Renaissance, the myth of Actaeon – the hunter's transformation into a stag hunted and killed by his own hounds as condign punishment for seeing Diana – engaged the attention of the Renaissance mythographers like Natalis Comes (Conti), the Emblem writers like Alciati, Sambucus and Whitney, the Neoplatonist philosophers like Giordano Bruno and the illustrators of Ovid. It is hardly surprising that the *apokatastasis* of Actaeon seized the imagination of the poets and playwrights of the period like Spenser, Sidney, Marlowe, Chapman, the love-sonneteers and, above all, Shakespeare. The Renaissance vogue of the myth is mainly Ovidian in origin; but, besides its sheer imaginative power as an instance of shape-changing magic, the episode lent itself to a variety of interpretative applications during the period and the bewilderingly wide range of suggestive possibilities of the myth came to be explored and exploited to a greater or less degree among them by the poets and dramatists. Before I go on to consider the striking dramatic variations which Shakespeare makes on the motif of Actaeon's 'translation', I shall briefly indicate the plethora of constructions put on it by the interpreters of the times and some of the suggestive force of the legend in and for itself.

The affinities of the Actaeon legend with the dominant metaphor of 'venery' and hunting in the vast body of late medieval and Renaissance love literature, together with the ubiquitous 'heart–hart' pun in the English love convention led the poets to invoke Actaeon's plight, directly or indirectly, often enough and perhaps made it convenient for them also to highlight the paradoxical nature of love and the reversals and inversions (not always comic) it could bring about by way of the transformation of the hunter into the hunted. Leaving aside the extreme instance of mythographic typological ingenuity which made one interpreter see a prefiguration of Christ's martyrdrom in Actaeon's fate (mentioned by Don Cameron Allen,[1] the availability to Shakespeare and his contemporary audience, in varying degrees, of the other learned as well as popular significances seen in the myth lends the Shakespearian uses of the myth, sometimes a telling ironical force and sometimes a rich ambiguity or ambivalence, both in terms of the total communication of words and stage picture together. If the legend promoted and was in turn promoted by the 'heart-hart' pun, an approximation, by the same argument, was made between Actaeon's horns and those proverbial ones of the cuckold in the popular imagination. A curious identity could suggest itself between the horned figure of Actaeon or for that matter an Actaeon-like horned figure on the stage and the performer of the horn dance such as the horn dance of Abbots Bromley or the horned figure employed in the popular skimmity ride as the target of public exposure and communal denouncement. As part of the general Renaissance moralising of Ovid's legends and an intricate ethical allegorising of their details, writers like Natalis Comes in his *Mythologiae* (Venice, 1581) and the Renaissance dictionaries of mythology explicated Actaeon's punishment as the wages of the sin of excessive physical passion, Actaeon's own libido eating him up, as it were, in the likeness of his hounds. The beastly degeneration is the result of animal passion; it is a slide-down in the great chain of being. This interpretation is the one adopted of the legend by Chapman in his 'Hymnus in Cynthiam', *The Shadow of Night*.[2] It is also the interpretation

1. *Mysteriously Meant: The Rediscovery of Pagan Symbolism and Allegorical Interpretation in the Renaissance* (Baltimore & London: John Hopkins University Press, 1970), p. 243.

2. *The Poems of George Chapman,* ed. Phyllis B. Barlett (London: OUP, 1941), pp. 35–9. See Douglas Bush, *Mythology and the Renaissance Tradition in English Poetry* (Minneapolis: the University of Minnesota Press, 1932), pp. 202–3, and Frances A. Yates, *The Occult Philosophy in the Elizabethan Age* (London: Routledge & Kegan Paul, 1979), p. 56.

adduced by the most well-known English Emblem writer, G. Whitney.[3] Whitney makes Actaeon's degeneration and destruction an object-lesson in lust and the punishment it brings. The continental Emblem writers, prior to Whitney, however, read the moral differently. To Sambucus, Actaeon's fate is a warning against the kind of wasteful expenditure and ostentation practised by those who are overfond of hunting, and to Alciati, it is a warning against the dangers of harbouring stolen property or criminals.[4] But the most enterprising and complex of the interpretations of the myth is Giordano Bruno's, put forward in his treatise of Neoplatonist love mystique, *De Gli Eroici Furori* (1584).[5] As the two modern English explicators of Bruno's almost visionary interpretation, what the myth connotes is the mystique of the love quest, the ultimate pursuit of the ideal Divine through its reflection in earthly love, the love of woman, the hunt for the vestiges of reflected Divine Glory on earth and the viewing of a glimpse of it by Actaeon in his act of seeing Diana bathing and finally, the pursuer of love becoming in the process the quarry pursued, an identification or at-one-ment achieved at the cost of death and destruction after which, and in fact in and through which, alone, according to the Neoplatonist assumption the fulfilment and unification in love are to be had. This mystical interpretation unfolded in Bruno's treatise, and also one very central to the main thesis of the work, which was published in England and dedicated to Sir Philip Sidney, just as the other moral interpretations of the Actaeon legend and its popular associations as well, could not have altogether escaped Shakespeare's notice or knowledge. Given Shakespeare's thorough mastery of the ins and outs of the love convention in general, evident in his subtle

---

3. *A Choice of Emblems,* Leyden, 1586, p. 15.

4. See Henry Green, *Shakespeare and the Emblem Writers* (London: Tribner & Co,1870), pp. 275–9, for these interpretations.

5. L. Williams, trans. Giordano Bruno's *De Gli Eroici Furori* under the title *The Heroic Enthusiasts*, 2 vols. (London: George Redway, 1887), Vol. 1, pp. 90–120. Frances A. Yates, *Lull and Bruno: Collected Essays,* Vol. 1 (London: Routledge and Kegan Paul, 1982), Ch. 5, pp. 180–209, and her *Giordano Bruno and the Hermetic Tradition* (London, 1964). John Charles Nelson, *Renaissance Theory of Love: The Context of Giordano Bruno's 'Eroici Furori'* (New York: Columbia University Press, 1958), Ch. 3, pp. 163–233, esp. p. 206.

handling of it, and given the 'half-ironical' dallying with Petrarchan and Neoplatonist assumptions and theories about love he makes in his *Sonnets*, *Venus and Adonis* and the comedies in general, and especially in *Love's Labour's Lost, A Midsummer Night's Dream* and also in *Romeo and Juliet,* Shakespeare's acquaintance with Bruno's interpretation of the Actaeon story can hardly be considered unlikely, though, as will be seen, his probable use of interpretation is 'more-than-half' ironical.

Besides making direct reference to the Actaeon idea in two of his plays, Shakespeare employs the idea allusively in terms of word and stage image alike in some other plays and exploits the associations of the Actaeon myth in similar fashion in yet other plays. To be sure, scholars between them have paid attention to many of these instances of Shakespeare's use of the legend individually. But the two scholars, the redoubtably learned John M. Steadman ('Falstaff as Actaeon: A Dramatic Emblem', *Shakespeare Quarterly*, 14 (1963), 231–44) and the medieval scholar Richard Leighton Greene,[6] in their illuminating analyses of the two episodes have paid only incidental or passing attention to other Shakespearian uses of the myth and hence had little occasion to point out the variety of these uses.[7] Moreover, in their preoccupation with one or the other of the interpretations or associations of the myth already cited by me earlier in this chapter, they fail to take note of the other possible interpretations of the myth. In short, Steadman's is a particularly 'learned', moral interpretation of Falstaff's appearance towards the close of *The Merry Wives of Windsor* in an Actaeon-like state with the 'buck's head upon him' (the First Quarto stage-direction) and his humiliation, and interpretation which pays little attention to the popular associations of the stage-picture and the stage-event in spite of its commendable alertness to the visual dimensions of the scene. At the other end of the spectrum, as it were, is Greene's penetrating perception about the allusions to the old custom or rural spectacle

---

6. 'Hamlet's Skimmington' in *Evidence in Literary Scholarship: Essays in Memory of J.M. Osborn*, ed. Rene Wellek and Alvaro Ribeiro (Oxford: The Clarendon Press, 1979), p. 1–11.

7. Also James O. Wood, 'Intimations of Actaeon in *Julius Caesar*', *Shakespeare Quarterly*, 24 (1973), pp. 85–8.

of the skimmington ride he uncovers in the scene of the play-within-the-play of *Hamlet* (the resultant suggestion being one of Hamlet taking Claudius out for a skimmity ride and thus exposing his guilt and shame in public). But Greene takes no cognisance of the Actaeon myth and its meanings in the 'learned' or 'middle-brow' tradition nor does he point attention to a scene like the curious one in *As You Like It* (IV.ii) in which Jaques has the Second Lord put the stag's head on the head of the First Lord who has killed the animal and they lead a dance very reminiscent of the Abbots Bromley horn dance. A brief examination of some of the Shakespearian scenes and situations concerned will at least help to synthesise the available findings and to see the typical inclusiveness and ambivalence which mark the playwright's deployment of the 'learned' and popular significances of the Actaeon myth in particular dramatic contexts and stage situations.

To proceed chronologically, apart from Shakespeare's incorporation of the associations of the Actaeon myth in the narrative structure and movement of *Venus and Adonis* with its basic patterns of reversals between the hunter and the hunted, the first extended and relatively straight use of the legend is to be found in the hunting scenes (II.ii. and II.iii) of *Titus Andronicus*. As Tamora the Gothic but now Roman queen and Aaron the Moor go through their assignation as the hunt is on 'in another part of the wood', and the villainous lot including the sons of Tamora plot their ruthless outrages on Bassianus and Lavinia, and Martius and Quintus too, Bassianus and Lavinia come their way; the two victims walk into the trap though they believe for a moment, and rightly, that they have caught Tamora and Aaron in their moment of illicit contact.

Enter *Bassinus* and *Lavinia*

Bassianus Who have we here? Rome's royal empress,
Unfurnish'd of her well-beseeming troop?
Or is it Dian, habited like her,
Who hath abandoned her holy groves,
To see the general hunting in this forest?

Tamora Saucy controller of our private steps!
Had I the power that some say Dian had,
Thy temples should be planted presently
With horns, as was Actaeon's; and the hounds

Should drive upon the new-transform'd limbs,
Unmannerly intruder as thou art!

Lavinia Under your patience, gentle empress,
'Tis thought you have a goodly gift in homing;
And to be doubted that your Moor and you
Are singled forth to try experiments,
Jove shield your husband from his hounds today!
'Tis pity they should take him for a nag.[8]

Titus Andronicus, (II.iii. 55–71)

The action of hunting including the hunting down of victims and the imagery of hunting and trapping develop in these two scenes of the play correspondences and mutual transferences which make for an active intercommunication of the 'figures-in words' and 'figures-in-action'. But it is no simple one-to-one correspondence or transfer between word and action. It is more of a deliberate ironical counterpoint between what is said and how it is said by way of speech on the one side and what is done and seen by way of action on the other—an effect of emblematic distancing and a technique of the play highlighted by Eugene Waith: 'The metamorphosis of violence in *Titus Andronicus*', *Shakespeare Survey,* 10 (1957, 39–49). In the 'flying' between Tamora, and Bassianus and Lavinia the Actaeon references are employed as though for mythological decoration and an ornamental presentation of the mutual antipathy between good and evil. Yet the bitter, all-too-real joke about Actaeon's and the cuckold's horns is driven home.[9] So is the equally bitter irony of Tamora being compared with Diana. Soon after these speeches, Bassianus is destroyed, and Lavinia is outraged and mangled, not unlike the way Actaeon was. The grim irony of the situation is enhanced by, and in fact owes itself in good part to the considerably innovative deployment of the Actaeon references.

8. The Shakespeare quotations in this article are from the Oxford Shakespeare, ed. W.J. Craig.

9. The cornuted husband is described earlier in the play thus: like Sir Actaeon he, with Ringwood at thy heels' (II.i. 120), and 'a secure and wilful Actaeon' (III. ii. 45).

Although Actaeon is not directly invoked in the hilarious concluding scene of *The Merry Wives of Windsor,*[10] it is forceful dramatisation of the Emblematic and perhaps to no less degree the popular associations of the Actaeon story. Steadman's article already cited is the definitive exposition of the Emblematic aspects of the scene; but while the motifs of beastly degeneration and the closing in of the attackers (the 'fairies' in place of the hounds in the Actaeon story) are fully brought out in Steadman's explication, we should not miss the fairly obvious irony of the use in reverse of the popular identification of Actaeon's horns with the proverbial horns of the cuckold with Falstaff's attempt to cuckold the citizens in his horned state bringing about his discomfiture. Moreover, the whole orientation of the scene, its pattern of action and movement is suggestive of folk customs and practices, and certain festive observances like 'hoodenings', mummings, dances around trees or 'yclepings'[11] and songs carried on at night with torches and tapers. The exposure of Falstaff the old lecher, though by no means an inamiable one, and the physical punishments he undergoes not the least of these being his having to lie prone (with no 'levers to lift' him) and the public humiliation he faces, do remind one of the skimmington ride performances put on to expose moral offenders in the village or town community; the target of attack was presented in the form of an effigy or an impersonator taking the guise of a horned beast often the deer, as Richard Leighton Greene shows in his article on *Hamlet* referred to earlier.

The scene in *As You Like It* (IV. ii) in which the First Lord is made to wear the head of the stag killed by him on his head as a trophy and to join in a dance and song is reminiscent of the horn dance such as that of Abbots Bromley; but the whole company after crowning the First Lord with the deer's (and the cuckold) horns at Jaques's instance would appear to close in on the figure with the deer's head and to 'bring him home' (ll. 10–15). The visual

10. The problem is that it does not have the *effect* of a public exposure and condemnation of Claudius. It convinces Hamlet and Horatio, the two only, of Claudius's guilt, if at all Hamlet really required to be convinced.

11. A brief account of these customs may be found in P.H. Ditchfield, *Vanishing England* (London: Methuen & Co, 1910), pp. 377–9.

impression presented at this point is that of an Actaeon-like horned figure, and the closing in on him by the company of 'forester-lords' is reminiscent of the 'Actaeon-deer' being closed in on in the illustrations of Ovid or the Emblem books. Janet Spens linked the scene to the Abbots Bromley dance and also this scene and the play to the Robin Hood play which were in evidence on the London stage in the closing years of the sixteenth century.[12] In Anthony Munday's near-contemporary Robin Hood play, *The Death of Robert, Earl of Huntington* 'after an off-stage deer hunt there comes Friar Tuck, carrying a stag's head, dancing'.[13]

The most familiar instance of Shakespearian allusion to the Actaeon myth also seems to be the one in which Shakespeare touches upon the ambivalence of interpretative meanings attaching to the myth.

Curio Will you go hunt, my lord?

Duke What, Curio?

Curio The hart.

Duke Why, so I do, the noblest that I have.
O! when mine eyes did see Olivia first
Methought she purg'd the air of pestilence.
That instant was I turn'd into a hart,
And my desires, like fell and cruel hounds,
E'er since pursue me.

(*Twelfth Night,* I.i. 16–24)

Douglas Bush wondered whether Shakespeare was making a conscious allusion to the Actaeon legend or merely indulging in a casual conceit.[14] The delicate and intricate play with the love convention, both Petrarchan and Neoplatonist, which Shakespeare makes in *Twelfth Night* and the way the play as a whole subsumes and surpasses the sophistications, the unrealities and also in a sense

12. *Elizabethan Drama* (New York: Russell and Russell reprint, 1970, originally published by Methuen, 1922), pp. 84–5; also in her *Shakespeare and the Tradition*, 1916.

13. I.ii. in *Dodsley's Old English Plays,* ed. W.C. Hazlitt, Vol. 8 (London: Reeves and Turner, 1874), p. 231.

14. *Mythology and the Renaissance Tradition in English Poetry,* p. 71, n. 11.

the indispensability of the 'game' of love and the mystique of love and virginity should alert us to the need for a multiple response to Orsino, his utterances and his predicament in the opening scene.[15] This figure is no caricature, nor is he a satirical portrait of one who is (in the often-resorted-to application of an Augustinian phrase) merely in love with being in love. It is *he* who uses nearly the whole gamut of the range of the fairly transparent conceits of love in this scene and later. The waggish 'character-mongering' critic who wondered if Orsino had ever so much as set eyes on Olivia or bestirred himself enough to step out of his palace to fall in love at first sight, let alone to pay court to Olivia, may have been right. Among the marks to know a lover exhibited by the Duke is a certain familiarity with the refinements as well as the commonplace elements of the tradition of love. The ambivalence or doubleness of response towards the character, which Shakespeare evokes, perhaps also invites us, his spectators and readers, to consider whether Orsino—so to speak—, in the process of perfecting himself as a paradigm of the love melancholic, had not also read his Bruno on 'The Heroic Enthusiasts' of love or at least got wind of his and other interpretations of Actaeon. The conceits quoted earlier may be taken as clichés put appropriately into Orsino's mouth; but the aspiration towards and also the cultivation if not the actual attainment of high sophistication in the form and convention of love can hardly be denied in his case. In and through Orsino and this particular utterance of his, Shakespeare perhaps makes contact with Bruno's ameliorative interpretation of Actaeon; the Emblematic degenerative interpretation would have little application in the Orsino context.

The ubiquitous 'heart–hart' pun apart, Orsino conceives and expresses his 'feeling' for Olivia in terms which would seem to go a little beyond the commonplaces of the Petrarchan paradigm and suggest the stance at least of fervour and 'enthusiasm' associated with the kind of love idealist envisaged in Bruno's treatise. The pride of place accorded to the eye as the purest in the hierarchy of the senses in the Florentine Neoplatonist love theories, is tacitly

15. C.T. Prouty, '*Twelfth Night*' in *Manner and Meaning in Shakespeare,* ed. B.A.W. Jackson (Shannon: Irish University Press, 1961) is an exploration of the relation of the play to the 'game'.

accepted by Orsino, and the attributes of *noblesse*, the purity and purificatory power of Olivia work the opposite way from the Petrarchan cliché of love as the pestilence or the plague all too easily caught. What is more, the moment he 'had sight' of Olivia, as Actaeon 'had sight' of Diana, he felt the longing for unification with the divine object of his love quest which started at the moment and was for divine transcendental perfection, the vestiges of which are found reflected in the image of earthly love. It is the drive towards the at-one-ment of the quester with what he seeks that converts the hunter into the hunted, as it happened in Actaeon's case, in Bruno's reading of the myth. The tenor of Orsino's utterance is more or less the same. The same tone at least filters through in Orsino's words and posture. Shakespeare does it all at least half at the expense of Duke Orsino and of the mystique of Neoplatonism in general and that of Bruno in particular.

How reminiscential in some of its imagery and circumstances the Dumbshow and the Mousetrap scene in Hamlet (III.ii) is of the skimmington-ride and the exposure to public shame of the sexual offender it was calculated to affect has been well brought out by Richard Leighton Greene. The imagery Greene bases his suggestion on is that of the horned deer (the imagery of 'a hunted male deer and of a pack of pursuing hounds', R.L. Greene, p.2) as a covert likeness for Claudius, with an implicit approximation of Claudius to an Actaeon figure. The idea of moral indictment and chastisement it entails has its reference to the Emblematic ethical interpretation of Actaeon as much as to the folk custom of the skimmington-ride. It is in consonance with the animal references used by Hamlet elsewhere in the play in relation to Claudius ('a satyr', I.ii. 140; 'a rat', II.iv. 23' 'a paddock, . . . bat . . . gib', III.iv. 190). The scene serves to corroborate the general impression given by Shakespeare's drama that it can effortlessly fuse suggestions emanating from apparently heterogeneous sources like the courtly, the learned–theological, the ethico–philosophical and the popular cultural and folk traditions into a homogeneous whole. If to Greene the scene carries associations of a skimmity ride, another scholar John C. Doebler who interprets some of the plays in terms of what he calls their iconic imagery finds in the scene of the Mousetrap a structural undergirding of the Augustinian idea of

God and Christ trapping Satan as if with a mousetrap and of the translation of the idea in the iconographical tradition (like the example of the Merode altarpiece).[16] It is Shakespeare's capacity to move in several worlds of cultural reference with equal ease and thus make the structure and texture of his plays a true interweave of these that gives room for both the 'tropical' and topical interpretation of the scene by Greene in relation to the folk tradition on the one hand and the 'tropical' ('trapically', the First Quarto reading; 'tropically', the Folio reading, *Hamlet*, III.ii. 249–50) interpretation by Doebler in relation to theology and iconography on the other.

There are indeed reminiscences of the Emblematic interpretation of the Actaeon story in the nemesis which overtakes Stephano, Trinculo and Caliban in *The Tempest* (IV.i.) as they are marching to execute their conspiracy against Prospero and are, in an anti-masque-like situation in the play, hunted down and out by a pack of hounds, disguised spirits, set on by Ariel with Prospero watching the whole show remaining invisible. The degradation of Stephano and Trinculo into an animal state in spite of Caliban's immediately preceding, incredulous apotheosis of the pair into the status of gods is well suggested in their scenes in the play. Prospero pulls himself up short, reminded all of a sudden of the advance of the conspirators. Ariel, however, has driven the trio hard enough so that they are all but drowned in a cesspool. They appear all wet, quite a pointed visual contrast to the mysterious way in which earlier in the play the garments of the shipwrecked king Alonso and his party as they come ashore are in a state of 'not a blemish, but fresher than before' (I.ii. 218–9). The trio yield to the temptation of the 'glistering apparel' hung out by Ariel, and the two men, though not Caliban, are guilty of theft. It is then that they are hunted down and driven out by the spirit-hounds, a condign punishment for their lustful designs on Miranda and their theft including the usurpation they plan as the mythographer Natalis Comes and the Emblem writers interpreted Actaeon's fate.

The range of the situations in which Shakespeare in the course of his plays, either directly or indirectly, invokes the image of

---

16. *Shakespeare's Speaking Pictures: Studies in Iconic Imagery* (Albuquerque: the University of New Mexico Press, 1974), pp. 96–105.

Actaeon is considerably wide. More remarkable is the range of variations Shakespeare makes on the myth and on the interpretative ideas and contexts which had come to surround the legend in his day. It may not be an exaggeration to say that Shakespeare in his use of the myth 'out-Ovids Ovid' by way of *his* metamorphoses of Actaeon. It was, after all, not for nothing that a contemporary of Shakespeare[17] as early as 1598, thought that the soul of Ovid was reincarnated in Shakespeare.

17. Francis Meres in his *Palladio Tamia.* See E.K. Chambers, *William Shakespeare*, Vol. 2, p. 194.

5

Books at Play

Books figure in Shakespeare's plays in various ways. There are the utterances by characters by a way of discussion on books and bookish learning in early plays such as *Love's Labour's Lost* (I.i) and *The Taming of the Shrew* (I.i.17–40), and in a late play such as *The Tempest* Shakespeare invokes books as the source of Prospero's magic and makes Caliban underscore the point shrewdly enough.[1]

Caliban There thou mayst brain him
Having first seiz'd his books . . .

. . . Remember
First to possess his books, for without them
He's but a sot, as I am; nor hath not
One spirit to command.

(*The Tempest*, III.ii.89, 91–4)

There is a fairly recurrent use of the book as metaphor or verbal image, especially for the human face or heart.[2] There are a few but very few instances of books and their authors being cited as authority by a character in support of what is being said, just short of

1. All citations from Shakespeare in this chapter refer to the text in *The Riverside Shakespeare*, ed. G. Blakemore Evans (Boston, 1974).
2. For example,
Lady Macbeth Your face, my thane, is a book where
Men may read strange matters.
(*Macbeth*, I.v. 62–3)
Olivia . . . where lies your text?
Viola In Orsino's bosom.

quoting chapter and verse, for example, Lord Say in *Henry VI*, Pt. 2 (IV.vii. 59–64) and Hector in *Troilus and Cressida* (II.ii. 164–7). Besides these three ways of invoking books, there is another significant figuring of books in the plays, the book as a stage hand-property and visual image, which captures attention, generates dramatic exchange and helps to build dramatic situation and movement. Here, we shall focus on the function of the book as visual stage image and its implications in the plays. As part of the background it may be kept in mind that the manuscript which was used as the theatrical prompt-copy was itself known in the parlance of Shakespeare's day as the book and the stage-manager was known as the bookholder, and indeed the play-text was termed 'book' from the time it left the hands of the playwright, as in the theatre and also at the stage of licensing and subsequent printing. The idea, it may be noted in this connection, has come to be emphasised in recent times that the books of Shakespeare, the play-texts, are not to be thought of in terms of any inviolable canonical, authorial fixity of status but in a manner which sufficiently allows for the role of theatrical collaboration and give-and-take in the formation of the play-text as the play-book and as the subsequently printed play in its Quarto and Folio versions. These factors will serve to reinforce an idea of the interplay, in several senses, of book and play as we consider the role of the book which figures as a physical or material phenomenon of stage property and as a stage presence in several plays.

A book is brought on as hand property which makes its presence felt in plays such as *Titus Andronicus* (IV.i. 1–77), *The Taming of the Shrew* (III.i, also I.ii. 137), *Henry VI, Pt. 3* (III.i.12), *Richard III* (III.vii. 95–108), *Julius Caesar* (IV.iii. 252 and 272–7), *Troilus and Cressida* (III.iii. 92–125), *Hamlet* (II.ii 167–8 and 191–204 and

---

Olivia In his bosom. In what chapter of his bosom?
Viola To answer by the method, in the first of his heart.
Olivia O, I have read it, it is heresy . . .
(*Twelfth Night*, I.v. 220–7)

See Ernest R. Curtius, 'The Book as Symbol in Shakespeare', *European Literature and the Latin Middle Ages*, trans. William R. Trask (New York, 1953), 332–40.

III.i.43) and *Cymbeline* (II.ii. 44–6). In these examples Shakespeare takes care to call attention to the property book in question, and the appearance of the book contributes to the ongoing drama, often both in the immediate and in the total context of the play. Also, the onstage presence of a book, the script as book or a playbook is implied in the rehearsal and the actual play-within-the-play scenes in *A Midsummer Night's Dream* and *Love's Labour's Lost*.

To take three examples which go together first, in the one, Richard Duke of Gloucester in *Richard III* (III.vii) in the run-up to his coronation as King, which he stage-manages with consummate Machiavellianism, comes to give audience thus: *Enter Richard (of Gloucester) aloft, between two Bishops* (s.d. III.vii.93). In the second example, ironically enough, it is the near-saintly King Henry VI, who gets killed by Richard Duke of Gloucester later in *Henry VI, Pt. 3*, who appears with a prayer book in hand (III.i.12). Henry VI has entered the English countryside from his exile in Scotland in disguise with the fond hope of a pastoral life of devotion *incognito* only to be found out and caught all too quickly, by a couple of deer-park keepers. In the third example of this kind, Polonius in *Hamlet* (III.i.43) thrusts a book of prayer in Ophelia's hands and bids her keep reading it as party of his scheme of 'loosing' his daughter to Hamlet for an encounter with him to be watched over by Claudius, Gertrude and himself. In these cases of the use of a book of prayer or the Book of books, the Bible, the common base is the received emblematic suggestion of the piety and devotion of the person appearing with book in hand. But what issues from Shakespeare's use of the visual signal of book in hand in all these cases is the dramatic effect of the ironical variations which the playwright makes on the conventional emblematic meaning. With King Henry VI the book in the hand is a direct enough marker of the devoutness of the king. But, lacking as he does kingly sagacity and capability, he becomes a hapless victim of *real politik* and miserably loses out in the power game. The unavailing nature of his devotion is part of the 'the true tragedy of . . . the good king', to adopt the play's Quarto title phrase, which is forcefully encapsulated in the episode. In the case of Richard Duke of Gloucester's ostentatiously unostentatious appearance, book in hand, in accordance with the script set and orchestrated by him and his colluder Buckingham earlier in the scene

(III.vii. 46–50), the hypocritical assumption of the garb of piety is much to the fore.

Mayor	See where his Grace appears, 'tween two clergymen.
Buckingham	Two props of virtue for a Christian prince, To stay him from the fall of vanity; And see, a book of prayer in his hand— True ornaments to know a holy man.

(*Richard III,* III.vii.95–9)

What interestingly comes through, as the suggestive element in this particular situation with all the more force, as in Richard's play-acting in general in the play, is the all but virtuosic relish of his in playing the role of the pious fraud. The book serves as a telling prop in this regard.[3] Giving the cue to Ophelia to 'read on this book' after putting it into her hands, Polonius himself makes a point of commenting on the put-up nature of the show, and his comment indeed 'catches the conscience' of King Claudius. This is much before the play of the Mousetrap, and leads him to make a significant confessional aside about his guilty deed. Claudius's statement is a clear signal to the spectator that the Ghost is an 'honest ghost' which should be taken at its word.

The play with book and book lesson in *The Taming of the Shrew* (III.i) is another variation on the use of the book for an ulterior purpose. The Latin text on which Lucentio gives Bianca a lesson is Ovid's *Heroides* which he makes an excuse of for his lesson in the Art of Love of the other Ovid. Apart from the comicity of such language lessons in Shakespeare in general (without a book in the

3. The six quarto editions of *Richard III* omit the two lines

    And see, a book of prayer in his hand
    True ornaments to know a holy man.

   But since they retain Buckingham's lines to Richard earlier in the scene

    And look you get a prayer-book in your hand
    And stand between two churchmen, good my lord—
    For on that ground I'll make a holy descant

There is no doubt that the staging included the book. The quartos' is perhaps a cut to shorten a very long play in the Folio version which is closer to what Shakespeare wrote; the quarto is only a little less long, though.

other cases), the impression conveyed in the present case is that the text can become a mere pretext, and it is also that if wooing by the book could take the form of sonneteering as in *Love's Labour Lost* it could take the form of reading sub-texts into the text under the pretence of reading. In the course of the lesson Lucentio's mind, rather Shakespeare's, goes to Ovid's masterpiece *Metamorphoses* from his *Heroides,* a work so central, at least in Golding's translation, to the Elizabethan and Shakespearian imagination and sensibility in a cross-associational reference to it (III.i. 53–4). Shakespeare's really no small grammar school Latin would have made Ovid accessible to him in the original.

It is hardly surprising then that among the books which Shakespeare brings on as hand properties the clearly identifiable ones are Ovid's. It is *Metamorphoses* which makes its appearance thus with prominent emphasis in the early play *Titus Andronicus* and once, but in a telling context in the late play *Cymbeline*. As has often been pointed out, the Ovidian spirit and influence is as strong (if not stronger) as the Senecan element in *Titus Andronicus*. What lends the play its quality is its 'metamorphosis of violence' (in Eugene Waith's phrase), of its Senecan horror piled on horror's head, through depiction in a vein of sensitised Ovidian conception and formalised presentation and of ornamental, rhetorical elaboration. Ovid's *Metamorphoses* in general and the myth of Tereus's rape and glossotomy of Philomel, his sister-in-law, in particular are remembered and alluded to several times in the play. Also the revenge of Titus on Tamora and her sons who rape his daughter Lavinia and cut off her tongue and hands is closely patterned on that of Tereus's wife Progne on Tereus for the rape of her sister Philomela. What is more, it is through the instrumentality of the book of *Metamorphoses* brought onstage as hand property in lurid fashion that Lavinia, raped and terribly maimed, with her tongue and both the hands cut off thus making it impossible for her to reveal the identity of the perpetrators of the horrid deeds, is at long last able to communicate and make Titus and her uncle Marcus discover the fact (IV.i). Lavinia enters giving chase to her nephew Lucius as he runs from her carrying a load of books for study. As he drops the books in the process, Lavinia searches for and picks up the boy's copy of Ovid's *Metamorphoses* which is what she is desperately after now. Frantically turning the leaves with her stumps, she lights on the page which depicts the rape of Philomela. Through her gestures and gesticulations, Titus and Marcus are able to understand what she yearns to reveal. The scene of the rape of Philomela in the midst of a hunting expedition in the woods is exactly like that of the rape of Lavinia.

Marcus See, brother, see how she cotes the leaves.

Titus Lavinia, wert thou surpris'd, sweet girl?
Ravish'd and wrong'd as Philomela was?
Forc'd in the ruthless, vast, and gloomy words?
See, see!
Ay, such a place there is where we did hunt
(O had we never hunted there!)
Pattern'd by that the poet here describes,
By nature made for murthers and rapes.
(*Titles Andronicus*, IV.i.50–9)

Of course, on the Shakespearian stage, any book, not necessarily a copy of Ovid's *Metamorphoses,* could have served as prop, as in all other cases. This is so if only because there was no scope on that stage for anything like a close-up of a small object like a book, especially in the context of the not-so-strong sight-lines of the relatively large stage and large theatre. What happens in *Titus Andronicus* from one angle is that in the play world as a heterocosm of life is literal reproduction of both myth and literature. Except that in Ovid's myth the revelation is made by the victim through a tapestry woven by her, Lavinia in the absence of hands uses the printed words in the book in lieu of the spoken word from her. On Marcus's suggestion, she writes the names of the wrongdoers on sand with a stick held in her mouth and guided by her stumps.[4] From another angle, Ovid's book turns out to be a speaking book and something also of a book of revelation. Indeed the revelation takes the form of an

4. The device of writing on sand may owe something to the practice which seems to have obtained in rural schools in Elizabethan England of pupils learning the alphabet and arithmetic by writing on sand. See J. G. McManaway, *The Review of English Studies*, 9 (1958), pp. 172–3. The practice, in fact, was not uncommon in rural primary schools in India till the early and middle twentieth century.

interesting anamorphism of the printed, written and spoken words. It is in line with the different kinds of use to which Ovid's book was put in the period. The classical pagan myths so memorably commemorated by Ovid also came to be both moralised and Christanised as part of the elaborate enterprise of Renaissance European mythography in poetry, drama, painting and thought.

In *Cymbeline* the villain Iachimo after smuggling himself into Imogen's bedchamber in a Trojan horse of a box ostensibly to be left in safe custody there steals out of it at night to do his voyeuristic 'blazon' of the items in the chamber and body of Imogen fast asleep, a mole on her left breast and all. He sneakily unfastens her bracelet to be produced to Posthumus as false trophy of his supposed sexual conquest of her. Iachimo specifies the details of the book Imogen has been reading and has left off with the leaf turned down at a crucial point in the book narrative before going to sleep.

> She hath been reading late
> The tale of Tereus, here the leaf's turned down
> When Philomela gave up.
>
> (*Cymbeline,* II.ii. 44–6)

It is Ovid's book, *Metamorphoses,* again, in all possibility some book present onstage as prop, just as the arras and wall hangings which decorated the stage façade of the Globe could have served for such furnishings of the chambers catalogued by Iachimo. We should appreciate the suggestive fit between the book and its crucial event of the rape of Philomela on the one side and the exact context in which Shakespeare brings it in. What Iachimo busies himself with at the moment is nothing short of a metaphorical or surrogate rape, except that it ultimately leads not to tragic revenge but to tragicomedic restoration. Such a pronounced use of Ovid's book as Shakespeare makes in his plays stands testimony to his deep absorption of Ovid and of the Ovidian spirit and the hold of Ovid on the Elizabethan literary mind. After all, that pioneer Shakespeare aficionado Francis Meres (*Palladis Tamia*, 1598) went so far as to suggest that Ovid's soul metamorphosed into Shakespeare's.

The unnamed books which spring into a short but intriguing presence onstage in *Troilus and Cressida* (III.iii. 92–125) and in *Hamlet* (II.ii. 167–8 and 191–204), as hand-held property, especially the former, serve as a striking example of the manifold ways the world has with books and books have with the world. Let us consider the *Troilus and Cressida* occurrence of the property book first.

Achilles . . . Here is Ulysses,
I'll interrupt his reading.
How now, Ulysses?

Ulysses Now, great Thetis' son!

Achilles What are you reading?
A strange fellow here
Writes me that man how dearly ever parted,
How much in having, or without or in,
Cannot make boast to have that which he hath,
Nor feels not what he owes, but by reflection;
As when his virtues, aiming upon others,
Heat them, and they retort that heat again
To the first (giver).

Achilles This is not strange, Ulysses.
The beauty that is borne here is the face
The bearer knows not, but commends itself
To others' eyes; nor doth the eye itself,
That most pure spirit of sense, behold itself,
Nor going from itself; but eye to eye opposed,
Salutes each other with each others' form;
For speculation turns not to itself,
Till hath travell'd and is mirrored there
Where it may set itself. This is not strange at all.

Ulysses I do not strain at the position—
It is familiar—but at the author's drift
Who in his circumstance expressly proves
That no man is lord of any thing,
Though in and of him there be much consisting,
Till he communicate his parts to others;
Nor doth he of himself know them for aught,
Till he behold them formed in th' applause
Where th' are extended; who like an arch
reverb'rate
The voice again, or like a gate of steel,
Fronting the sun, receives and renders back
His figure and his heat. I was much rapt in this,

And apprehended here immediately
Th' unknown Ajax.

(*Troilus and Cressida,* III.iii. 92–125)

Ulysses carries and pores on the book, the whole exercise being a stratagem of his calculated plan to exert a subtle pressure on Achilles to pull him out of his sulk in his tent and to make him come forward to meet Hector's challenge. Ulysses's citation and annotation of the author is a subterfuge to rouse Achilles into action, and Ulysses gives the screw its final turn by evoking a picture of the unknown Ajax's vauntingly bestirring himself towards the exploit of taking up Hector's gauntlet. Ulysses clinches the issue further through his subsequent discourse on Time (III.iii.145–89), the second bravura utterance, aria-like, of his discourse after his earlier speech on Degree (I.ii. 75–137) which is also an instance of a grand received idea, a master narrative being deployed towards a political end.

For all this, the idea which Ulysses quotes from his author and poses to ponder quizzically is a significant commonplace of Platonic and Neo-platonist philosophical thought, the axiomatic belief that a human being's gifts such as beauty, valour and talents of different kinds can realise themselves or even recognise themselves only through a process of inter-subjective and often mutual interaction. The idea is none the less true and important for its being a commonplace of thought of the times or for the characteristically Ulyssean manipulative use to which it is being put in the context. Editors suggest that Ulysses's author, whether a 'strange fellow' (in Ulysses's deliberately provocative characterisation of him) or 'not so strange' (according to Achilles the ready acceptor of the idea), could be Plato or Cicero or that the idea may be part of the general climate of opinion of the times with no specific author meant. However that be, Ulysses's play with the book is an object-lesson in the use of books for covert control and for a kind of smooth, ineluctable indoctrination and hegemonisation. It makes us wonder whether the postmodern perception that the book is an instrument of power in this sense and manner was not already Shakespeare's. He seems to have been aware of what a hegemonising agency could do with books even as he was well aware of the other uses of the book.

In *Hamlet* a property book is pressed into service the first time round in the hands of Hamlet (II.ii) before the item appears in Ophelia's hands (III.i) as she keeps 'reading on this book' at Polonius's instance when Hamlet enters to speak his most famous soliloquy.

Enter Hamlet, *reading on a book.*

Queen	But look where sadly the poor wretch comes reading.
Polonius	. . . what do you read, my lord?
Hamlet	Words, words, words.
Polonius	What is the matter, my lord?
Hamlet	Between who?
Polonius	I mean, the matter that you read, my lord.
Hamlet	Slanders, sir; for the satirical rogue says here that old men have grey beards, that their faces are wrinkled, their eyes purging thick amber, and plum-tree gum, and that they have a plentiful lack of wit, together with most weak hams; all of which, sir, though I most powerfully and potently believe, yet I hold it not honesty to have it thus set down, for yourself, sir, shall grow old as I am, if like a crab you could go backward.
Polonius	(*Aside*) Though this be madness, Yet there is method in't.

(*Hamlet,* II.ii. 168 and II.ii. 191–205)

The question is not so much whether the 'satirical rogue' which Hamlet reads and cites from is Juvenal or Stephano Guazzo *(Civil Conversation)* or Erasmus *(In Praise of Folly)* or some other book. Basically it is that Polonius's enquiry about what he is reading gives Hamlet another opportunity for satirical improvisation; he takes occasion as it comes time and again to play the satirist as he does to Ophelia on women in III.i. But there is more to it. True, Hamlet recounts the satirical author's portrait of old age somewhat like Jaques's portrayal of it in his Seven Ages of Man speech in *As you Like It* (III.vii. 157–66), and thus makes the cap fit old Polonius. But Hamlet takes care to undo the satire in riddling fashion even as he uses it, saying that it is not fair on the part of the author to set it down cynically thus. In the process young Hamlet, significantly, shows himself capable of placing himself in the old age situation which is that of his interlocutor. Due allowance made for the admixture of mad banter, deliberate or inevitable, we could see Hamlet changing places with Polonius in his imagination for the nonce with that much of empathy. Though Hamlet does say 'these tedious old fools!' as soon as Polonius starts leaving a few lines later, Hamlet's saying more 'no' than 'yes' to the satirist's attitude makes for an access of incipient outgoingness on his part especially when we consider how critics have diagnosed Hamlet to be too full of himself. His fascinated contemplation of old age and his half-tolerant, though still half-contemptuous view of it anticipates his contemplation of skulls in the graveyard scene towards the close of the play. Thus it forms part of the pattern of Hamlet's preoccupation with death, his 'death-consciousness'. A line of gradation may be traced from his contemplation of old age, provoked by the satirist's ridicule, to his final coming to terms with death.

In *Julius Caesar* towards the end of the quarrel scene (IV.iii) between Brutus and Cassius, there is a display of the book to some notable effect.

Brutus . . . .
Look, Lucius, here's the book I sought for so;
I put it in the pocket of my gown.
(*Julius Caesar,* IV.iii. 252–3)

and

Brutus . . . .
Let me see, let me see, is not the leaf turn'd down
Where I left reading. Here it is, I think.

Enter the Ghost of Caesar.

How ill this taper burns! Ha! Who comes here?
(*Julius Caesar,* IV.iii. 273–5)

As he settles for the night after his exchange and reconciliation with Cassius, Brutus looks for the book he has been reading and finds it in his own pocket. As Lucius, his boy, with sleep overpowering him, sings and plays on the lute for him, Brutus opens his book at the page where he had left off earlier. No sooner he does so than does appear as though on cue Caesar's ghost. In the atmosphere of eerie uneasiness and the guttering candle, as the sleeping Varro, Claudius and Lucius cry in their sleep, the ghost appears producing the impression that the opening of the book by Brutus conjures it up.

These examples occurring across the canon demonstrate Shakespeare's consummate theatrical art in evoking with the book effects of rich dramatic life and power. What is more, the examples are such as to bring home to the spectator or reader a recognition of the manifold roles of books in general and of the multiplicity of functions and purposes they serve. Books are a mode of revelation of different kinds and degrees. They could often serve as an instrument of power, a tool of manipulation and a means of hegemonisation which takes its target unawares as it were. While the book as speculative instrument is done justice to in the dramatist's way with it, he would seem to go much farther beyond and display an intuitive grasp of the use of books and knowledge with a hidden agenda as it is called, which phenomenon comes to be highlighted in postmodern thought and cultural criticism. It is no less important to note that Shakespeare was alive to other uses as well as what may be called the uselessness of books in certain situations. We do not know if Shakespeare got to hear about the use of his own book, his first fruit, *Venus and Adonis* mentioned in one of the *Parnassus* plays, by young gallants sleeping with a copy under the pillow. However, Shakespeare and young Shakespeare at that, was well aware of the unprofitability of book learning and citation of authority when it comes to brass tacks at times. In *Henry VI, Pt. 2* (IV.vii.) Lord Say, caught in the clutches of Jack Cade and his rebel gang, tries to reason with them and in order to placate them in an attempt to save his head he quotes from a school-text of the times, Julius Caesar's *Commentaries,* Caesar's praise of the country of Kent and its inhabitants, as Cade and his rebels are Kentish Londoners.

> Hear me speak, and bear me where you will.
> Kent, in the Commentaries Caesar writ,
> Is term'd the civill'st place of all his isle:
> Sweet is the country, because full of riches;

> The people liberal, valiant, active, wealthy,
> Which makes me hope you are not void of pity.
> (*Henry VI, Pt. 2.* IV.vii. 59–64)

But the fine words and their authority are entirely lost upon Cade and his men who are avowedly up in arms among other things to kill all the literates in the population, and Lord Say pays with his head.

Given such deep insights and an inclusive awareness on his part about the uses and impact of books, it is natural that Shakespeare exhibits enough signs, inevitably indirect, of reservations, if not a healthy skepticism about books. His attitude to books can be said to have a duality about it, as many things with Shakespeare would seem to have. Breathing as he did the Renaissance climate of enthusiasm for books, he knew enough of his books and brought so much more away from those books he knew than anyone else could ever dream of doing. It is not for nothing that T.S. Eliot said that Shakespeare could gather so much more about history from Plutarch's *Lives* (North's Plutarch) than all the books that the British Museum could supply. Shakespeare knew his many narrative and dramatic sources, the novellas and plays and the relevant non-dramatic poetry, Holinshed and Hall if not other chroniclers and Renaissance political writers, his predecessor and contemporary playwrights, Seneca, Cintho and Guarini if not Euripides in translation and Plutarch. He knew his Spenser and Chaucer and thinkers like Montaigne, and his grammar school education and later reading familiarised him among other things with Horace, Cicero, Ovid and perhaps also some Renaissance Italians and Neoplatonists such as Giordano Bruno. He knew how to take what he wanted from travel writing, ephemeral literature, instruction manuals and encyclopedic compilations and such curious lore as Harsnelt on witchcraft and exorcism and Mouffet on sericulture. Most of all, his familiarity with the Book, the Bible (among other Bibles especially the turns of phrase and idiom as well as the thought in the early English translations, Tyndale and Coverdale), and his absorption of these fed unobtrusively into the plays and their idiom. And, after all, for long the Bible and Shakespeare were paired as books of premier status in the Anglophone world.

But if Shakespeare borrowed he repaid with usury. He is no bookish playwright like Ben Jonson or Webster whose writing in his plays is a thickly inlaid mosaic of reminiscences and quotations, buried and overt. It is interesting that the plays such as *Titus Andronicus* and the *Taming of the Shrew* and characters such as Brutus and Hamlet though not exactly Ulysses and Imogen (in which cases Shakespeare invokes the book as a tiny stage property), have something academic about them. But Shakespeare himself, besides his reading, would have acquired a number of ideas and perceptions through a process of cultural osmosis in whatever contacts and conversations he had with others, and all these contributed to the astounding exploration of endless ideational possibilities, which marks the plays. Nor should we forget that it was his intuitive genius which, as it explored and exploited the medium of the total language of the theatre comprising all its verbal, visual and material resources as well as its own inner resources, could achieve what it did achieve.

For all the quiet pride of Shakespeare in his profession of playhouse and playwright, he did not in his own lifetime want to collect them in a book. His interest and role in the publication of the play quartos and his sonnets was perhaps minimal or less than so. He did not want to call his plays 'works' as Ben Jonson did when he published his plays and poems in a collected edition in 1616, provoking a gibe against him over it from Thomas Heywood. Indeed, while the play manuscript was called 'book' in theatrical parlance and at the licensing and printing stage, the published plays were not recognised as real books then. They were books that were no books, for instance, for Thomas Bodley when he endowed the Bodleian Library at Oxford. The plays were not catalogued as part of the holdings though interestingly these found their way in there. Shakespeare did not take books too seriously though he recognised their value and the ramifications of their power and force. Berowne's statement in *Love's Labour Lost* (I.i. 86–7):

> Small have continual plodders ever won
> Save base authority from other men's books

taken together with the King of Navarre's remark in reply:

> How well he's read, to reason against reading!

may be taken as in a way indicating Shakespeare's point of view. The perception of the late Milton expressed through the words of Christ to Satan in *Paradise Regained* was also Shakespeare's:

> many books,
> Wise men have said are wearisome; who reads
> Incessantly, and to his reading brings not
> A spirit and judgement equal or superior
> (And what he brings what needs he elsewhere to seek?)
> Uncertain and unsettled still remains,
> Deep versed in books and shallow in himself
> Crude or intoxicate collecting toys
> And trifles for choice matters, worth a sponge,
> As children gathering pebbles on the shore.
> (Milton's *Paradise Regained,* Bk. 4, 321–30)

Milton echoes a sentiment as old as the Ecclesiastes, 12, but it is Milton's celebration of books in his early *Areopagitica* in which he describes a book as the 'precious life-blood of a master spirit' etc. that is oft-quoted.

As a code it may be noted that in *The Tempest* Prospero's final farewell to magic which he now would give up includes a farewell to his books, the books he relied on to learn and work his magic

> . . . deeper than did ever plummet sound
> I'll bury my book.

Not that we should resort to the old allegorisation of Prospero as Shakespeare and his bidding adieu to magic as Shakespeare's farewell to drama (there was no such at that point). But Prospero's cultivation and use of the book as power and his later rejection of it is broadly paradigmatic of Shakespeare's dual attitude to books, a recognition of their value and power and at the same time a keen alertness to the implication of the different uses of books and an attendant salutary mistrust of them. Certainly Shakespeare could use the book as a means of his theatre magic.

6

Stage Movement as Stage Moment

As in dance, and as in the celluloid medium, movement on the stage is part of drama's business, but as in modes of dance and in kinds of films the emphasis accorded to, and the quality and extent of resort to movement would differ from playwright to playwright and depend on the kind of drama. Shakespeare, characteristically enough, makes a judicious use of several kinds of movement of actors as characters across the stage in accordance with the requirement of dramatic action and encounter and with the exigencies of the stage. Movement is entailed in the battle scenes, those of swordplay, fencing and duelling, and in those few, not many, episodes of pursuit and chase, etc., which occur in the plays. There are also several instances of either conventional or formal movement such as characters 'passing o'er the stage' or moving in a procession, which are part of the theatrical spectacle. Indeed, in an early play like *Romeo and Juliet* (end of I. iv. Q2 s.d. 'They march about the stage'),[1] Shakespeare uses the old stage convention, as in Sanskrit drama, of a character or characters walking from one end of the stage to the other and back to indicate the movement or journey from one location to another. However, there is a class apart in the movement entailed in the entrances of characters and in the instances of address in the ongoing action of character to character in their developing relationship. There are many cases of such movement related to the entry of a character

1. References to the plays are keyed to *The Riverside Shakespeare*, Gen. Ed. G.B. Evans (Boston, 1974).

onto the stage and to encounter between characters, which make a dramatic point and striking theatrical sense. Such instances deserve a close look, and we may consider some examples.

We may do well to keep in mind a couple of factors as we look at instances. First, the largeness of the stage of the Globe or any Elizabethan public playhouse stage. The recent excavations around the site of the Globe prior to the building of the new replica Globe, and at the site of the Swan theatre, led us to wonder if the largeness of the dimensions of the theatre as a whole was not earlier exaggerated in historical reconstruction. Yet the relative largeness of the stage with reference to the auditorium is not put much in doubt. What such a large stage called for was a manipulation of its large coplanar space and, as occasion demanded, the space available in another plane, the upper acting level or the 'balcony' and 'windows'. Shakespeare exploits both horizontal and vertical space with implicit sureness of touch and with economy. We may not have authentic knowledge of by whom and how exactly the actual disposition or 'blocking' of characters and the siting of action on the stage was taken care of in the Elizabethan theatre. But we could surmise that a master playwright like Shakespeare could well anticipate the look a play will wear on the stage while writing it. He could thus incorporate in the play, almost effortlessly, the necessary and desirable movement, the accompanying utterances as well as the pattern of disposition of characters onstage in a visualisation of the staging. Generally the spot where the main action is set will be in a part fairly centrestage and closer to the auditorium than to the stage façade. It meant that a character had to enter the stage through one of the two or three doors and walk quite a number of paces to reach the action spot. It also meant that the door served as a reference-point to the action as entries and exits had to be through the doors for the most part. This exigency called for a number of 'look where he/she comes' sort of deictic indications in the speeches and also what are called 'covering' utterances necessary to preclude 'dead' or silent moments on the stage. But Shakespeare's 'covering' of entry movement by characters in many cases goes far beyond merely serving such theatrical utility, and becomes an artistic opportunity.

Secondly, we have to be wary of going by the marking of entrances of characters in the text in most of the older editions of the plays still in use. The more recent editors show greater alertness in the choice of the point of entry of characters and set an 'Enter' s.d. after what should be the right line. These latter do so because they pay more attention to the Folio and the Quarto s.ds. in this regard than their predecessors did. But the newer editors are not consistent in their attention to how the entry would have been staged in the Shakespearian theatre. The older editors, following the tradition starting with the pioneer eighteenth-century editors like Rowe who were victims of the fallacy of the proscenium stage assumptions and approach, used to mark the entry s.ds at the wrong points and repeated the 'within' directions of their predecessors which had been inserted with a naturalistic bias at places where these are not called for. At the same time, while mindfulness of the Folio and the Quarto marking of entries is generally of help in the matter, it is not without complication. At times, variations exist between the F and Q entry markings; besides, the entry markings in a particular Quarto or in the F lack in consistency of attention to actual staging practice, and hence turn out to be vague. In addition, there is the problem of the 'massed entries' directions in the F text of plays such as *The Two Gentlemen of Verona*, *The Merry Wives of Windsor* and *A Winter's Tale*, plays presumably printed from the version provided by the scribe Ralph Crane. Such 'massed entries' were probably based on the prompt-book used in the theatre where the prompter would list all the characters required for a particular scene irrespective of whether they enter at the beginning or at subsequent points, in order to keep them ready, leaving it to the individual actors to enter at the beginning or later in the scene according to their 'cue' which they would in any case know from their memorised 'parts'.

With these background factors in mind, we may start examining the movement involved in particular entries and in certain specific encounters of characters where drama results out of such movement in good measure. Taking up entry movement first, we may begin with some *Measure for Measure* entrances.

Duke . . . .
I pray you tell me, hath any body inquir'd
for me here today? Much upon this
time I promis'd here to meet.

Mariana You have not been inquir'd after, I have sat here all day.

Enter Isabel.

Duke I do constantly believe you. The
time is come even now. I shall crave
your forbearance a little. May be
I will call upon you anon for some
advantage to yourself.

Mariana I am always bound to you. *Exit.*

Duke Very well met, and welcome.
What is the news from this good deputy?

. . . .

Duke 'Tis well borne up.
I have not yet made known to Mariana

Enter Mariana.

A word of this. What ho, within, come forth!
I pray you be acquainted with this maid,
She comes to do you good.

(*Measure for Measure,* IV.i. 16–27, 47–51)

As the Duke is in conversation with Mariana, Isabel makes her appearance through one of the stage doors at l. 20, but the Duke meets her only at l. 25 at which line Mariana makes her exit evidently through another door. The Duke had been waiting for Isabel to arrive and meet Mariana and give her details about the assignation with Isabel which Angelo has planned for the night. The details, it is interesting to note, are made known to the audience by Shakespeare through Isabel's report to the Duke-friar, and not through the private meeting of Isabel with Mariana who, according to the 'bed-trick' planned by the Duke, would take Isabel's place. That meeting takes place offstage. After listening to Isabel, the Duke-friar calls forth Mariana with 'What ho, within! come forth' at l. 49. But Mariana, in F's direction, has already made her entry at l. 48 for the reason that the boy-actor would take that much space of time at least to pace across to the Duke and Isabel. Even a recent editor such as the Riverside one takes the s.d. for Mariana's entry forward after l. 49, following Rowe. However, in the non-illusionistic or conventionalistic Shakespearian theatre the 'within' need not literally be within the stage. Mariana is already visible on the stage. The momentary glimpse that the spectator has of both Isabel and Maria first at a distance from each other leads up to their coming close to each other in their first brief onstage meeting and their exit together to settle the details and precautions relating to the 'bed-trick'.

Provost I would do more than that if more were needful.

Enter Juliet.

Look, here comes one; a gentlewoman of mine.
Who falling in the flaws of her own youth,
Hath blister'd her report, She is with child,
And he that got it, sentenc'd; a young man
More fit to do another such offence
Than die for this.

Duke When must he die?

Provost: As I do think, tomorrow
[*To Juliet*] I have provided for you. Stay a while
And you shall be conducted.

(*Measure for Measure*, II.iii.9–18)

The Provost's 'covering' speech to the Duke-friar for the entry of Juliet is six lines long and by the time he turns to her from the Duke it is two more lines. Juliet in her state of advanced pregnancy takes her own time to make it to the spot where the Duke and the Provost stand. The comment of the Provost on her condition and on the fate of Claudio her lover is full of sympathy and consideration for both, though not without its male-chauvinist dig at Juliet, and it shows his real attitude of resentment against the cruel statute which requires a young man to die for getting his lady love with child. This is in spite of his being the head of the prison. Also, in such instances the entry movement has a way of becoming a 'still' or part close-up of a character so that the character appears frozen for a moment in the spectator's view and both the spectator's view and response are guided by the 'covering' speech.

A similar instance but with a difference is to be found in the entry of Mistress Overdone the Bawd at I.ii.42.

Enter Bawd.

Lucio	Behold, behold, where Madam Mitigation comes.
1 *Gent*	I have purchas'd as many diseases under her roof as come to—
2 *Gent*	To what, I pray?
Lucio	Judge.
2 *Gent*	To three thousand dolours a year.
1 *Gent*	Ay, and more.
Lucio	A French crown more.
1 *Gent*	Thou art always figuring diseases in me, but thou art full of error. I am sound.
Lucio	Nay, not (as one would say) healthy, but so sound as things that are hollow. Thy bones are hollow, impiety has made a feast of thee.
1 Gent	[*To Bawd*] How now, which of your hips has the most profound sciatica?

(*Measure for Measure,* I.ii. 42–50)

Evidently, the middle-aged bawd Mistress Overdone walks in limping slowly and with difficulty, stricken as she is with the venereal diseases which is the very topic of the discussion 'covering' her entry. The harsh realities of metropolitan and suburban sex trade and low life are brought forward in correspondence with parallel happenings at other social levels in the play, and put in their place in the scheme of things.

An example from *As You Like It* (IV.i.26) of a telling interrelationship between an entry movement and the 'covering' utterance in the ongoing stage dialogue may be considered.

Jaques Yes, I have gain'd my experience.

Enter Orlando.

Rosalind And your experience makes you sad. I had rather

have a fool to make me merry than experience to make me sad—and to travel for it too!

Orlando Good day and happiness, dear Rosalind!

Jaques Nay then God buy you, and you talk in blank verse.
(*As You Like It*, IV.i. 26–31)

Orlando enters to meet his 'love' appointment with the shepherd youth 'boy-Rosalind', walking with the impatient hurry of an enthusiastic lover.[2] During the while, Rosalind clinches her withering sarcastic deflation of Jaques's fashionable pose of what he diagnoses as the traveller's melancholy. Her words suggest that she would prefer the company of a fool to that of a much-travelled melancholic. The 'fool' may apply to Orlando who is her fool in a sense or, to go one better, as Rosalind thinks ahead, the reference could be to a baby born to her by Orlando, 'fool' being a not uncommon term for an infant in Elizabethan English. For, does not Rosalind, not long after her first meeting with Orlando in I.ii., say in response to Celia's question,

---

2. An intriguing exception to the rule of synchrony between the pace, slow or fast, of the character who enters and the length of the 'covering' utterance is to be found in *Romeo and Juliet* (II.vi.15). Juliet enters to Friar Laurence and Romeo already onstage waiting for her to arrive and for her union with Romeo to be solemnised in secret by the Friar.

Friar Laurence Therefore love moderately, long love doth so;
Too swift arrives as tardy as too slow.
Enter Juliet.
Here comes the lady; O! so light a foot
Will ne'er wear out the everlasting flint.
A lover may bestride the gossamer.
That idles in the wanton summer air,
And yet not fall: so light is vanity.

Juliet Good even do my ghostly confessor.

Though the Friar's words indicate that Juliet comes tripping along fast, the boy actor takes the space of five lines, ironically true to the Friar's 'Too swift arrives as tardy as too slow.' The ensemble suggests the motto of *festina lente* (hasten slowly) which the Friar invokes in his words here and in his earlier counsel to Romeo: 'Wisely and slowly they stumble that run fast' (II.iii.94).

> 'But is all this (her sadness) for your father?': 'No, some of it is for my child's father.'
>
> (I.iii. 10–11)

A particularly striking instance of the kind of synchronisation we have been considering is the entry of Gloucester 'with a torch' at l.109 of the storm scene in *King Lear* (III.iv).

Lear . . . .
Off, off, you lendings! Come, unbutton here.

Enter Gloucester *with a Torch.* (F)

Fool Prithee, nuncle, be contented, 'tis a naughty night to swim in. Now a little fire in a wide field were like an old lecher's heart, a small spark, all the rest on's body cold. Look, here comes a walking fire.

(*King Lear,* III.iv.109–14)

The F marking of the entry of Gloucester, torch in hand, seems more appropriate to the staging than the Q marking of it after l. 114 or that of many recent editors at l. 113. Lear, the Fool, Kent and Edgar as mad Tom huddle together against the tender mercies of the blowing storm and the cold in the dark of the night. At the point at which Lear tears off his clothes in his madness, Gloucester enters with a torch in order to bring succour to Lear. The Fool in his own way cautions Lear against exposure to the cold and expresses his longing for at least 'a little fire' for whatever it may be worth. His similitude of the fire of lust in an old lecher's heart being outmatched by the coldness, the impotence of all the rest of his body and his calling the figure of Gloucester 'a walking fire' as Gloucester comes zig-zag from a distance, groping and looking here and there in the torchlight for Lear and his companions, set themselves in mutual illumination. Gloucester walking with a moving spot of light in hand is the only relief in the enveloping darkness, both in a literal and a metaphorical sense, however much ultimately unavailing Gloucester's help to Lear might be. The reference to the 'old lecher' may have an applicability to Gloucester whose lust in his younger days brought about the birth of his bastard son Edmund who plots against him unknown to Gloucester. The oblique moral comment by way of a momentary hit of the

Fool's witticism should not be pressed, for it would be insensitive to pursue such a high moral line, in the Shakespearian dispensation. A strong imaginative impression is thus evoked at this theatrical moment in the play.

It is interesting to watch the little drama in the simultaneous entry of Ophelia through one door and exit of Reynaldo through another, and Polonius's movement between the two in *Hamlet* (II.i.), the movements occurring at l. 70 according to both F and Q2.

Polonius ... you have me, have you not?
Reynaldo My lord, I have.
Polonius God buy ye, fare ye well.
Reynaldo Good my Lord.
Polonius Observe his inclination in yourself.
Reynaldo I shall, my lord.
Polonius And let him ply his music.
Reynaldo Well, my lord.

Exit Reynaldo. *Enter* Ophelia.

Polonius: Farewell. How now, Ophelia,
What's the matter?

(*Hamlet*, II.i.65–72)

Polonius bids Reynaldo farewell as though he has ended at long last his long and lingering instruction to him on how he should spy on Laertes in Paris. But, as Reynaldo walks towards the door, Polonius walks after him as if to prolong his interminable session. That makes Reynaldo stop and turn back to Polonius with the response 'Good my lord'. Polonius speaks his ambiguous instruction, 'Let him (Laertes) ply his music'. Reynaldo leaves through the door saying, 'Well, my lord'. And Polonius bids him farewell now for real and walks immediately towards Ophelia who has entered through another door and who comes rushing to her father 'affrighted' by Hamlet's behaviour. There is thus little need to 'cover' her entry. Similarly, a good effect of theatre can be traced in the entry onstage of Antony and the Roman messenger and in the exit, at the very next moment, of Cleopatra with her companions although till that point in the scene she had been clamouring to meet Antony. In characteristic caprice, she leaves, implicitly refusing to meet him, at the end of the second scene of *Antony and Cleopatra* (I.ii).

The inconsistency in the use of the 'massed entries' convention in the F text of *A Winter's Tale* has resulted in a few entry directions left in in the play for characters to enter in mid-scene as, for example, the scene of the three Gentlemen's narration (V.ii). These entries show that the characters do not need a 'covering' of their movement from the door to the characters onstage. The case is similar with entry directions in *Cymbeline* and *The Tempest*. This factor, however, slight and minor it may be, lends credence to the possibility that the playwright had his mind's eye on the smaller stage in the more intimate Blackfriars' playhouse, though surely the plays were also given at the Globe and adapted themselves well to the public playhouse in the manner, so to say, of Shakespeare's plays in general having adapted themselves to staging in different venues.

We may now go on to consider some examples of onstage movement which do not strictly involve entry or exit. *Hamlet*, curiously enough, is a play which involves several instances of active movement. Among these are Hamlet's almost athletic movement across the stage with his father's Ghost, his movement with Polonius's corpse, his movement in the graveyard and his leap into Ophelia's grave and his fencing movements in the final scene. If these are part of the action in an obvious sense, Hamlet's encounter with Ophelia immediately after his 'To be or not to be' soliloquy (III.i.) is remarkable for the dramatically revelatory movement it involves for Hamlet. The King and Polonius in their 'lawful espials' watch the encounter without leaving the stage at all according to the Q2 directions. In response to Ophelia's returning of his love favours Hamlet launches into one of his powerful satirical outbursts, severely and repeatedly warning Ophelia and exhorting her to protect her chastity and commands her to enter a nunnery. Hamlet harps on this, driving home the word 'nunnery' as many as five times. His whole series of angry and bitter outbursts are punctuated not only by repeated 'farewells' (four times) but by the onstage movement of froing and toing from and towards Ophelia (three times). It provides a dynamic picture of distraction, sad disillusionment and *weltschmerz* on Hamlet's part and of Ophelia's bewilderment and sorrow as a reaction. The whole consort, utterance and action, is powerful in its communication. Though the word 'nunnery' is invoked in the main in the primary sense, the lurking undertone of meaning, 'brothel', in the use of the word in Elizabethan English and in its occurrences in the drama of the period, is also present as a hovering expression of Hamlet's disgust.

In *As You Like It* the meeting of Rosalind and Orlando immediately after he vanquishes Charles the wrestler and the springing of love at first sight between the two is effectively dramatised through the lingering movement back and forth of Rosalind with reference to Orlando and the stillness of Orlando who stands surprised and dumb-stricken by love.

Rosalind Gentleman,
Wear this for me; one out of suits with Fortune
That would give more, but that her hand lacks means.
Shall we go, coz?

Celia Ay. Fare you well, fair gentleman.

Orlando Can I not say, I thank you? My better parts,
Are all thrown down, and that which here stands up
Is but a quintain, a mere lifeless block.

Rosalind He calls us back. My pride fell with my fortune,
I'll ask him what he would. Did you call, sir?
Sir, you have wrested well, and overthrown
More than your enemies.

Celia Will you go, coz?

Rosalind Have with you.– Fare you well. *Exit.*

(*As You Like It*, I. ii. 245–6).

After handing Orlando a chain, a love token in the guise of a victory trophy, Rosalind half-heartedly turns to go from him, leaving Orlando standing stock-still and wondering why he is so. Rosalind, who makes as if to go, turns back and moves to Orlando on the excuse that he is calling her back, forgetting her pride and making an indirect love confession. Celia pulls her back after this with: 'Will you go, coz?' This last gesture of almost pulling the companion and the accompanying movement and expression 'Will you go?' recurs, interestingly, several times in *As You Like It* in love situations.

Rosalind	Go with me to it ('my cote') and I'll show it to you; and by the way you shall tell me where in this forest you live. Will you go?
Orlando	With all my heart, good youth.
Rosalind	Nay, you must call me Rosalind, Come, sister, will you go? *Exeunt.*

(III.ii. 430–5)

Rosalind takes Orlando in hand offering to cure him of his love melancholy for Rosalind by making him play a game of make-believe imagining her in male guise to be his Rosalind and paying court to her every day at the rendezvous of her cottage. Celia has all along stood still watching the preceding long exchange and the striking of the deal of the love-game with wonder. Now, she is struck dumb and still at it all, and Rosalind has to shake her from her muse, pulling her to go (walk) with them. Celia is again in a similar situation, this time she herself being overpowered by love at first sight for Oliver at IV.iii.182.

In *Henry IV, Pt.2*, there occurs Falstaff's affectedly and lumberingly brisk walking movement, his page in tow, when confronted by the Chief Justice. The Justice's servant sticks to Falstaff like a bur, pursuing him, however hard Falstaff may feign deafness on his part. Cornered by the Justice, Falstaff tries to wriggle himself brazenly enough using diversionary verbal tactics and more or less gets away with it. This is the only occasion in the two parts of the play of an ambulant Falstaff exercising his agile wit. In the Gadshill robbery scene in the first part, though according to the F s.d. Falstaff 'runs away' leaving behind the booty they had gathered from the travellers, when surprised by the Prince and Poins who rob the robbers, the Prince's immediate description of the action we have seen is

> . . . Falstaff sweats to death,
> And lards the lean earth as he walks along.
>
> *(Henry IV, Pt.1.* II.ii.108–9)

This is, however, contradicted by what the Prince later tells Falstaff to his face to call his bluff:

> . . . Falstaff, you carried your guts away as
> nimbly, with as quick dexterity, and roar'd for

> mercy, and still run and roar'd, as ever I heard
> bull-calf.
>
> (II.iv. 258–1)

This leaves the staging of the 'running' of Falstaff at Gadshill to the resources and discretion of the actor.

Other examples of notable onstage movement of characters in Shakespeare are Iago's movements from and to Othello in the central seduction scene and in the scene of the eavesdropping of Othello on the mime (to Othello) directed and enacted by Iago with Cassio and Bianca. The movement, 'like a lapwing,' of Beatrice on one side and of Hero and Ursula on the other as the latter deliberately contrive Beatrice's 'noting' or overhearing of their praise of Benedick and of his love for Beatrice, for Beatrice's benefit (*Much Ado*, III.i.).

Also, there are a few occurrences of cleverly manipulated movement which are worth noting. Jaques with his refrain 'ducdame' in the songless song he speaks in *As You Like It* (II.v) draws his onstage listeners to come crowding around him curious to know what is 'ducdame', the deliberately nonsensical tag used by Jaques. Amiens asks the question. Pat comes Jaques's answer that 'it's a Greek invocation to call fools into a circle'. In his forum speech on the dead Caesar, Antony not only makes movements of descent while he speaks, astutely inciting the Roman citizens and making them crowd around Caesar's body to form a ring as he displays it, wounds and all, as a master-stroke of demagoguery.

Another kind of movement can be seen in *Antony and Cleopatra* (III.xi) where Antony in his discomfiture of defeat in the sea-battle and Cleopatra who put him on to it, 'sit down' in grief at opposite ends of the stage and are prodded by their associates into meeting each other, while Cleopatra, supported by Iras, makes a shuffling movement towards Antony. There are also a few instances of a pointed exploitation of vertical movement, characters descending from an upper acting level to the 'platform' stage, apart from a few instances of the descent of 'gods' in scenes of theophany (Wilson Knight's term for it). Such descents are brought forward with economy by Shakespeare. The central confrontation between Bolingbroke and King Richard II takes place with Bolingbroke on the platform stage and Richard appearing on the balcony 'on the walls of Flint Castle'. Bolingbroke's emissary, Northumberland, goes between the two and the two levels. And, finally, King Richard comes down 'like Phaeton' to meet Bolingbroke in the 'base court' thus providing a stage crystallisation of the Fall of the King (*Richard II*, III.iii). Incidentally, there is the fall of Prince Arthur from the prison wall to his death in *King John* (IV.iii), and there is also the memorable 'fall' of Gloucester from Dover Cliff in *King Lear*, where the fall involved turns out to be a rise to self-knowledge for Gloucester. A curious and rather deliberately theatricalised vertical movement is that of the dying Antony's body being lifted up laboriously by Cleopatra and her maids from the lower stage to the upper level (*Antony and Cleopatra*, IV.xv.37: 'They heave Antony aloft to Cleopatra').[3]

Stage movement is one of the important visual dimensions of drama of which Shakespeare is absolute master as of its verbal and aural–oral elements and constituents. Also the instances of stage movement looked at so far show that the visual stage phenomenon is set in an active relationship of both receiving and giving with the associated words and speech. The words spoken in synchrony with it serve to bring home how the theatrical moment in question looks both before and after in the total movement of the play, and is not merely a moment for the sake of the moment or movement. Such theatrical moments, an ensemble of the visual and the verbal, often link with the themes of the play in question; and themes, once much canvassed in criticism not so long ago and not much regarded now, have none the less a place in the Shakespearian story.

---

3. There is the famous descent of Romeo from Juliet's chamber window, presumably with the help of a rope ladder, in *Romeo and Juliet* (III.v.42) as well as the real fall of Prince Arthur to his death (*King John,* IV.iii.8).

7

Whatever Happened to Reynaldo?: Vanishing Characters

The curious phenomenon of absconding characters in Shakespeare has elicited little attention but for occasional comments in editorial annotation and perhaps an essay or two.[1] The readily and widely recognised instance is that of Lear's Fool with Adam in *As you Like It* making a second. But there are also several other characters across the plays, minor figures as these may be, whose disappearance raises questions of varied interest. These are instances very different from cases like Mercutio in *Romeo and Juliet* or Mamilius in *The Winter's Tale* who get 'killed off' early enough in their plays' course, leaving a critic wondering in the first case whether the playwright 'killed off' Mercutio since the extravagance of his rhetoric was endangering the play. This dropping of characters by the wayside as in the instance of Adam puts them under a sort of erasure in a manner which makes for possibilities of meaning and suggestion at several levels. A no-nonsense approach which regards the dramatist's dropping of characters as no more than a simple use-and-throw procedure would be either an oversimplification or a misapplication of Occam's razor. True, a practical dramatic economy governs Shakespeare's dispensation of his characters in this as in other respects. Yet when we look at the

1. R.A. Dave's essay, 'Shakespeare's vanishing characters,' Vikram Chopra, ed. *Shakespeare: Varied Perspectives* (Delhi: B.R. Publishers, 1996) deals with some examples from a highly metaphysical point of view. Quotations in the present paper are keyed to the old Oxford Shakespeare, ed. W.J. Craig (London: Oxford University Press, 1974).

considerable range of the occurrence of the *figura abscondus* in the plays, we could see that Shakespeare's way with these characters relates to a multiplicity of factors in addition to or apart from the exigencies of casting and of doubling, of the actor resource of his theatre. The requirements of doubling and saving of the limited number of available actors overall for roles do have something to do with Shakespeare's practice of dropping characters, but these do not explain, much less would seem to determine it.

It is not as though such characters register as absent presences in their plays after their disappearance in the manner of Julius Caesar or Antony in *Antony and Cleopatra*. Nor are such dramatis personae much missed by any of the other characters. And also the reader or spectator may not miss the missing figures so quietly dispensed with by the playwright that in the tempo of the play's movement their absence is scarcely felt or noticed, except that in the final encore the missing character actor would be seen joining the ceremonial bow on the sage. None the less, the spectator's play-long amnesia of the figures would lift subsequently, and some of the intriguing aspects of the character's vanishing trick and of the dramatic–theatrical ropes behind it would call for attention. The instances cover a range of gradation from those which apparently or really answer to the out-of-sight-out-of-mind formula through those either exemplifying points of dramatic structure and balance or suggesting sociological implications to the ones with a whole complex of many-layered significance.

In contrast to the persistence till the end of the induction frame in *The Taming of a Shrew,* the Christopher Sly Induction in Shakespeare's *The Taming of the Shrew* remains a mere prologue, and the lively induction figure of Sly is practically made to fade out of the play proper even as it starts, the Lord, his household retinue, the induction frame etc. vanishing into thin air. Granting possibilities like *A Shrew* being a quarto version of Shakespeare's play instead of being a source and the closing of the play with the Sly Induction frame having been there originally in Shakespeare's play but left out for whatever reason in the Folio text, the original staging of the play could have either accommodated the presence of the Induction personages of Sly, the Lord and company as silent spectators on stage throughout or could have started with the cleaning of the stage by these characters. If, however, it was the practice of the Induction figures to station themselves on the upper acting area as in *The Spanish Tragedy,* Sly and company would have sat through the performance as prime albeit silent spectators, and their presence with a deafening silence would produce a strange effect with the character being there and not being there at the same time. If Sly and company simply cleared out of the stage, among other things, it would be a clearing of the stage by Sly the tinker, and the alehouse figures, on the one side, and the Lord and his household on the other for the main play which is something of a middle-class citizen drama if not a sort of anticipation of city comedy. And the Induction actors would in that case double as actors in the main play.

Duos and trios of subsidiary characters occur in many of the plays. Shakespeare occasionally employs the device of a quiet, insidious blotting out of one or more of the members of these groups, who very often function as alter egos or echoes of each other. Salerio and Solanio in *The Merchant of Venice* are split images of a single character function. Dramatis personae like these who are more functions and less or little by way of persons get dropped out with hardly any occasion caused of their being missed. It is not so in the case of characters who turn out to be persons as well as functions. Solanio, however, according to Dover Wilson's witticism, is but Salerio with a cold. Perhaps, the nasal twang in the name warrants it. The pair put in as many as four important, sustained appearances together for considerable stage time. But the playwright by stages eases out Solanio, giving a separate stint to Salerio in two different scenes first in II.vi. and later in III.ii though in III.i. the two pair together in between for a key encounter with Shylock. Although the omnibus s.d. for the trial scene (IV.i) does not list either, Salerio does put in his appearance in the scene, although curiously, taking on the role of the court usher, and making just two short announcements. We may suspect that the short scene III.iii in which the gaoler brings the imprisoned Antonio in the company of Solanio to meet and make a vain plea to Shylock is one in which the actor of Salerio doubles as the gaoler.[2] The entry of Antonio, first

2. The law of re-entry need be no bar to the re-entry of the actor of Salerio donning the gaoler's uniform though he appears in III.ii as messen-

seen as an under-trial prisoner to Shylock, flanked by Solanio, his companion and by the gaoler played by the actor of Salerio, Antonio's second companion, would have a telling effect. For the two are his customary companions and parasites. The gaoler remains silent, and Solanio after this makes his exit from the play. Shylock's gibe at the gaoler sounds like a coded give-away to remind the audience that the actor of Salerio is playing the part.

> I do wonder,
> Thou naughty gaoler, that thou art so fond
> To come abroad with him at his request.
>
> (III.iii. 8–10)

It is hence almost a fading out by degrees of both from a garrulous role through a graded silence into a limbo.

Flavius and Marullus in *Julius Caesar*, Bernardo and Marcellus in *Hamlet* and Demetrius and Philo in *Antony and Cleopatra* are characters with whom their plays open but are 'put to silence' for practically the rest of the play. Different factors alongside similar considerations would seem to work behind these occurrences of the pattern of paired dropped characters. The disappearance of the Roman tribunes Flavius and Marullus is called attention to in *Julius Caesar* whereas that of absconding characters in other plays is hardly noticed in their course. The two begin the play with their confrontation of the artisan commoners of Rome over their holiday celebration of Caesar's triumph; their stance of a patrician disapproval of the plebeian apotheosis of Caesar, and the artisans' partial attempts at self-assertion though they disperse yielding to authority, besides the sheer dramatic force of an encounter they carry, make the point about the political conflict underlying the Roman situation, though the political gets overlayered and subsumed by the personal and the psychological in the course of the conspiracy of liberation and its aftermath. Marullus's and Flavius's act of the disrobing of the images of Caesar, and iconoclastic political gesture, we learn subsequently from Casca, earns the wrath of Caesar.

---

ger bearing Antonio's letter to Bassanio. He and the others could well leave the stage to Bassanio and Portia a few lines earlier than the end of the scene. Exits are not consistently marked.

> Marullus and Flavius for pulling scarfs
> off Caesar's images, are put to silence.
>
> (I.ii. 290–2)

In Plutarch the two are only stripped of their tribuneship by Caesar for their act. Shakespeare makes it a case of 'the rest is silence' with (them) in more than one sense. He hints, somewhat mysteriously, at the political liquidation of the two, making it thus a portentous suggestion of political violence. The associates of Brutus and Cassius, except for Lucius and Lucilius who are personal servants, like Decius Brutus, Casca, Ligarius, Metullus Cimber and others either get killed or get dropped by the playwright to be presumed to have been killed by the mob or by Antony and party. So much so that in the second half of the play Brutus and Cassius have a practically new and large enough set of associates. Clearly the actors who played the tribunes and the fellow conspirators in the first half would double as the associates of Brutus, Cassius, Antony and Octavius in the later part of the play. This would serve to promote an overall impression of a large cross-section of people involved in the fortunes of Rome, with the available players in the company.

Such double casting possibilities would not arise in the case of Caesar's wife Calphurnia who, after her two appearances in I.ii. and II.ii., neither returns to the play nor gets mentioned. There are interesting correspondences between her scene with Caesar (II.ii) and Portia's with Brutus (II.i.). While however, Portia makes her appearance again (II.iii.) and later her death by suicide gets reported twice over with emphasis (IV.iii.), with Calphurnia the rest is silence after her silent bystander's role in the triumphal procession scene (I.ii.) except for her monosyllabic 'Oh, my Lord' to Caesar's call 'Calphurnia', and her well-articulated argument with Caesar in her attempt to persuade him not to venture forth to the Capitol in II.ii. If Caesar's wife is forgotten in his will read out by Antony it is in the same way as Shakespeare's wife is 'forgotten' in his will but for the settlement of his second-best bed on her, that is, for the reason that in Elizabethan law the widow was entitled to a share in the husband's property even without a testamentary bequest. But in the play Caesar's wife is forgotten and is little missed while Caesar operates as an absent presence till the end.

Bernardo, Marcellus and Francisco keep guard in the liminal region of Elsinore and start the action of the play setting the interrogative mood of the play with their questions as guardsmen's challenge. But for Marcellus's watching and witnessing function in the scenes of Hamlet's encounter with his father's ghost, these characters are clean dropped by the playwright so much so that Marcellus and his other two companions do not enter the enclosed world of Hamlet's Elsinore and only serve to usher the spectator into it.

The framework of viewing-cum-commenting through which Antony and Cleopatra are introduced in the opening scene of their play is provided by Demetrius and Philo who at the end of the scene leave the play for ever. Again, in a play of swelling numbers of minor characters, soldiers and messengers who keep coming and going, the players of Philo and Demetrius would have roles enough to double later in the play. In a sense, the detachment from the play of these two commentator-figures as well as of another observer-character Mecaenas (II.ii.iv. and vi), besides the distancing of himself from Antony by Enobarbus the Chorus figure, would reinforce the mode of disengagement in which the whole play and the main characters would seem to be couched.

Reynaldo in *Hamlet* is in some ways a class apart among characters who put in a single appearance and then are heard no more like Curan, the courtier in *King Lear* (II.i.) who gives Edmund an update on court rumours about the impending war between Albany and Cornwall for whatever these are worth, and departs from the play. At first sight, as Reynaldo appears in II.i. to take instructions from Polonius on how to spy on Laertes in Paris, it may look as though Reynaldo is more than a sounding board for Polonius's doddering circumlocutory improvisations on how exactly to keep a tab on Laertes and

> With windlasses, and assays of bias,
> By indirections find directions out.
>
> (II.i. 65–6)

Nobody later in the play, nor the spectator, spares a thought for Reynaldo after his exit at the end of II.i. Events move swiftly enough and Reynaldo in the play's time scheme would have hardly a chance to report to his master back from Paris on Laertes. Yet on

Laertes's sudden return leading an abortive uprising against King Claudius, as revenge for the death of his father, Polonius, Claudius it is who speaks at length, though in order to place and inveigle Laertes into agreeing to a fencing match with Hamlet, about the golden report on Laertes ('a masterly report', IV.vii. 95) he has got not from Reynaldo but from Lamord the Norman horseman *par excellence.* Yet, at least, in one perspective in which the play has been seen, the question has been asked what reports Reynaldo brought to Polonius about Laertes. Laura Bohanan the anthropologist reports[3] how the tribal elders in the Tiv in West Africa when very interestedly listening to and absorbing the story and account of the play *Hamlet* given to them were particular about knowing what message Reynaldo sent to Polonius on Laertes. The character's role is through the comico-satirical turn between him and Polonius to serve to bring home Polonius's penchant for indulgence in espials not always lawful and which finally costs his life as he is stabbed behind the arras in Gertrude's chamber. Incidentally, the name of the Steward who is the confidant of the Countess of Rousillon in *All's Well* is Rinaldo.

Old Adam's disappearance from *As You Like It* midway through the play has often been noted. The character who does 'much business appertaining' in the early parts of the play and performs as a distinctive visual presence, goes out of the play and is scarcely missed by any one including the love-lorn Orlando who owes a good deal to his servant-benefactor. In Lodge's source romance *Rosalynde* Adam the loyal and affectionate servant is remembered till the end when he is rewarded by the restored Duke who appoints him chief of the guard. In the play there is the suggestion (in I.i.) of a paired contrast between Adam and Dennis the henchman servant of Oliver, the latter an eminently forgettable figure after his single appearance. After taking the initiative and showing a great deal of enterprise capped by the self-sacrificing gesture of parting with his life's savings for the sake of Orlando, and accompanying him to the Forest of Arden, Adam speaks his penultimate speech in the play as he is about to collapse in his famished state.

3. Laura Bohanan, 'Shakespeare in the bush', James P. Spradley and David M. McCurdy, ed. *Conformity and Conflict* (Boston: Little Brown & Co., 1997), p. 30.

> Dear master, I can go no further. O!
> I die for food. Here I lie down,
> and measure out my grave. Farewell,
> kind master.
>
> (II.vi. 1–3)

If it is a premature farewell, it is only just a little premature when Adam makes a last appearance, at the Duke's banquet, carried by Orlando on his back at the end of Jaques's 'seven ages of man' speech and he could say no more than a few words of thanks.

> I scarce can speak to thank you for myself
>
> (II.vii. 169)

and that is the last we see or hear of Adam in the play. The old tradition propagated by Rowe that Shakespeare as player played the role of old Adam in *As You Like It* may well be true. If Shakespeare–Adam cut himself off from the play by II.vii., it could be that he deliberately did so for several possible reasons. After all, the playwright remembered the third son of Roland de Boys mentioned in the very first scene and had him brought on as messenger towards the close of the play to convey tidings that the usurping and invading Duke Frederick had undergone a conversion at the hands of an 'old religious man' in Arden and had given up the dukedom back to the elder Duke. If Shakespeare chose to elide Adam, it was after he gave himself considerable opportunities of significant theatre action as the player of the role. By the point in the play (II.vii.) when Adam registers his stage-presence as the 'venerable burden' (in the Duke's phrase) of Orlando, not only does the stage-image of the figure on Orlando's back at once counter and also in a way confirm Jaques's cynical depiction of old age. Similarly, his active movements and youthful gestures till he is laid low by hunger and exhaustion go together in their own way to suggest the effect of a presentation of the stages of life (as in Friedrich's painting 'The Stages of Life', 1835), as after all Adam has passed through these stages. Adam's final appearance is set in visual and ideational juxtaposition to Jaques's concluding words in his speech, and it is with a certain appropriateness that he goes into 'mere oblivion (II.vii. 165).

Moreover, it is possible that the player-playwright after doing Adam doubled as William the shepherd to provide a foil to Touchstone's bamboozling wit in the latter's encounter with him. The hint for such a possibility is there in the play with the dramatist-actor's Christian name, and his Arden association by birth.

Touchstone	. . . Is thy name William?
William	William, sir.
Touchstone	A fair name. Was born I' the forest here?
William	Ay, sir, I thank God

(V.i. 22–6)

Shakespeare may thus have gone out of the play as Adam to come back as William. Yet another reason may be that after Adam has served his turn his presence may have been rather incongruous, in terms of considerations of class and of age alike in the later part of the play where the magician uncle and 'an old religious man' are invoked only as unseen figures in the distant background.

The most well-known example of the vanishing character in Shakespeare is the Fool in *King Lear.* It is often suggested that, if the Fool slinks out of the play after the crucial storm-scenes, it is because his voice of practical prudence, wisdom and wit by then has had its untrammelled play and has made its impact on the audience as much as on Lear though he be in his state of madness, and hence the Fool's function is fully served.

The Fool, in this sense, has little to do after he has performed his key role in the intensification of the tragic predicament of Lear, and also of Kent as Caius and of Edgar as mad Tom; this has been sufficiently achieved by the effect of the grotesque (so well brought out by Wilson Knight) created among the Fool's 'foolery', King Lear's madness and Edgar's improvisations on the state of madness and possession. Whatever the Fool may do or say after that, would be in a fashion anticlimactic. So it is that he bids adieu from the play, saying, meaningfully

> And I'll go to bed at noon

(III.vi. 92)

and thus pointing up the total inversion of values in the handy-dandy situation of the world of the play and of Lear at that moment.

Almost as often as it is discounted, the idea has been proposed that the Fool vanishes out of the play for the reason that the actor who played him also doubled as Cordelia. The idea has its attractiveness in view of the piquancies of correspondence such a practice could generate in the theatrical dynamics of the play, and the case has been argued well for it recently by Richard Abrams.[4] However, we can be pretty sure that Robert Armin who played the Fool's role with great distinction in Shakespeare's company could not have functioned also as a boy-actress playing Cordelia. Furthermore, for aught we know, Armin would hardly have undertaken the further strain of another role like Cordelia, which though it does not occupy too much of stage time is a demanding enough one. It could well have been played by the specialist boy-actress in the tragedies, John Rice or someone else. Hence the argument from doubling exigencies cannot account for the disappearance of the Fool from the play. Also, with the play in its later half passing more and more into a climate of war and politics and of politico-ethical confrontations, the Fool would have not much opportunity of playing his role of commentator or re-accentuator and would thus not quite fit in. In the situations towards the close of the play when, in the words spoken by Edgar or Albany:

> Speak what we feel, not what we ought to say
>
> (V.iii. 336)

the fool has little or no function. Our speculations about the appearing and disappearing role in which Shakespeare casts quite a few of his minor characters should not certainly lapse into the kind of critical atavism which leads us either into attempts *a la* Mary Cowden Clarke at the reconstruction of these characters' pre-dramatic fate, or worse, into enquiries into what these characters would be or become in their post-dramatic career after their exit from their plays. It is a different matter if critics who laughed at the old practice of speculating about the boyhood, girlhood, or youth

---

4. Richard Abrams, 'The double casting of Cordelia and Lear's fool,' *Texas Studies in Language and Literature,* 27 (1985), pp. 354–68.

of characters, curiously took it upon themselves to study and pronounce their postdramatic, often eschatological destiny. True, the vanishing lines of all actors as characters and of characters as actors, be they in the category of vanishing characters, or not, meet in the tiring house of the theatre and the world if not the bourne from which no traveller returns. Yet, though not for the duration of the dynamics of the theatre action, later on recall, the spectator or reader often notices what strikes him or her as the premature final exit of some of the characters discussed. The impression they leave springs from a particular tonal effect or shade of the art of dramatic creation and theatrical execution. It could at times or often be a considered stroke of the theatre-poet as part of his elicitation and manipulation of audience response. Shakespeare could retain the Ship captain who takes charge of Viola's female attire at the beginning of *Twelfth Night* till the very end where though he does not put in a stage appearance we hear of his having been put in custody by Malvolio and being ordered to be released to enable him to bring Viola's maiden attire. If the same Shakespeare lets drop certain characters, it is not a forgetful negligence of loose threads. It is a subtle blotting or procedure of erasure. This procedure works its effect in such a way that putting the characters concerned *sous rature* uncannily highlights them or brings them into relief. It is all the more so in the case of characters who develop dimensions as persons even as they serve as functions. To put it another way, the erasure effected by the vanishing rod the playwright wields in their cases makes the spectator grasp and savour the fictionality and the reality of these characters with his or her 'multiconscious apprehension' all the keener for it.

8

'Single-speech Hamiltons' and 'Shadows'

Thanks to the interest coming to be shown in recent years in the subaltern and the liminal by quite a few cultural political critics on the one hand, and on the other, thanks to the illuminating attention accorded to 'bit parts in Shakespeare' by a critic like M.M. Mahood in her book of that title from the angle of the theatrical dynamics and other implications of these, really minor characters in Shakespeare would in a way seem to be in the process of coming into their own, critically speaking. It may perhaps be worth attending to some curious categories of these bit parts. There are some across the plays whose parts are shortest of the short; a single speech of a few lines or sometimes no more than a single line. There are several more who make a single appearance and are seen no longer in a play, a kind of one-off figures. And there are a few who are only seen appearing and not heard speaking at all; such roles were known as 'shadows' in Elizabethan theatrical parlance. All such incidental figures are common in drama in general, and Shakespeare introduces them basically as cogs in the machine. Not all such merely functional characters evoke any particular interest. But certain of these, despite their fleeting role, dressed as they are in their little, brief authority, dramatically speaking, seem to develop a certain piquancy, a noticeable resonance and a certain accession of theatrical energy. They do so by virtue of the difference they make to the course and movement of the play and of the suggestions of 'looking before and after' emerging in and through them both in their immediate context and in the play's theatrical dynamic.

The more interesting instances of single-speech and single-show characters are Mercade in *Love's Labour's Lost* (V.ii.724); the

English ambassador in *Hamlet* (V.iv.), the Justice in *Measure for Measure* (III.i), Peter of Pomfret in *King John* (IV.ii.154); Jaques de Boys in *As You Like It* (V.iv.158); the Priest in *Twelfth Night* (V.i.155); Francisca (*Measure for Measure,* I.iv.2); the Captain in the Folio *King Lear* (V.iii.35) and, 'with a difference' Francisco (*The Tempest,* II.i.120). There are many not particularly significant instances such as Leonardo in *The Merchant of Venice* (II.ii.189), and Helen (*Cymbeline,* II.ii.2). Then there are several single gentlemen who arrive as messengers or missive-bearers on the scene and the First, Second and sometimes Third Gentlemen who perform choric or mediate functions, besides the messengers designated as such who come and go in the plays, these last very frequently in a play like *Antony and Cleopatra* and the numbered citizens. All these are mostly 'functions', except perhaps the First Citizen in *Coriolanus.* There are also the god-in-the-machine-like figures such as Hymen (*As You Like It,* V.iv.132), Juno in the Masque in *The Tempest* (IV.i.102), Jupiter in *Cymbeline* (V.iv.93) and Diana in *Pericles* (V.ii.241) who make a single appearance and a single utterance. But they are a class by themselves, and make for revealing theophanies as Wilson Knight pointed out. It may be worthwhile to look at some of the interesting instances of 'single-speech Hamiltons' in detail.

Even as Mercade bursts upon the scene in *Love's Labour's Lost* (V.ii.721) and starts delivering the message of the King of France's death, the Princess would have guessed, presumably as the audience on stage and offstage did, the news of her father's death from the mourning black which Mercade would wear (supplying, incidentally, one of several variations on the motif of the black in the play). So she completes Mercade's verse-line and message.

Mercade	God save you, madam!
Princess	Welcome, Mercade. But that thou interrupt'st our merriment.
Mercade	I am sorry, madam; for the news I bring Is heavy in my tongue. The king your father—
Princess	Dead, for my life!
Mercade	Even so; my tale is told

Berowne Worthies, away! The scene begins to cloud.[1]

(*Love's Labour's Lost*, V.ii. 721–9)

Mercade's arrival marks the surprise advent of reality breaking in into the enclosed world of the studious academy of the King of Navarre and company which has already got transformed into love's academy, and also into the teasing game world of the Princess and her companies. The name Mercade with its spelling variation Marcade suggests both 'Mar-Ardadia', a dislocator of the world of pastoral and romance and Mercury, the messenger-god. The character's arrival effects a sudden shift in the climate and paves the way to the unusual conclusion of the play in which, as Berowne puts it,

> Our wooing doth not end like an old play;
> Jack hath not Jill . . . .
>
> (V.ii.882–3)

The figure is an interrupter not only for the long-drawn-out charade of the lords and the ladies with its gender war of love but the pageant of the Nine Worthies. The pageant itself ends with a twist, that of an excess of reality by way of the sudden surfacing of the problem of Amado–Hector's affair with Jacquenetta and his rival Costard–Pompey's challenge which, comic as it is, almost serves as a precursor to the dislocating effect produced by Mercade's appearance. He takes on the significance of something like an emblem book item suggesting the intrusion of death into the pastoral world of ease and pleasure, the *et in Arcadia ego* motif. As the motto-like ending lines of the play say it,

> The world of Mercury (Mercade?) are
> harsh after the songs of Apollo.
>
> (V.ii. 938–9)

Surprised by love earlier in the play, Navarre and his companions are at the end jolted into a confrontation with the harsh realities of the world from their retreat and into the prospect of a twelve-month-long penance of a wait. Yet, such an ideational progression

1. Quotations from Shakespeare in this article are keyed to the old Oxford Shakespeare, ed. W.J. Craig.

commonly traced in the play is put in a different perspective by the ending epigram (which was printed, without a speech prefix, in bold letters in the Quarto). The assertion provides a strong intimation of the experiential validity of the pastoral, even as the play points out its complexities as well as the inadequacies of withdrawal. Shakespeare's theatrical stroke is to have used Mercade as an economical and effective dramatic shorthand for his multiple purposes.

The uncanny prophet of gloom, Peter of Promfret, who makes a single appearance in *King John*, brought to the presence of the king by Falconbridge, makes a witheringly portentous single phrase utterance to be led away to prison and subsequent execution. He is the kind of theatre figure and voice that would make a strong impact, however momentary, on the spectator (*King John,* IV.ii). The situation is one of King John in the process of being engulfed by bad news from all quarters: besides the death of Arthur lying on his conscience there is news of the death in France of his mother, of the French invasion of England under the Dauphin, and of the revolt of the lords and nobles against him. At the moment Falconbridge enters, Peter the prognosticator in tow, to give John further bad news to the effect that besides the alienation of the estates of the clergy and the nobility from the king, the third estate of the commons is

> . . . strangely fantasied,
> possess'd with rumours, full of dreams,
> Not knowing what they fear, but full of fear

and produces Peter with the words:

> And here's a prophet that I brought with me
> From forth the streets of Pomfret, whom I found
> With many hundreds treading on his heels:
> To whom he sung, in rude harsh-sounding rimes,
> That ere the next Ascension-day at noon,
> Your highness should deliver up your crown.
>
> (*King John,* IV.ii.144–52)

In straight answer to the King's angry 'twice-thouing' question

> Thou idle dreamer, wherefore didst thou so?
>
> (l.153)

the awesomely grumpy prophet stands his ground and speaks up in stern, ringing tones, in his sole utterance in the play

> Foreknowing that the truth will fall out so.

John dismissively calls him 'an idle dreamer' and orders Hubert to throw Peter in prison to be hanged precisely on Ascension day as 'fit' punishment.

Shakespeare develops with effective brevity a passing reference in Holinshed to a 'hermit' of York, who was hanged 'together with his son', when the day that he had predicted to be ominous for John passed off without any great damage, into a notable little cameo of a character who comes once and goes but not without leaving his impress. King John might seem to forget him but really cannot. He cannot but remember the strange prophet immediately after the surrender, albeit momentary, of his crown to Cardinal Pandulph, in a gesture of reconciliation and submission to the Pope to get him to persuade the French to lay down arms. The cardinal soon hands King John back his crown.

> *King John* Is this Ascension-day? Did not the prophet
> Say that before Ascension-day at noon
> My crown I should give off? Even so I have;
> I did suppose it should be on constraint;
> But, heaven be thank'd it is but voluntary.
>
> (*King John*, V.i. 25–9)

The prophecy comes true but not without a certain equivocalness, apparently characteristic of prophecies as a rule, and yet it comes home forcefully. In one deft passing stroke Shakespeare seems to make the fleeting figure of Peter the ballad-making prophet, bring in his trail suggestions of the popular voice, the crucial significance of the crown in the history plays, especially the crown which lies so uneasy on King John's uneasier head, and furthermore, suggestions of a curious intermixture of the preternatural and the Christian religious (Ascension Day). Peter's presaging is in line with, and by way of capping it all in, the vein of portents and foreboding running in the early histories upto King John. It is not for nothing that Hubert, when he returns quickly after jailing the prophet, recounts so vividly how the country has witnessed the ominous phenomenon of five moons on the sky at a time and is also agog with prophecies (*King John*, IV.ii.181–202). When Cardinal Pandulph and King John enter at the start of V.i., the crown is apparently already in the cardinal's hands, as the king enters with him saying:

> Thus have I yielded up into your hand
> The circle of my glory
>
> (V.i. 1–2)

And the cardinal hands the crown back saying:

> Take again,
> From this my hand, as holding of the Pope,
> Your sovereign greatness and authority.
>
> (V.xi. 3–5)

Whatever ambivalence is seen to underline the Prophet's single-phrase utterance, even more strongly marks King John's relationship with the Pope and the clergy all the way from the cardinal to the monks at Swinstead Abbey. It is a relationship portrayed by Shakespeare from a point of view so different from that of the rabidly Protestant play of John Bale on King John.

The sudden stage appearance of Jaques de Boys, the second son of 'old Sir Rowland' towards the very close of *As You Like It,* with practically his lone single speech, is as if it were a performative utterance by proxy of the now abdicating usurper Duke Frederick. It serves to complete the movement of comedy in the play with economy, with both a forward-looking celerity and a harking back to the beginning so characteristic of Shakespeare's endings. The spectator hears about Jaques de Boys from Orlando at the very opening of the play:

> My brother Jaques he keeps at school,
> and report speaks goldenly of his profit.
>
> (*As you Like It,* I.i. 5–6)

But in the play it is the other Jaques who takes over. And Jaques de Boys, the Oliver favourite, materialises on the scene only at the very end to announce himself hard on the heels of the multiple weddings solemnised in the presence of Hymen and the series of revelations, recognitions and reunions, somewhat in the fashion of another god on the machine. He brings news to the whole company about how Duke Frederick who came to the 'skirts' of the Forest of Arden marching an army with intention to kill the banished senior Duke, his elder brother, underwent a sudden miraculous conversion on

> . . . meeting with an old religious man,
> After some question with him, was converted
> Both from his enterprise and from the world;
> His crown bequeathing to his banish'd brother,
> And all their lands restor'd to them again
> That were with him exil'd.
>
> (*As You Like It*, V.iv. 167–72)

His advent and utterance brings to completion the pattern of regenerative repentance, and transformation, recognition and reunion, and restoration in the music of the play's close. It is interesting that with the arrival of this Jaques, the satirical Jaques withdraws himself from the scene and the play saying that he would go to philosophise with the convertite Duke Frederick. In terms of theatre, the newcomer Jaques perhaps supplies the lack of a dancing companion to the Duke in the final dance at the close, as the whole company dance their way out of the play. The 'fictional reality' of what the report of Jaques de Boys conveys and brings about is curiously verbally foreshadowed in the instant fiction created by Shakespeare for Rosalind in her forest encounter with Orlando in III.ii. 357–67, 446–7. Rosalind tells Orlando that 'she-he' lives in the 'skirts of the forest like a fringe upon a petticoat', and that she had the cultivated accent of 'an inland man' since 'an old religious uncle of mine taught me to speak' and also taught her about his bitter experience of the love of woman in his youth. Rosalind also tells Orlando that she could cure him out of his love for Rosalind by counsel and make him, as she did with an earlier client of hers:

> forswear the full stream of the world,
> and to live in a nook merely monastic.

The last is exactly what the usurping Duke Frederick finally does. In the satirical Jaques's words,

> The duke hath put on a religious life
> And thrown into neglect the pompous court.
>
> (*As you Like It,* V.iv. 188–9)

Jaques de Boys' appearance leaves the impression of a rounding off of the play through a process of recall and restitution and this comedy hastens to its happy resolution.

The priest in *Twelfth Night* whom Olivia brings to lead her and Sebastian (taken by her for Cesario) with dispatch to the altar to be wedded in secret (IV.iii) and whom she later has to summon to bear testimony to the wedding (V.i) plays a curious little 'bit part' noticeable in several respects. When he enters the stage to the monologising Sebastian, led by Olivia, he is a sort of voiceless 'shadow', meekly and alacritously taking orders from Olivia about performing an instant stolen wedding for Olivia and Sebastian. The irony, as Dover Wilson pointed out, is that Olivia weds Sebastian exactly in the chantry set up on purpose to pray for her father's soul, thus breaking her vow of a seven-year mourning for her father and of absolute withdrawal from male company, and the chantry priest is the officiating clergyman. To be noted also is the telling juxtapositional closeness of the first appearance of the chantry priest (IV.iii) to the comic ministrations of Feste the clown (in the guise of Sir Topas the priest) to Malvolio in the dark house in the previous scene (IV.ii). Part of Feste's ventriloquist playing of the role of Sir Topas the priest is his play with disguise, the gown and the beard, and with the assumed darkness of the stage during the encounter with Malvolio. On the stage, for aught we know, the same gown if not the beard may have been the chantry priest's also except that the actor of the chantry priest will be taller than Robert Armin who probably played Feste. The hints are there in the words of Feste and Maria.

Feste Well. I'll put it on and I will dissemble myself in 't; and I would I were the first that ever dissembled in such a gown. I am not tall enough to become the function well.

(*Twelfth Night,* IV.ii. 5–8)

and

Maria Thou mightst have done this without thy beard and gown: he sees thee not.

(*Twelfth Night,* IV.ii. 69–70)

When the chantry priest appears in the final scene of recognitions and reunions and ultimate union of hearts, called in by the desperate Olivia, the 'holy father' finds a tongue once and for all and pronounces his testimony with a public address of authority and dignity so different from an earlier all-too-private role. The sole utterance he makes in the play bespeaks these qualities:

> A contract of eternal bond of love.
> Confirm'd by mutual joinder of your hands,
> Attested by the holy close of lips,
> Strengthen'd by interchangement of your rings;
> And all the ceremony of this compact
> Seal'd in my function, by my testimony:
> Since when, my watch hath told me, toward my grave
> I have travell'd but two hours.
>
> (*Twelfth Night*, V.i. 160–67)

He thus vouches for what he, like Olivia, takes to be the wedded state of the young Cesario, the object of attention at that moment in the whole assembly. He stays on stage till the last and is a silent witness to the proceedings including the 'natural perspective' of the truly wedded Sebastian, the look-alike twin of Viola-Cesario and Viola-Cesario materialising together on the scene. Thus his mere presence provides a certain holy sponsorship and auspices to the final recognitions, reconciliations, and the union of the Duke and Viola. The priest's speech serves, moreover, to underscore the idea of the sanctity of matrimony and of the ceremony of the wedding, an idea which is, as a rule, a keynote of the music of the close and indeed of the progression of Shakespeare's comedies. The priest speaks only too much in character as a man of religion of late medieval and early Renaissance times when he computes time in terms of the progress of his life towards death. But he does so with the intriguing difference that he sports his watch, then modern enough for one thing and for another a rather expensive item of wear at the time. This suggests a kind of showing off and indeed Queen Elizabeth is said to have prided herself on her possession of one. All this has the effect of lending the semblance of a person to this character function.

Making due allowance for the important factor of ambivalence attendant on it, we should note the presence in *Measure for Measure* of the reminiscences of religious and scriptural ideas and phrases and the role of the friars with the incognito Duke as friar centrestage in this regard and the monastic in general. However all this occurs alongside the place bawds and bawdry houses and the loss of maidenheads and heads have 'in the story'. Isabella, the central figure, appears in the guise of a novice about to enter a nunnery, and makes her first entry in the company of Francisca. The latter is the only full-fledged nun in the play who puts in a brief single-show appearance as if at the end of her preliminary initiation and briefing of Isabella about the discipline and austerities of the Franciscan nunnery of 'poor Clares' (I.iv. 1–14). Isabella does protest too much her ready willingness and active seeking of even a severer regimen, in response to Francisca's query whether she did not think the privileges accorded to nuns large enough. It is at that moment that Lucio comes to knock at the door of the nunnery in search of Isabella about her brother Claudio's predicament to seek her intercession to Angelo on his behalf. Francisca retires from the scene and the play after leaving it to Isabella to answer the door:

> *Francisca* It is a man's voice, gentle Isabella,
> Turn you the key, and know his business of him:
> You may, I may not, you are yet unsworn.
> When you have vow'd, you must not speak with men
> But in the presence of the prioress:
> Then, if you speak, you must not show your face,
> Or, if you show your face, you must not speak.
> He calls again. I pray you, answer him.
> (*Measure for Measure,* I.iv. 6–14)

(Though the s.d. 'Exit' is not in the Folio, she does make her exit, one of the many instances of the omission of the exit direction in the Shakespearian playtexts.)

A telling overall visual and ideational effect is contributed to by this stage image of Francisca in her conversation with Isabella probably now with her novice cap on, together with the appearance of Friar Thomas at the beginning of the play and Friar Peter towards the close as a kind of confidant of the Duke, not to mention the Duke as Friar. The idea of the discipline of the strict religious orders is intriguingly juxtaposed in the play with the strict discipline of and discipling by Angelo, on the one hand, and, on the other, with the license of the bawdry world and with the quotidian morals of the likes of Claudio and Juliet, and Mariana, and the passing First and Second Gentlemen (I.ii), with Lucio 'a fantastic' in between on this scale.

The captain in *King Lear* (V.iii.27) to whom Edmund gives the written but unspoken command, jointly issued by him and Goneril, to kill the imprisoned Cordelia and Lear appears only once and speaks no more than a half-line of monosyllables:

> I'll do it, my lord.
>
> (*King Lear*, V.iii. 35)

in the Folio text. But in the Quarto he has two more lines:

> I cannot draw a cart nor eat dried oats;
> If it be man's work, I will do it.
>
> (*King Lear*, V.iii. 39–40)

According to the Folio, he takes one look at the command and unflinchingly and callously agrees to execute an unwarlike command without any scruple. The grim harshness of it all is more effectively communicated through this by itself rather than in conjunction with otiose justification in the quarto lines of the captain.

Francisco in *The Tempest*, an attendant lord of the 'court party' of Alonso, Antonio and company in the play, presents an interesting instance of a character who is a regular in all the several 'court party' scenes but has only a single speech once, and in a subsequent scene a single half-line, and no more. Through his silent presence, as a non-participating observer for the most part, he registers himself as a *punctum indifferens* and his voice in his only speech (II. i. 120–9) comes through as one of sane calm and assurance and sound observation. He studiously refrains from joining or countenancing the teasing game against the garrulous Gonzalo that Antonio and Sebastian relentlessly play, though his immediate companion Adrian does so marginally. It is Francisco who expresses the strong belief that Ferdinand has survived the wreck in a speech which is among other things a striking evocation of a master-swimmer's stroke and feat, worthy of the very best sports-commentator.

> *Francisco* Sir, he may live:
> I saw him beat the surges under him
> And ride upon their backs: he trod the water,
> Whose enmity he flung aside, and breasted

> The surge most swoln that met him his bold head
> 'Bove the contentious waves he kept and oar'd
> Himself with his good arms in busy stroke
> To the shore, that o'er his wave-worn basis bow'd
> As stooping to relieve him. I not doubt
> He came alive to land.
>
> (*The Tempest*, II.i. 120–9)

And it is Francisco who marvels with an observer's relish at the sudden vanishing of the spirits in strange shapes which bring in and spread in 'an excellent dumb discourse' an inviting banquet before the famished court party, the banquet that is to tantalise them subsequently; in his half-line

> They vanish'd strangely.
>
> (*The Tempest*, III.iii. 40)

There are numerous instances in Shakespeare of attendants swelling the scene as part of a king's or noble personage's customary appendage and also soldiers in scenes of battle where supernumerary actors take these minimal 'shadow' parts. As the revealing s.d. in the Folio of *A Midsummer Night's Dream* (V.i.126), clearly a s.d. of theatrical origin:

> *Enter* (Tawyer *with a* Trumpet *before him*) Pyramus *and* Thisbe *and* Wall *and* Moonshine *and* Lion

shows, servants in the theatrical company and stage-hands would have chipped in to play these roles. For Tawyer was a servant in Shakespeare's company already in service at the time of the performance of *A Midsummer Night's Dream,* and who died c. 1625. Yet there are a few instances where 'shadows' in a way distinguished themselves on account on their participatory function in plays. Some of these are interesting and in cases problematic for several reasons—Philostrate in *A Midsummer Night's Dream* in the Folio text but not so in the Quartos, and the jailor in *The Merchant of Venice.* These are to be distinguished from certain major characters who turn into silent stage presences, e.g., Isabella towards the close of the last scene in *Measure for Measure* or Silvia towards the close of the *Two Gentlemen of Verona.*

The idea of the revels in the name of those specially commissioned for the occasion of the wedding of Theseus and Hippolyta serves not only as a framework for *A Midsummer Night's Dream* but also as a governing motif of the festive comedy. Philostrate, the master of the revels to Theseus, is seen at the very start of the play entering with the couple, and he is commanded by Theseus to go and call up the festive spirit and, implicitly, to commission the revels to make the celebrations.

Theseus Go, Philostrate,
Stir up the Athenian youth to merriments;
Awake the pert and nimble spirit of mirth;
Turn melancholy form to funerals;
The pale companion is not for our pomp.
(*A Midsummer Night's Dream,* I.i. 11–15)

And Philostrate makes his exit after registering his silent presence, once for all in the Folio text of the play. But in the Quarto version Philostrate reappears to play his role as a master of the revels by reading out to Theseus the list and details of the 'devices' on offer for performance on the wedding night and also introduces the play of 'Pyramus and Thisbe' as master of ceremonies. In the Folio text, however, it is Egeus, father of Hermia, who played the unrelenting spoilsport by opposing his daughter's love and who, now a reconciled parent, takes on the functions of the master of the revels. Both the alternatives seem to have been actual stage practices, as both the Quarto and the Folio texts according to textual scholars show signs of theatrical provenance. Most modern editors follow the Quarto and bring in Philostrate in Act V. It could be that at a point of time the actor of Philostrate became unavailable for the full role, and an actor who could fit the role only as a 'shadow' stood in for him at the start of the play, and the Folio reflecting that practice, substituted Egeus for Philostrate's sustained and active role in the final scene. There is also the possibility, though only slight as the text involved is the Folio, and not a Quarto, that the editors Heminge and Condell felt that they should not give the chance to Philostrate being 'deciphered' (in Ben Jonson's term) as the real-life counterpart of the contemporary master of the revels in Britain, and therefore made do with Egeus.

The jailor who appears in *The Merchant of Venice* (III.iii) leading Antonio out in the company of his associate Solanio in order that Antonio may meet Shylock and himself make a last plea to him for mercy does not speak a word. But he is paid considerable attention to by Shylock, thus evoking attention to him on the spectator's part. There is a good possibility of the player of Salerio, the *alter ego* of Solanio, the other constant companion of Antonio having doubled for the nonce as the jailor. He later reappears in the court scene ostensibly as companion to Antonio but actually to play some sort of an usher in the court. The piquancy of the joke of the actor of Antonio's other companion now appearing as the jailor of Antonio, with the two flanking Antonio (now a prisoner), exactly as they did earlier on in the play, is more than hinted at in the words put into Shylock's mouth.

Shylock Jailor, look to him: tell not me of mercy
This is the fool that lent out money gratis
Jailor, look to him.
. . . .
I do wonder,
Thou naughty jailor, that thou art so fond
To come abroad with him at his request.
(*The Merchant of Venice,* III.iii. 1–3; 8–10)

The actor of Salerio who appears in III.ii would have had time enough to make his exit in that scene in advance of the end of the scene leaving Bassanio and Portia in private, in order to appear as jailor for the next scene.

Overall, the impact made by such characters as may be called 'single-speech Hamiltons', at times with no more than a cryptic single line as their speaking part and also by 'one-off' figures who are 'shadows' or mutes without speaking parts at all, adds a certain depth and a subtle new dimension to the plays where they occur. Trivial and negligible as these functional figures would seem, they at times both gather and radiate significances worth noting. In a theatre where doubling was in practice such parts would have lent another opportunity for players to exhibit their versatility if not virtuosity. Or, such parts may have been conceived by Shakespeare with a particular player of his troupe who may have had a sort of special penchant for such appearances, somewhat akin to what in present day film parlance is called 'guest appearances'.

9

The Shakespeare Inset and its Poetic of Illusion

In this chapter we shall look at certain scenes and situations and passages across the plays which are in the nature of inserted or inset 'performances' and study them especially from the point of view of the ideas of the name and nature of dramatic illusion and its functions and effects which may emerge in these. Of course, a play itself is a 'performance' but what we shall choose for consideration are set 'performances', set within the plays, some representative examples of several kinds of such 'insets'. One obvious kind comprises the plays-within-the-play and pageants such as the ones in *Love's Labour's Lost*, *A Midsummer Night's Dream*, *Hamlet* etc. A second kind, that of improvisatory theatricals at short or no notice, is instanced by the role-playing and role-exchanging charade between Hal and Falstaff (*King Henry IV, Pt. 1*, II.ii). A third category is enactment of an elaborate illusory action, the most remarkable instance being Edgar's 'staging' of the scene and 'action' of Gloucester's 'jump' and fall from Dover Cliff. A fourth category consists of ventriloquist role-playing and play-acting for the nonce indulged in by individual characters, for example by Hubert in *King John* (IV.ii. 185–202) and Ulysses in *Troilus and Cressida* (I.iii. 142–84). I categorise as 'insets' these several kinds of 'performances', or 'devices' as the Shakespearian or Elizabethan parlance would have it, which for all their textual and contextual functionality and embeddedness in the play's structure, stand out in some relief and draw our attention. These are to be regarded not so much as sewn-on purple patches, but as modes of theatrical play and life and of rich and deep thematic and meditative import. (These instances have occasionally been styled 'insets' in commentary. But the phrase 'Shakespearian inset' has also been used to denote rhetorical or lyrical utterances with a noticeable afflatus such as Ulysses's 'degree' speech in *Troilus and Cressida* by Francis Berry in his book on *The Shakespearian Inset* of some decades ago.)

The 'insets' I wish to deal with give an immediate impression of an abundant play of theatrical sense, great virtuosity and often hilarious wit. Frequently these reflect a complex play with levels of illusion, which explores as it exploits the layeredness of illusion. Such multiplicity of strata of illusions, more frequently, brings up the question of the relationship between modes of illusion and modes of reality, and, more particularly, the intricate intercommunication between illusion and reality. What I try to enquire into is some of the implications which these 'insets' in their varied ways and orientations may be seen to enfold in their dynamic process of drama. These point towards shifts in levels of illusion in drama, the interplay and interrunning of illusion in drama, the interplay and interweaving of illusion and reality, especially for an emerging (albeit implicitly so) conception of the nature of the effect and sense of the kind of reality produced by drama and the theatre. In the present chapter I would like to focus on these rather than the 'performance' aspects and other facets of the Shakespeare 'insets' such as the ways in which these reflect certain attitudes and assumptions of the profession of theatre on the part of the playwright.

Perhaps it is particularly worthwhile if not timely, to consider if and how the 'insets', as the plays themselves do, convey an abiding and active sense which drama and the stage and theatre could evoke and communicate, of the nice if also perilous balance of illusion and reality, of the theatricality and reality or verisimilitude, of the art and artifice and the ultimate truth-to-life. It is important not to miss that Shakespeare brings home in piquant fashion as much the reality of the illusion of drama (and by a sort of synecdochical extension the reality of the illusion of life) as the illusioned status of drama and the stage and the illusoriness of life and the world. ('We are such stuff as dreams are made on'). If 'all the world's a stage' in the potent theatre-of-the-world metaphor which was a forceful commonplace of Shakespeare's day, the stage-world or play-world, conversely, could 'incarnate' or realise the world-stage. Shakespeare and his theatre, participating as they did in the 'popular dramatic tradition' (modified as this concept of S.L. Bethell's may now stand by Robert Weimann and sceptically queried by some cultural critics of recent years) imbibed a keen 'multiconsciousness' (in Bethell's memorable term) which made for a simultaneous and active apprehension of drama as illusion and drama as reality. It is this unique impression of reality conveyed by drama and the stage, so well highlighted by Abhinavagupta and other aestheticians in the Indian tradition, which we are ultimately alerted to in any close examination of the 'insets' in the plays of Shakespeare. Such a sense of reality evolves in and through the course of an exposure, and sometimes a probing, of the exigential and essential elements of illusion which inevitably go to the making of drama and theatre, and thus earns itself. In our contemporary critical situation, on the one hand, there is the postcultural criticism, with its assumption of a divorce between the world or drama and literature on the one side and the world and its realities on the other (and a consequent emphasis on the non-reality of both). On the other hand, there is the cultural criticism which tries to annul the boundaries between the world of drama, theatre and literature on the one side and sociopolitical and economic realities of the world on the other. The balance which one might seek between these two tendencies of collapsing together or of sharp compartmentalising of drama and the world is to be found in what one may call the implied poetic of dramatic illusion of the Shakespeare 'inset' and the Shakespeare plays.

Let us start our examination of instances with a look at Edgar's curious stage management of Gloucester's fall from Dover Cliff in *King Lear*. Edgar plays several quick-change roles in one person in the scene, and weaves a series of subtle webs of illusion around his unrecognising father Gloucester in which to entrap him. He does this for Gloucester's good and by way of a psychological, albeit humouring, shock therapy for him. One of the most striking points about the episode is an apparent, teasingly ironic coalescence in the theatrical dynamics of the scene of the 'timeless' and 'spaceless' stage of Shakespeare's day, of the non-illusionistic or conventionalistic illusion of that stage and theatre with the non-illusionistic illusionism practised by Edgar as surrogate playwright and stage manager for the nonce. So much so that the spectator in *that* theatre is likely (at least initially) to take the scene and picture of Dover Cliff evoked by Edgar through word images for real in terms of the conventionalistic orientation of the stage of the times. At least, there is room for a certain ambivalence in this regard. Shakespeare's superimposition and interweaving of two non-illusionistic illusionisms into a potentially tantalising double-illusion in the scene is a metadramatic or metatheatrical comment on the why and how of and on the force of dramatic illusion, and on the lines of partition, sometimes thin enough, that divide illusion and delusion. In this perspective, the episode serve as as a potent object lesson in the poetic of theatrical illusion. In fact, it turns out to be a kind of exemplification of the important modification which Coleridge made to Johnson's theory of dramatic illusion about the spectators being always in their senses and knowing full well that the stage is but a stage and the characters are but actors. Coleridge posited a willing suspension of disbelief on the spectator's part as a desideratum for giving the creatures of dramatic imagination a semblance of truth and reality. It is only such a deliberately willed credence to what happens on the stage that would make for adequate audience response and participation and would also distinguish the play of illusion from mere delusion.

The blinded Gloucester is taken in by the serial, quick-change play-actings of Edgar, and by his contrivance of an elaborate and grotesque game of make-believe of Gloucester's fall from the tall overhanging cliff, of his miraculous preservation and of the devil tempting him to take the suicidal plunge, and hence is a victim of delusion, although well-meant. The spectator who is responsive, however, would not initially forejudge that either Edgar is leading Gloucester elsewhere than Dover or that Edgar is making it all up about the cliff, the view from it and the fall. Instead, to spell out rather laboriously a single, spontaneous act of the mind, he or she would take the hints amply provided in Edgar's words and gestures and Gloucester's initial doubts. Thus the spectator would on that basis respond by an instinctive and instantaneous reorientation of the 'willed suspension of disbelief', and by coming to recognise and savour the make-believe of Edgar for what it is, a well brought-off make-believe and not believing it after the fashion of Gloucester.

It is better to have before us the passage in good part. Here goes the quotation:

Gloucester When shall I come to the top of that same hill?
Edgar You do climb up it now; look how we labour.
Gloucester Methinks the ground is even.
Edgar Horrible steep:
Hark! Do you hear the sea?
Gloucester No, truly.
Edgar Why, then your other senses grow imperfect.
By your eyes' anguish.
Gloucester So may it be, indeed.
Methinks thy voice is alter'd, and thou speakest in better phrase and matter than thou didst.
Edgar You're much deceiv'd, in nothing am
I chang'd
But in my garments.
Gloucester Methinks you're better spoken.
Edgar Come on, sir: here's the place:
stand still,
How fearful
And dizzy 'tis to cast one's eyes so low!
The crows and choughs that wing the midway air
Show scarce so gross as beetles; half way down
Hangs one that gathers samphire, dreadful trade!
Methinks he seems no bigger than his head.
The fishermen that walk upon the beach
Appear like mice, and yond tall anchoring bark
Diminish'd to her cock, her cock a buoy
Almost too small for sight. The murmuring surge,
That on the unnumber'd idle pebbles chafes,
Cannot be heard so high, I'll look no more,
Lest my brain turn, and the deficient sight
Topple down headlong.
Gloucester Set me where you stand.
Edgar Give me your hand; you are now within a foot
Of the extreme verge; for all beneath the moon
Would I not leap upright.
Gloucester Let go my hand
Here, friend 's another purse; in it a jewel

Well worth a poor man's taking . . .
. . . Go thou further off;
Bid me farewell, and let me hear thee going.

Edgar Now fare you well, good sir.

Gloucester With all my heart.

Edgar Why do I trifle thus with his despair
Is done to cure it,

Gloucester O you mighty gods!
This world I do renounce, and, in your sights,
Shake patiently my great affection off;
If I could bear it longer, and not fall
To quarrel with your great opposeless wills,
My snuff and loathed part of nature should
Burn itself out. If Edgar live, bless him!
Now fellow, fare thee well. (He falls)

Edgar Gone, sir farewell.

(*King Lear*, IV.vi)

The whole episode in itself and also in the context of what follows in the long scene (IV.vi), the meeting of mad King Lear and blind Gloucester, Edgar's encounter with and slaying of Oswald with Edgar assuming yet another identity in a series of role changes, evokes the whole gamut of the range of emotions from the absurd and the comic and the grotesque if not the farcial through certain turns of surprise and physical movement and heroic action to deep pathos and tragic feeling. The audience would not fail to note Edgar's virtuouso-like stage-management of the event and his function as a 'point-of-view' character in the rest of the scene.

The story goes that once the great eighteenth-century actor Garrick, in order to entertain his company at a dinner, started improvising and performing the role of a person holding an infant in his arms, continued for some while as though fondling the imaginary child in various ways and discoursing with it, and then in a sudden coup d' theatre-like action tossed it out of the window with the result that almost the whole company felt a real shock and were aghast, with outbursts of distress. The actor of Edgar's utterances, with the word-scenery painted by Shakespeare, creates an impression of the reality of Dover Cliff and the fall strong enough to convince Gloucester and just about have the spectator also be duped like Gloucester. Edgar's words about the effect of the 'conceit', the evocation of imagination, he has produced as being too real or rather too strong on Gloucester, are one among several signals to the spectator that he is playing a game of make-believe. Lear's telling phrase later in the scene, 'this great stage of fools' (IV.vi.188) self-reflexively glances at the particular stage moment in which it is spoken and cross-references itself to the staging of Gloucester's fall by Edgar, even while it radiates its larger general significations. Shakespeare may be said to explore the non-naturalistic conventions of his stage, or rather make an exploratory–creative use of these, and of the possibilities of ambivalent response to these. In the process he lets us know how an entirely subjectivised experience of an objective one like Gloucester's attempted suicide through a steep fall and his miraculous escape, an internalisation of an exterior phenomenon, could be communicated so effectively through the idiom of his set of stage conventions. It is not for nothing that Shakespeare's presentation of Gloucester's despair in and through the fall from Dover Cliff in now subjectivising, now apparently objectifying terms, influenced Hopkins in one of the most moving of his 'terrible sonnets', 'No Worst, There is None', an anguished adumbration of religious despair:

> O the mind, mind has mountains, cliffs of fall,
> Frightful, sheer, no—man—fathomed. Hold them cheap
> May who ne'er hung there. Nor does long our small
> Durance deal with that steep or deep.

In terms of the staging conventions of his theatre, Shakespeare places the question whether Gloucester falls from the cliff or not ever so gingerly in doubt. The streak of nagging uncertainty about the game is felt by Edgar himself when he momentarily fears that Gloucester might have fallen dead out of his 'conceit'. In Peter Brook's production of the play in 1962 Gloucester swooned as he fell and revived after his encounter with Edgar now in another *persona*. In several ways, the whole episode in its theatrical process is, among other things, something of a metadramatic exploration of the nature and power of stage illusion and the sort of reality it calls up.

An implied poetic of dramatic illusion may be traced in *A Midsummer Night's Dream* in the rehearsals for the play about 'Pyramus and Thisbe' and the actual performance of the play by Quince, Bottom and the company of artisans on the nuptials of Theseus and Hippolyta, what with the intervention in the former by Puck with his 'translation' of Bottom with an ass's head, and the interventions in the latter by the lover-companions of Theseus. In this 'dream' play of Shakespeare's, the play of illusions created by fairy-magic with sleep and dream and changes of love-loyalties as its mode of operation sets up instructive correspondences with theatrical illusion which, besides being the *raison d'etre* of the main play, is a question raised in the rehearsals and performance of 'Pyramus and Thisbe'. The fears expressed by the artisans, Quince, Bottom and Snug, about their roles in their play before the Duke being taken too much for real by their court audience and giving a fright and hence offence, point to one extreme of an imbalance of response to stage illusion. If that is so, the mocking and sceptical interruption and expostulations with which the court spectators bombard the artisan performers in the course of the actual performance, though in a way partly justified by the slip-ups of the actors, constitute the opposite extreme of an imbalance of theatrical response, a refusal of engagement and a withholding of the modicum of a 'willing suspension of disbelief'. Through a kind of a dialectic between such extremes of engagement and disengagement is suggested the need for a right intermixture of perceptions of illusion and reality. Though the others in his company find little more than an occasion for their sport in the play presentation at the expense of the artisans, Theseus patronises it with a certain warmth, though he also does not refrain from laughing at the inadequacies of the actor-presenters. The comic elan of the play within is kept up throughout, with such bunglings of the actors as when Thisbe kills herself with the butt-end of a dagger. (An allusion to it in a children's company play of 1607 by Edward Sharpham, *The Fleir*, refers to this stage business. And it may as well apply to Pyramus's killing of himself; as in *A Midsummer Night's Dream* itself, Philostrate tries to dismiss the idea of commissioning 'Pyramus and Thisbe', telling his Duke

> And tragical, my noble lord, it is;
> For Pyramus therein doth kill himself.

> Which when I saw rehear'd, I must confess,
> Made mine eyes water; but more merry tears
> The passion of loud laughing never shed.
> (V.i.66–70)

However, Theseus not only chooses the play but gives it a receptive response. To Hippolyta's comment:

> This is the silliest stuff that I ever heard
> (V.i.214)

he interjects:

> The best in this kind are but shadows, and
> The worst are no worse, if imagination amend them.
> (V.i.255–66)

Though Hippolyta's riposte to this:

> It must be your imagination then, and not theirs.
> (V.i.217)

has its point, the idea well emerges that even the best of stage enactment by the best of players would fail to convey a sense of reality or versimilitude if the spectator does not bring to bear an imaginative sympathy, the right kind of audience response and participatory engagement on what he or she witnesses. The term 'shadows' suggests the opposite of reality, an emptiness and lack of substance, 'nothing' in Philostrate's parlance, but, more interestingly, as a specific reference to actors in theatrical terminology the term 'shadow' denotes a walk-on, silent 'bit part'. That would imply that even the best of actors would come through little better than 'shadows' in this sense if the audience do not accord them a proper response.

A similar metatheatrical enquiry into the nature of dramatic response is built into the presentation and reception of the Pageant of the Nine Worthies which occurs towards the end of *Love's Labour's Lost*. It is true that the performers for the nonce of the pageant, the comic types, the braggart, 'fantastical, soldier Armado, the pedant Holofernes, the curate Sir Nathaniel, Costard the clown and Moth, Armado's boy, are bungling amateurs. At the least provocation, many of them dry up and forget their part. But in the ruthless heckling and relentless mockery of the prince's companions and their avoidance and deliberate refusal of any 'willing suspension of disbelief' underneath all the exuberant and enjoyable comicity and word play they expose themselves in their basic unfairness. The princess's response, like that of Theseus in *A Midsummer Night's Dream*, points up the contrast. As performers of the lover's masque of the Muscovites to their lady loves, as a wooing game, earlier in the play (V.ii. 155–264), the prince and his companions experienced, if anything, a worse discomfiture than the performers of the Nine Worthies. The interruptions have the effect of breaking the illusion or dispelling it before it is called up, in and through sudden eruptions of the realities relating to the participant actors who are exposed to be perhaps more than 'a little p'erparted'. There is warrant enough in Holofernes' protest:

> This is not generous, not gentle, not humble!
>
> (V.ii.629)

The weaving of the pattern of the sudden breaking in of reality into the circle of illusion is akin both to the prince and company being surprised by love in the metaphorically enclosed grove of academy into which they withdraw and finally, to the dire reality of the outer world breaking in, through Marcade's entry and announcement of the King of France's death, into the love game comedy of the play and into the already dislocated and disoriented world of the pageant. To adopt the closing lines of the play, *Love's Labour's Lost*, the words of Mercury may be harsh after the songs of Apollo, but such clashes or even telescopings are very much part of the larger reality of life.

In the case of both the presentations, the pageant in *Love's Labour's Lost* and the dislocation of the essential but delicately varying, if not quivering, balance of consciousness of the actors as characters, and of the characters as actors such double or multiple awareness was characterised by S.L. Bethell as 'multi-consciousness', as we have already noted. The active dynamics of 'multiconsciousness' on the part of all the parties to the dramatic transaction alike, the playwright, the actors and the audience, could be exploited in a variety of ways. It could also and often did take the form of a deliberate dramatic self-consciousness or self-conscious theatricality which led to the mechanics and the artifice of the theatrical process themselves being covertly or overtly called attention to and enlisted as participants in the subtle and yet instinctive operations of 'multiconsciousness'.

The diverse modes of the interrunning of different kinds and degrees of both illusion and reality which mark the plays in general and the Shakespeare inset in particular include the sort of such crisscrossing to be found in the charade between Prince Hal and Falstaff in *King Henry IV, Pt. 1*(II.ii) and in 'The Mousetrap', the play-within-the-play in *Hamlet*. In the enactment of the interview of Hal with his king father, meant to be a rehearsal with a difference of the actual interview later (III.ii), between Hal and Falstaff, Falstaff first plays the king and Hal plays himself which latter makes for a coincidence of make-believe and reality. At the Prince's instance they switch roles and Hal, impersonating the king, delivers a damning tirade against Falstaff with Falstaff feigning not to recognise who the target of the attack is. But Falstaff soon starts appealing imploringly albeit half-jocularly against any banishment by the King. But Prince Hal, now in the role of the King, asserts with laconic severity and sternness of tone and voice:

> I do, I will. [*A knocking heard*]

It is a grim precursor and portent of the reality of the banishment of Falstaff to take place the moment Hal assumes the role of the King after his coronation as King Henry V at the end of *King Henry IV, Pt. 2*. In the theatrics for the nonce, Hal's monosyllables are echoed by a knocking at the door heralding the arrival of the Sheriff and his men in search of the fat robber, the knocking suggesting the invasive ingress of reality into the make-believe world of play and game.

In the presentation of the 'Murder of Gonzago' or 'The Mousetrap' in *Hamlet*, the dumb show depicts in good measure the story of the lives of the Elder Hamlet as king, his queen Gertrude and also Claudius, and the play within advances up to the point at which in the play one Lucianus, the King's nephew, poisons the sleeping king in order to obtain his crown and his queen. It is only at that point that Claudius gets overpowered by his recognition of too much closeness to reality in the illusion for his comfort, of Hamlet's awareness of the skeleton in his cupboard, and above all of the possibility of Hamlet becoming his slayer in revenge. Dover Wilson made the Claudius of his edition of *Hamlet* literally look the other way in the course of the dumb show, but perhaps Shakespeare's Claudius had only metaphorically to look the other way to hear the prick of conscience without betraying any outward reaction. In any case, Shakespeare would have liked his play-within-the-play to progress as Hamlet's mirror test of guilt at least for a while before it is brought to an abrupt close at the King's behest.

A Shakespeare inset which raises many possibilities with its multifarious and varied play and exploration of layered illusion is to be seen in *Troilus and Cressida* (I.iii.142–84). It is Ulysses's elaborately detailed and queerly engaged acting out of the theatrics going on according to him, between Achilles and Patroclus in their isolation in the former's tent. It occurs in the Greek council scene and follows almost on the heels of the once-too-often-quoted and too-often invoked exhortation by Ulysses about the irrefragability of 'Degree'. After offering his diagnosis that the Greek warriors' failure to penetrate Troy or win a decisive victory is the growing disdainment of 'Degree' among them, that is, the 'neglection of degree', Ulysses illustrates what he considers to be the prevailing debunking of the great by his leisurely citation of how Achilles and Patroclus parctise such debunking. The inset should be quoted in good part at this point to facilitate our discussion.

> The great Achilles, whom opinion crowns
> The sinew and the forehand of our host,
> Having his ear full of his airy fame,
> Grows dainty of his worth, and in his tent
> Lies mocking our designs. With him Patroclus
> Upon a lazy bed the livelong day
> Breaks scurril jests,
> And with ridiculous and awkward action—
> Which, slanderer, he imitation calls—
> He pageants us. Sometime, great Agamemnon,
> Thy topless deputation he puts on
> And, like a strutting player, whose conceit
> Lies in his hamstring, and doth think it rich
> To hear the wooden dialogue and sound
> 'Twist his stretch'd footing and the scaffoldage,—
> Such to-be-pitied and o'er-wrested seeming,
> He acts thy greatness in:—and when he speaks.
> 'Tis like a chime a-mending; with terms unsquar'd

> Which, from the tongue of roaring Typhon dropp'd,
> Would seem hyperboles. At this fusty stuff,
> The large Achilles on his press'd bed lolling,
> From his deep chest laughs out a loud applause;
> Cries, 'Excellent!' 'tis Agamemnon just
> Now play me Nestor; hem, and stroke thy beard,
> As he being drest to some oration'.
> That's done;—as near as the extremest ends
> Of parallels, like as Vulcan and his wife.
> Yet good Achilles still cries, 'Excellent!
> 'Tis Nestor right. Now play him me, Patroclus,
> Arming to answer in a night alarm'.
> And then forsooth, the faint defects of age
> Must be the scene of mirth; to cough and spit,
> And with a palsy—fumbling on his gorget,
> Shake in and out the rivet; and at this sport
> Sir Valour dies; cries, lo! enough! Patroclus;
> Or give me ribs of steel; I shall split all
> In pleasure of my spleen . . . '

The first of a whole series of piquant ironies abounding in the passage with its simultaneous illusion-mongering and illusion-baiting is that it is a *tour de force* of near-unparliamentary, comical instance theatricals indulged in by Ulysses at the solemn conclave of the Greek war council, the presiding members being the sage and serious Agamemnon and the grand old Nestor. The wily Ulysses ultimately aims at bringing Achilles, his *bete noire*, more than a peg or two down if not debunking him. Ulysses performs a feat of having it both ways, crying out on debunking and vicariously practising it himself with impunity, and brings it off. It is an obstreperously theatrical staging-out of the staginess of what Ulysses alleges to be the improviso acting between them of Achilles and Patroclus.

The venerable figures supposedly caricatured are none other than Agamemnon and Nestor, and the caricatures in the name of enacted report are acted out with enormous relish and style by Ulysses under the very nose of Agamemnon and Nestor in the august assembly. Playing the hamstring player that Patroclus is, Ulysses struts for the moment in an impersonation of Agamemnon, frettingly footing the stage for an effect of sound and fury, creating the 'wooden dialogue', in something like 'King

Cambises' vein.' Ulysses ventriloquises the applauding response of Achilles to such poor hemming and hawing imitation as presented by Patroclus. More than Ulysses, Shakespeare would seem to achieve many ends in his speech for Ulysses who 'in one person plays many roles'. At a primary level, the playwright–dramaturgist provides a demonstration of *an exemplum ad horrendum* of what sorts of crude, positively bad hamstring acting may be current and are to be guarded against. Secondly, he suggests a distinction between true imitation and mere caricature in so far as acting is concerned. Ulysses apparently has in mind a similar distinction between laudable and desirable emulation and a mere apeing of mannerisms, foibles and follies. Shakespeare also implicitly raises the question whether the stage representation of the great really serves to enhance public regard and to give an impression of power and glory. A good deal of new historicist and cultural criticism in recent years has stressed this aspect of Shakespearian and related drama as providing a display of royal power and authority and its promotion through direct 'gaze' and subtle, indirect techniques. Yet we have evidence that Sir Henry Wotton wrote in a letter in 1614, in which he reported the fire at the Globe during a performance of *King Henry VIII* that the play made 'greatness very familiar' if not ridiculous. So it is possible that certain stage representations could have the effect of exposing the feet of clay of demi-gods. The presentation on the stage of the living monarch by an actor was avoided, and in the sole instance of such presentation having been attempted in 1604, where the living King James I was sought to be portrayed in his previous avatar as James VI of Scotland, in a play entitled *The Tragedy of Gowrie*, the play had to be withdrawn within a week on a Privy Council order.

Shakespeare also seems to be making more than one point about the deliberately overt, self-conscious theatricality, gaining vogue in the new children's companies at the time of *Troilus and Cressida*. He may be glancing at such emphasis on theatricalism, on calculated bombast and on deliberate parody of the old big bow wow mode of stage presentation as was to be found, for example, in the plays of John Marston. Thus a considerably complex, implied poetic of theatrical conception and practices on the part of Shakespeare may be traced to underlie Ulysses's pastiche performance.

From the examples of several kinds of the Shakespeare inset we have considered, as also from other examples not considered here, certain inferences may be drawn. What Shakespeare brings to the fore in these is the fascinating interplay between the worlds of illusion and of reality. No simple compartmentalisation or stark contrast between illusion and reality will be adequate to the complexities of interpenetrative relationship between the two. Shakespeare rather brings home almost at once the force of the illusion of reality and of the reality of illusion. Such an interpenetrative intercommunication comes through in various ways in terms of the disjunctions and conjunctions of illusion and reality which often mark the Shakespeare inset. We move between the worlds with amazing speed, ease and instinctiveness of accommodation. To put it another way, the different worlds or worlds-within-worlds or levels of reality are in a dynamic relationship with one another, with constant quick oscillation and reorientation or rather of electronic simultaneity or instantaneity of change and reordering. Such a dynamic 'both/and' logic of the double or multiple world of illusion-cum-reality could perhaps be diagrammatically indicated by adopting and modifying Luce Irigaray's Venn diagram for 'both/and' logic thus:

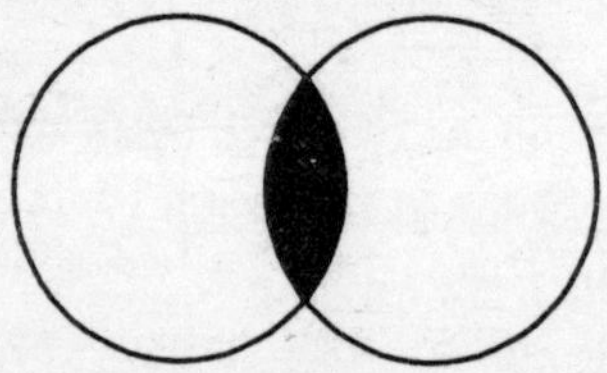

The two (as in the diagram) or more circles or spheres of illusion and reality may be imagined as in active gyration and interpenetration, the state of gyration suggesting the dynamic dialectic between illusion and reality.

The basic factor here is the strong, inalienable impression of reality with which Shakespeare makes dramatic illusion at its most characteristic impinge on us, and he does this also through the insets we have been considering showing how fallacies, inadequacies, bunglings and misdirections of conception, communication and response in theatrical experience can mar the impression, which, as Maurice Morgann wisely said with regard to Shakespeare, is the fact, the reality. The impression is one of luminous reality, of the 'golden world' which Sir Philip Sidney spoke of as delivered by the poet as distinct from the quotidian brazen world. It was exactly this kind of apprehension of the world of drama and poetry as one of luminous, noumenal reality, as marked by *avabhasa* and hence carrying an 'idealistically real' quality, which our prime Sanskrit aesthetician Abhinavagupta advocated in his *avabhasavada*. Such a special luminous order of reality should be distinguished from the *abhasa*, the 'realistically ideal' quality he attributed to the quotidian phenomenal world. It is the special force, power and validity and above all, relishability of dramatic or literary illusion, its uniqueness and irreplaceability and indispensability, which require to be constantly borne in mind in the postmodern critical situation of discounting or denying it through the tendency of flattening drama and literature into name-what-you-will sociology, politics, or whatever or into yet another discourse among discourses.

10
The Profession of Playhouse and Player in the Shakespeare Inset

Shakespeare's implicit, unfussy commitment to drama and theatre as an institution and his exclusive allegiance to the Chamberlain's men who later became the King's men, as their star playwright, sharer and one of their actors, carries a suggestion of a notable professionality, a governing sense of which marks all his plays early and late. True, a self-deprecatory attitude may be read into the utterances in his Sonnets such as

> Alas! 'tis true I have gone here and there
> And made myself a motley to the view
>
> (Sonnet 110, ll. 1–2)

> O! for my sake do you with Fortune chide
> The guilty goddess of my harmful deeds,
> That did not better for my life provide
> Than public means which public manners breeds.
>
> (Sonnet 111, ll. 1–4)

However the lines are at the most an expression of a passing mood which has to be understood in the context of the address to the Friend; what emerges when we consider Shakespeare's career, profession and life as a whole is a tacit, happy, and not to mention profitable, engagement with playwriting, the playhouse and playing. His career synchronised with the phenomenal growth and flourishing of the professional commercial playhouse. More importantly, it coincided with the acquisition by the institution of not only social respectability but a political space and strikingly, alongside it, a rapport with the court if not the sovereign, and with almost all sections of the general community, despite the then prevalent puritan and other antitheatrical prejudice. Such a development was contributed to in no small measure by Shakespeare's association with his theatre which can be said to rank highest among the companies of the times in many respects. It was the time when several categories of people associated with the now fully institutionalised theatre gained status besides material prosperity. The professional actor especially acquired a sense of identity, a kind of social recognition and esteem and above all a certain dignity in place of the earlier indignities he was subject to, as Muriel Bradbrook showed in her book *The Rise of the Common Player* (London, 1964). An expression of Shakespeare's apprehension of aspects of this ongoing development with regard to the theatre in his time may be traced particularly in the insets across the plays, such as the play-within-the-play and other inserted, enacted performances where there are frequent contexts for such reference. The chapter takes a look at the implications which such insets in the plays carry in this regard.

An abiding sense of Shakespeare's quiet pride, and also faith, in the presentational resources of his stage and theatre and in the talents and accomplishments of his actors, which facility informs his drama as a whole, would seem to come through especially in the insets referred to in several plays. First, there is an irony apparently directed against amateur acting and dramatics and in favour of the professional drama and acting. Secondly, there runs a suggestion of both the problems and deficiencies of court drama as against public theatre drama. There is also an implied contrast made between the tradition of the gild, artisan actors of late medieval religious drama and the popular moralities and the actors of the early years of institutionalised London public theatre, on the one hand, and the professional actors and acting of Shakespeare's theatre. Yet, perhaps the irony should not be taken as entirely one-sided; it also cuts both ways to some extent. Also, Shakespeare takes every opportunity to defend and assert the dignity of the professional player. Above all, with his informing sense of the legitimacy of the profession of theatre and of acting to the fore in his insets, Shakespeare takes occasion frequently to raise, in terms of the processes and dynamics of the inset 'devices' or performances, issues and questions of acting, verse and delivery, of the attitudes and assumptions in regard to stage conventions and properties and of audience response and of the kind of 'multi- consciousness' which should govern the whole enterprise. We may look at some examples of the Shakespeare inset and see what issues regarding the modes, mechanics and processes of play presentation onstage are implicitly raised in these.

The difficulties, and indeed the perils and disasters that amateur drama is heir to and the difference and superiority of professional drama such as Shakespeare's are amply indicated in the insets in *Love's Labour's Lost* and *A Midsummer Night's Dream*, and suggested in the charade between Prince Hal and Falstaff in *Henry IV, Pt.1*. In *Love's Labour's Lost* both in the Muscovite masque of the King of Navarre and his cohorts and in the pageant of the Nine Worthies the calculatedly and wilfully hostile reception accorded to the performances in the respective cases spoils the show to the general comic effect primarily intended by the playwright. But the comic effect is also at the expense of amateur theatricals. The efforts and trouble which the amateur performer has to go through in learning and memorising their 'parts' and lines and in the stage delivery are underscored. In an age when memory was actively cultivated, sheer habit and practice would have made the task not so formidable for the repertory theatre player to whom it would be second nature to speak his lines 'audaciously'. ('Audacity' and 'audaciously' were the terms used in the then different sense, by Shakespeare, Thomas Heywood in his *Apology for Actors* and also Milton later, to denote the quality of fluent, bold and clear enunciation.) The actor was generally 'perfect' in this respect. That is why the actor who forgets his part is cited as an example of extreme discomfiture. Boyet reports how the king and company instructed and prepared Armado's page, Moth, to act as their herald in the Muscovite masque:

> Their herald is a pretty knavish page,
> That well by heart hath conn'd his embassage;
> Action and accent did they teach him there;
> 'Thus thou must speak, and thus thy body bear'.
> And ever and anon they made a doubt

> Presence majestical would put him out . . .
>
> (*Love's Labour's Lost*, V.ii. 97–102)[1]

Moth in the actual enactment is unable to resist his bafflement by the concerted adverse response of Boyet, the Princess and her companions despite his brave attempt. And he is 'out' of his part.

> *Moth* They do not mark me, and that brings me out.
> *Berowne* Is this your perfectness? Be gone, you rogue!
>
> (V.ii. 173–4)

But the king and his companions' masking enterprise despite their sedulous conning and delivery is pitifully rebuffed by the princess and her friends.

The Nine Worthies' pageant, planned and 'fitted' by the pedant Holofernes with himself, the curate Nathaniel, Costard the rustic, Armado the 'fantastic' and Moth his page, the village types thus intending doubling or trebling the parts meets with no better fate. Costard, however, steals the show with his performances, 'armed as Pompey', and more with his interventions on his own. He could say

> ... I hope I was perfect. I made a
> little fault in 'Great'.
>
> (V.ii. 559–60)

Nathaniel the curate gets much put out by interruptions and is forced to retire, with Costard commenting:

> A conqueror, and afeard to speak! run
> away for shame, Alisander!

but adding, with sympathy,

> There, an't shall please you; a foolish
> mild man, an honest man, look you, and
> soon dashed! He is a marvellous good
> neighbour, faith, and a very good bowler;
> but, for Alisander,—alas you see
> how 'tis,—a little o'erparted.
>
> (V.ii. 579–85)

---

1. Quotations from the old Oxford Shakespeare, ed. W.J. Craig, 1974 reprint.

The schoolmaster Holofernes presenting Judas Maccabeus the prophet himself and Moth as Hercules 'in minority' as a child, in spite of his competent delivery and presentation, schoolmaster that he is, is subjected to a battery of verbal harassment by the king's companions and Boyet. He retires retorting:

> This is not generous, not gentle, not humble.
>
> (V.ii. 628)

Incidentally, in contrast to the adverse response of Navarre and his court, when Queen Elizabeth in the course of one of her triumphs across the country found a village schoolmaster drying up totally awestruck by the presence in his attempt to read a welcoming address to her, the Queen picked up the paper from him and herself read it out for him. Armado the fantastic in his role as Hector meets a worse fate than Holofernes, concerned as he is in several ways. The pedant and the fantastic are both addicts to the word, though the wrong way round:

> *Moth* They have been at a great feast of
> languages and stolen the scraps
>
> *Costard* Oh! They have lived long on the
> alms-basket of words.
>
> (V.i. 39–42)

Yet their verbal fluidity is of no avail, when they attempt dramatic utterance. Shakespeare would seem to suggest that the shaping and enunciation of the dramatic word demands unique skills on the part of both playwright and player.

Similarly, in *A Midsummer Night's Dream* Quince the carpenter rattles off the Prologue to 'Pyramus and Thisbe' which he directs and stage manages, without punctuation or pauses or proper linkages. It is as though Shakespeare the professional has the point raised and discussed by Theseus and his companions for some space (*A Midsummer Night's Dream*, V. i. 118–28). No wonder Hamlet exhorts the First Player:

> Speak the speech, I pray you, as I pronounced it to you,
> trippingly on the tongue; but if you mouth it as many of our
> players do, I had as lief the town-crier spoke my lines.
>
> (*Hamlet* III.ii. 1–4)

Falstaff's attempt to speak in the part of King Henry IV in his charade with Prince Henry, 'in King Cambises' vein,' though he has his fan as actor for the nonce in Mistress Quickly, is not much of a success in role-playing, provoking the prince to assume the role himself and give his to Falstaff. (*King Henry IV*, *Pt. I*, II.iv. 482–3). Incidentally, Shakespeare, through Falstaff's phraseology here, is able to parody the euphuistic style of Lyly in his plays as well as in his romance.

Tackling dramatic speech, especially verse-speaking, is always a challenge, as the problems which arise in the rendering of verse in the case of even the very best actors in the flourishing present-day Shakespearian theatre often shows. But probably Shakespeare's actors in his day probably could meet the challenge.

Shakespeare has in mind the tradition of the court drama of the 1580s, mainly represented by Lyly's comedies, especially in *The Two Gentlemen of Verona* and *Love's Labour's Lost*. In the first he makes an ironical exploitation of the friendship convention dear to Lyly and in the latter the conception and presentation of Armado and Moth has ironical reference to Lyly's *Endymion*. It is not so much of a relationship of influence as reaction. As the leading force behind the public playhouse tradition, Shakespeare and his theatre vindicated this tradition, and it is noteworthy that his company came to perform their public theatre plays at court regularly and often before the ruling monarch; they came to be in the good books of the Privy Council. In the insets in *Love's Labour's Lost* and *A Midsummer Night's Dream* the risks of mounting a play and playing at court are hinted at. Though the fears of the artisans in their rehearsals (I.ii. 73–84) about the lion-like roaring causing offence by frightening the ladies at the court and hence resulting in the hanging of the artisans are ludicrous. Behind it there is the problem of the player's risk of incurring the court's displeasure. Let alone the theory that Shakespeare's *A Midsummer Night's Dream* was intended for court performance at a court wedding, Shakespeare's drama and company would keep their head on its shoulders if not hold the head high, successfully negotiating between the twin perils of censorship and of licence. The lone instance of Queen Elizabeth's anger at a particular performance of *Richard II*, put up by his supporters on the eve of the Essex rebellion is an exception to this rule. And even in this case no punishment or disadvantage whatever to the company ensued.

The artisan players with Quince the carpenter for their leader and Bottom the weaver as their star performer, and their rehearsals and production of 'Pyramus and Thisbe' in *A Midsummer Night's Dream* remind us of the strong old late medieval tradition of the trade gilds' artisan members performing the Mystery plays and the Moralities. By Shakespeare's time the tradition of the Mysteries had been practically suppressed in the new climate of the Reformation, although the boy Shakespeare could well have seen one of the very last enactments of the Mystery cycle at Coventry in 1571. For aught we know, the artisan actors in the heyday of the tradition could have been competent enough to do justice to the dramatic qualities of many of the Mysteries. However, Shakespeare writing for the public playhouse actors at a time of the coming of age or real arrival of the professional actor, could well have not thought much of the old practice of amateur artisan acting. By the same argument, he unfavourably contrasts with his playhouse productions and practices, the early plays and their actors in the initial years of the London playhouse, the late seventies and eighties of the sixteenth century, as ironical digs at ''Ercles' vein' and 'King Cambises' vein', espoused by Bottom and Falstaff for their acting, and at the lumbering fourteener lines of that drama, with Bottom going one better than the fourteener proposing to make it 'eight and eight' (*A Midsummer Night's Dream*, III.i. 26).

In the matter of playhouse practices and conventions and stage conditions in general Shakespeare institutes in his insets an implicit ironical contrast which sometimes cuts implicitly both ways. Quince the director-manager of 'Pyramus and Thisbe' in *A Midsummer Night's Dream,* has the 'parts' ready and written up for his actors; he 'fits' them and will also get a bill of properties ready. Quince says:

> This green plot shall be our stage, this hawthorn-brake our tiring-house, and we will do it in action as we will do it before the duke.
>
> (*A Midsummer Night's Dream,* III.i.3–7)

By the same argument, Falstaff sets out on the charade of impersonating King Henry IV to the Prince, saying:

> . . . this chair shall be my state, this
> dagger my sceptre, and this cushion
> my crown

evoking the prince's retort:

> Thy state is taken for a joint-stool,
> thy golden sceptre for a leaden dagger,
> and thy precious rich crown for a
> pitiful bald crown!
>
> (*King Henry IV, Pt. 1,* II.iv. 419–25)

In such instances, the contrast with the vastly superior resources of the Shakespearian professional stages also implies a correspondence at another level. That aside, far from being 'a bare board', as it was once thought, the Shakespearian stage whether that of the Globe or the earlier Theatre, was colourfully equipped especially in its stage-façade for all its being a non-illusionistic and hence conventionalistic theatre, as the design of the New Globe in London now demonstrates. In the matter of stage properties and stage adjuncts and ornamentation the Shakespearian theatre must have, if anything, compared favourably with Henslowe's Rose Theatre and proved superior. It is not surprising that Shakespeare mockingly introduces the comic improvisations of the Lion and the Wall in 'Pyramus and Thisbe'. The attempt of Quince to ensure moonshine in the Duke's chamber on the performance night is meant to expose the absurdity of realism taken to its extreme. By the same argument, when Bottom suggests a prologue, in order to reassure the ladies and keep them from fear, to the effect

> . . . I, Pyramus, am not Pyramus,
> but Bottom the weaver: this
> will put them out of fear.
>
> (*A Midsummer Night's Dream,* III.i. 19–22)

it raises thoughts about the cruciality of the inherent quality of the 'multiconsciousness' governing the whole popular tradition of drama including the Shakespearian theatre, the quality which S.L. Bethell wrote about in 1944 (*Shakespeare and the Popular*

Dramatic Tradition). The awareness and consciousness on the part of the spectator of 'the actor as character' and 'the character as actor' at once may be missed by some involved in the dramatic transaction or may be disturbed or dislocated as by Bottom. Such a double consciousness would have been second nature to the citizens and villagers who witnessed the mysteries enacted by their artisan and craftsman neighbours in their day. Such multiconsciousness, Shakespeare seems to imply, has to arise and operate spontonaeously and instinctively. It is his sureness of touch and finesse in exploring the heritage of this 'multiconsciousness' which enables Shakespeare to use the stage-world similitude most meaningfully, and to exploit modes of self-conscious theatricality in his later plays. Or for example, when he reminds his *Hamlet* audience that Burbage who played Brutus in *Julius Caesar* is Hamlet now and the player of Polonius was Julius Caesar in the earlier play.

Polonius I did enact Julius Caesar
I was killed i'the Capitol;
Brutus killed me.

Hamlet It was a brute part of
him to kill so capital
a calf there.

(*Hamlet,* IV.ii 104–12)

It is true that in *Henry V*, through the self-apologetic Chorus utterances by way of admitting the inadequacies of his stage to represent the epic scenes of great battles or for that matter, the sea or horses, Shakespeare craves the indulgence of the audience.

On this unworthy scaffold to bring forth
So great an object; can this cockpit hold
The vasty fields of France? Or may we cram
Within this wooden O the very casques
That did affright the air at Agincourt?

(*Henry V*, First Chorus, ll. 10–14)

This repeated request of the Chorus to 'eke out our performance with your mind' is Shakespeare's way of not only or merely disarming disbelief and evoking a willing suspension of it on the part of the spectator but a signal of a confidence that with the existing resources of theatrical language effectual dramatic communication will be established. A similarity may be found in the way the present-day viewer with the awareness of the unseen hand of com puter graphics at the back of his mind responds to the performance on the television or cinema screen where, for example, a few soldiers in the filming are made to appear as thousands on the screen in a battle scene.

In *A Midsummer Night's Dream* Theseus avers with tolerant indulgence towards the players of 'Pyramus and Thisbe' that even 'the best in this kind are but shadows.' It is an admission and a warning that even the gifted professional actors may fall short. However, if anything, Shakespeare's success is partly owing to his confidence in his actors and in their theatrical and stage practices. For instance, the overzealousness of Bottom to take on many roles, if not all, in the play being planned (I.ii.) besides the simple ridicule intended behind it, carries the stage problem of 'fitting' an actor and some in double, or treble roles. The Shakespearian playhouse developed good working traditions in this respect. Though the idea advocated by T.W. Baldwin once of the actors being cast on certain habitual 'lines' or special kinds of roles for them may not be valid, in all probability the actors did not take on too much and a judicious use was made of doubling dictated by the limited number of professional players available in the company. This went alongside the versatility of the Shakespearian player. Burbage appears to have been remarkable in this regard. He also played the lead role which was acted by Alleyn earlier when older plays such as *The Spanish Tragedy* were revived by Shakespeare's company. The elegy to him notes his amazing versatility. The average professional actor, though not attaining very high levels of accomplishment, would avoid such clumsiness in stage business which Shakespeare seems to have mockingly implied in Thisbe in 'Pyramus and Thisbe' stabbing herself with the butt-end of her dagger, a clumsiness mocked at later at a second level in Edward Sharpham's *The Fleir* (1607), a self-consciously theatrical exercise of a play carrying parodying reminiscences of situations and utterances in earlier plays. Through Hamlet's instructions to the player, Shakespeare underscored such common vices the actor was prone to such as the intrusive gags of the clown or the fool such as Tarlton's the adoption of postures, gestures and tones of ranting, etc. 'out-Heroding Herod'.

In general, Shakespeare's attestation of the dignity of the actor and of his status and legitimacy in society comes through in the insets. He was himself also an actor, although we know little about his acting career except for a tradition that he played old Adam in *As You Like It* and the Ghost in *Hamlet*, and the fact that his name figures in the players' lists of a couple of Ben Jonson plays of his company. Shakespeare's line in Sonnet 87:

> In sleep a king, but waking no such matter

taken with an epigram of his contemporary John Davies of Hereford, 'To our English Terence, Mr Will. Shakespeare':

> Some say (good will) which I, in sport, do sing,
> Had'st thou not plaid some kingly parts in sport,
> Thou had'st bin a companion for a king.
> And, beene a king among the meaner sort.
> (*The Scourge of Folly*, 1611, 76–7)

would suggest his acting of kings. Whether in the early *The Taming of the Shrew* or in *Hamlet*, there is an assiduous insistence that a dignified and hospitable treatment should be accorded to the players as guests:

> *The Lord* . . . take them to the buttery,
> And give them friendly welcome every one;
> Let them want nothing that my house affords.
> (*The Taming of the Shrew*, Induction, ll.102–4)

and

> *Hamlet* . . . Good my lord, will you see the players well bestowed? Do you hear, let them be well used; for they are the abstracts and brief chronicles of the time. . . .
>
> *Polonius* My lord, I will use them according to their desert.
>
> *Hamlet* God's bodikins, man, much better; use every man after his desert, and who should 'scape whipping? Use them after your own honour and dignity. . . .
> (*Hamlet*, II.ii.553–63)

The enjoined warmth and courtesy in the reception of the actors, the affection with which Hamlet responds to the players and his keen remembrance of the particular roles and speeches of the actors in their plays as well as *The Shrew* Induction Lord's command and his recollection with admiration of a certain Soto the wooer's role 'aptly fitted and naturally perform'd', by a particular player'– all these bespeak not only the characters' love of the stage but Shakespeare's warmth of feeling and fellowship towards the actors. No wonder his fellow actors Heminge and Condell were the ones who edited and brought out the plays in folio, the First Folio (1623) years after his death and that Shakespeare remembered them in his last will and testament.

Shakespeare's fellow-feeling for the actor-community would seem to extend to travelling troupes as well. The troupes in the two plays mentioned are examples. True, he takes occasion in *Hamlet* (F) to bemoan the challenge of the newly revived boys' companies, felt by the 'great Globe itself', forcing the actors onto the road in search of playing venues. But that does not point to any prejudice against travelling players. Travelling troupes from London visited Stratford fairly regularly in the 1580s, and it has recently been also suggested by E.A.J. Honigmann in his *Shakespeare: the Lost Years* (Totowa, N.J: 1985) that Shakespeare perhaps began his theatre career by joining one such travelling troupe elsewhere as actor when he was attached to a noble household. If true, this cannot of course be taken as the only factor, making for his sympathy and fellow-feeling for travelling actors. For, according to a tradition started by Shakespeare's fellow actor William Beeston, Shakespeare was a schoolmaster in the country in his youth but his portrayal of schoolmaster characters in the plays is hardly complimentary.

Shakespeare's handling of his boy-actors and his attitude towards them deserve some attention. He perhaps made the subtlest and most effective and fruitful use of the convention of the 'boy-actress.' But what is interesting is that as well as exploiting in several ways the androgynous potentialities of the boy-actresses, he could enable, almost inspire them to execute their roles in accordance with their talents, with natural ease, vivacity, the right economy of effort, and effectiveness. No wonder an English traveller expressed his admiration for the performance of young girls in female roles in an Italian play which he saw in Italy, saying that he was pleased that the girls performed their roles as naturally as the 'boy-actresses' on the English stage of the time. Also, Shakespeare refrains from using the boy-actors for producing the kinds of deliberate incongruity, parody, disorientation and distortion of scale dear to a playwright like John Marston who wrote mainly for the children's companies. For aught we know, Shakespeare's company did not treat their boys with the harshness sometimes discovered in the way the child-actors were recruited and treated by the children's companies.

On the whole, Shakespeare's dramatic career is a story of happy collaboration between himself as playwright, as part owner of his company and its actor, on the one side, and his company, its playhouses and its players, on the other, not to mention his various satisfied audiences. With these last, he had a rapport and none of the reservations and occasional displeasure entertained by playwrights like Ben Jonson. It was almost a model of healthy partnership, a camaraderie, that made for mutual enrichment and creative cross-fertilisation. Shakespeare himself is not known to have instructed his players in rehearsals in the way Ben Jonson is recorded to have done, and Ben Jonson seems to have had a reputation as a good instructor. But we can safely presume Shakespeare to have enjoyed free and ready lines of communication with his actors. To an extent, Shakespeare seems to have intended certain character roles and parts for particular actor-colleagues of his vestigial. 'Enter' stage directions as well as other evidence amply show this. His was an exclusive bond of loyalty to his company, in contrast to the practice of other playwrights. He refrained from taking to the writing of court masques, though he incorporated some masque elements in his last plays and though his public playhouse plays were performed at court and at noble households at regular intervals by the company. All this stands testimony to Shakespeare being not only the complete man of his theatre but every inch a man of his theatre. A most striking factor about Shakespeare the poet-playwright is the sustained unity between the poet-dramatist, the playhouse sharer and the actor in Shakespeare.

To sum up, the Shakespearian insets may be said to afford intimations of his convictions and attitudes regarding matters and issues of the professional theatre, its ways of functioning and practices and above all its place in society and its impact on the court and on the general population from more or less the whole spectrum of which the theatre-going though not the play-reading public, was drawn (despite the thesis to the contrary, as regards this last, of a critic like Ann Jennalie Cook). Shakespeare's keen aliveness to the material and physical conditions of the stage is particularly to be noted in the context of materialist criticism of Shakespeare which, while placing all its stress on the material conditions of art and literature, does not sufficiently take into account the mutual entailment of these and the art of drama.

That Shakespeare distanced himself from the idea of drama for the court and of the court, is only slightly less interesting than the fact that the court often enough invited his company to perform there and that the Privy Council order for the closure of the London theatres after a performance of *The Isle of Dogs* in the Swan in 1597 exempted his company. Evidently, his drama all along evoked on the part of the court a high degree of receptiveness, though not altogether untinged with wariness. More particularly, Shakespearian drama could well negotiate the hurdles of censorship through fine negotiation. It was a discreetness which was not a meek acceptance of curbs that made art tongue-tied, so much so that censorship did not exactly suppress drama, contrary to the assumption by some scholars that it was a formidable factor. An acquaintance with Shakespeare's apprehension of the reception of drama, as implied in the response of the onstage audiences to performances within the plays, may help clarify our critical discussion of the question. The Shakespeare insets as well as the plays embody an implied poetic of dramatic illusion and play reception. The central emphasis is on the indispensability of 'a willing suspension of disbelief' (to use Coleridge's classic expression). The insets implicitly raise the question of the effect of the representation of personages of greatness such as kings and heroes of legend, a question often canvassed in cultural politics.

On the whole, Shakespeare seems to have had an unobtrusive awareness, an innate grasp and a certain anticipation and accommodation of the dimensions, pressures and pulls of factors of power, ideology, and sociopolitical practice. It is all too obvious that this is why contemporary cultural–political criticism has seen so much of these dimensions in Shakespeare and other drama, as it is obvious that Shakespeare could hardly help responding to sociopolitical challenge. However, it is perhaps not to state the obvious to say that Shakespearian drama in particular seems to have responded to factors of power, ideology and socio-politics in indirect and often delicately poised, nuanced but effective ways. What we have to do is to find out by our proper directions these indirections rather than be content with working out direct and one-to-one correspondence, often reductionist in the result.

11

The Impugnable as Inexpugnable: Censorship and Shakespearian Drama

In what may be viewed as a collateral if not concomitant development of the vogue enjoyed by cultural political criticism of Renaissance drama and literature, there has been a rekindling of scholarly and critical interest in the question of censorship in relation to the Renaissance English drama. For example, there have been several recent book-length studies[1] of the matter, besides articles and the earlier examinations of the records of the English court's successive Masters of the Revels, Sir Edmund Tilney and Sir George Buc in Elizabethan and Jacobean times in this regard. These studies have, no doubt, served to bring to the fore the political dimensions of the Shakespearian theatre as an institution in general and to alert us to the political factors such as may have operated in and around particular plays which attracted the censors' attention. However, illuminating as these studies are, these would seem to have addressed and interpreted the figuring of the material under the shadow of censorship in the plays, and the censoring event and its outcome, either with the assumption that

---

1. Richard Dutton, *Mastering the Revels: The Regulation and Censorship of English Renaissance Drama* (Iowa City: University of Iowa Press, 1991); Janet Clare, 'Art made tongue-tied by authority', *Elizabethan and Jacobean Dramatic Censorship* (Manchester: Manchester University Press, 1990); Annabel Patterson, *Censorship and Interpretation* (Wisconsin: University of Wisconsin Press, 1984).

the theatre was inherently complicit with the Establishment and thus was 'always already' hegemonised by the powers that were or on the premise that the drama and the theatre had radical potential and tendencies and could often take an oppositional role, now in covert, now in relatively overt fashion. Roughly, these two critical attitudes in their orientation could be categorised as the new historicist assumption that basically the Shakespearian theatre and drama were willy-nilly an agent and an instrument of power, and the cultural materialist or oppositional criticism's view of plays and playwrights as sites and voices of questioning of authority, received opinions and traditional social and moral values. An examination of a few representative instances of Elizabethan plays which were provocations to the censor and of the impact of the censoring action on the plays, playwrights and the theatre would go to show that the situation which obtained cannot be viewed with such all but mutually exclusive 'either/or' assumptions and that, often, it could be seen to be one more of a 'both/and' multiplicity in varying degrees from case to case. The material liable to be censored often functions in the plays of the time in a double-edged manner in several ways. So much so that it is not only that the sensitive material provokes the action of the censor's scissors on itself and thereby could achieve a *success de scandal* for the play. Also, even as the material risks and faces trouble, it finds ways of sometimes escaping action and sometimes resuscitating and reincarnating itself and thus surviving as a sort of hardy perennial.

That such a two-fold status of sustaining or risking proscription and at the same time managing to achieve recuperation marks material in Renaissance English plays, and indeed the theatre and drama of the period as a whole as an institution, can be gathered from a brief consideration of certain examples. There are the censorship attentions that the play of *Sir Thomas More* came in for and the play's response, the involvement of Shakespeare's *Richard II* with Queen Elizabeth and the court as well as with Essex's followers, the possible disapproval at the hands of the authority evoked by passages in *Hamlet* and *King Lear*, both in their Quarto versions, the notorious and all but compulsive proneness that the plays of the boy company, the Children of the Chapel, exhibited in the first decade of the seventeenth century, and the telling instances of

Middleton's *A Game at Chess* (1624) and Massinger's *The Roman Actor* (1625). The power vested with the Master of Revels to censor whatever in the plays may be regarded by him as 'heretical, seditious, or unseemly for Christian ears,' for one thing, left as much room for so much matter to escape the net of censorship as for the apparently long and strict arm of censorship to seize hold of it. For another, as the evidence of the Henslowe papers shows,[2] theatre owners and theatre managers like him could, through periodical payments of cash and periodical entertainment of Tilney, succeed in averting his censoring of plays. Ironically enough, the city fathers for their part tried to bribe Tilney to induce him to restrain the players. Thirdly, while it is true that governmental repression, more than the general strong wave of Protestantism with the iconoclastic campaign it entailed, led to the ceasing of the active tradition of the Mystery and Miracle plays which was current till around the middle of the sixteenth century, the Puritans' and city fathers' opposition to the playhouses could not come in the way of the phenomenal flourishing of the theatre and drama precisely because the monarch herself, her successor and the court patronised it. Furthermore, in all probability as Margot Heinemann and Martin Butler have shown in their books, the Puritans and the citizen community leaders came to patronise the theatre in such a manner that several plays and playwrights could seem to have taken an oppositional and anti-court stance and function, and, more interestingly, they could generally do so without incurring the displeasure of the powers that were.

In the case of *Sir Thomas More* one of the very few plays of the period of which the original manuscript is extant we have on the manuscript the instruction of Tilney the censor written in that the whole scene of the 'III May Day' riots of the London populace be left out, the one in which the native citizens expressed their resentment against foreign artisans in London for their haughtiness by rising in rebellion and trying to kill them and burn down their houses.

---

2. R.A. Foakes and R.T. Rickert, eds. *Henslowe's Diary* (Cambridge: Cambridge University Press, 1961), p. xxviii and n.5.

> Leave out the insurrection wholly and the cause thereof and begin with Sir Thomas More at the mayor's sessions (a successive scene) with a report afterwards of his good service done being sherieve [sic] of London upon a mutiny against the Lombards only by a short report and not otherwise at your own perils.[3]

Tilney also ordered the amendment of a passage in another scene which carried fairly direct topical references to the discontents and outbreaks of rioting among sections of the London population in 1592–3,[4] which were directed against the foreigners in the city. In this collaborated play Shakespeare seems to have come to have a hand, apparently at this stage, and the scene he contributed which is now generally accepted to be in his own handwriting, called Hand D in the playscript by the bibliographical scholars, portrays the confrontation of the leaders of the rioters with More as the Sheriff of London, accompanied by the Earl of Shrewsbury, the Mayor and a few officers, and More's successful persuasion of them to give up their plan. This Shakespearian scene was meant to take the place of the original objectionable scene of staging of the riots. But the point that emerges in a consideration of the scene is that it is still in the Shakespearian form a rioting scene just short of the actual riot. Though the design of the scene is mainly oriented to More's skilful handling of the crowd, his play of rhetoric and moral suasion, the rioting action is invoked in telling enough detail in the very speeches through which More turns away the wrath of the rioters and practically quells the riot. The verbal evocation of the rioters' proposed acts of defiance, violence and destruction is strong enough to the extent that the scene may be said to have it both ways.

---

3. Quoted from the *Revels History of Drama in English*, Vol. 3, p.45.
4. The date of the play of *Sir Thomas More* is not known for certain. The consensus favours 1592–4, though J.M. Nosworthy argued for a date circa 1601–2 ('Shakespeare and *Sir Thomas More*', *RES*, n.s.6, 1955, pp. 12–25). Scott McMillin, *The Elizabethan Theatre and the Book of Sir Thomas More* (Ithaca: Cornell University Press, 1986) dates the censor's and subsequently Shakespeare's, intervention 1592–3 and T.H. Howard-Hill, ed. *Shakespeare and Sir Thomas More* (Cambridge: Cambridge University Press, 1989) suggests 1593–4.

You'll put down strangers,
Kill them, cut their throats, possess their houses

(ll.119–20)

. . . by this pattern
Not one of you should live an aged man
For other ruffians, as their fancies wrought
With self-same hand, self reasons and self right,
Would shark on you, and men like ravenous fishes
Would feed on one another.[5]

(ll.82–7)

Apart from this, Shakespeare had himself portrayed the Jack Cade rebellion in lurid detail in *2 Henry VI* (Act IV), and the play for aught we know did not attract censorship action. Around 1592–3, the period to which *Sir Thomas More* may be assigned, there was the anonymous play *The Life and Death of Jack Straw* which carried scenes from the Peasants' Revolt and vigorous utterances by the character of John Ball in justification of the revolt. It held the stage, and its quarto appeared in 1594 and then again in 1604. Evidently, the topicality lent to that play by the civil disturbances in London in 1592 did not attach any objectionability to that play.

Shakespeare later also portrayed scenes of encounter between representatives of the common people in the form of the plebeians of Rome briefly in the opening scene of *Julius Caesar* and rather more extensively in *Coriolanus*. Let alone the oblique connection of the scene in *Julius Caesar* with the artisan apprentices and their love-and-hate relationship with the theatre, through the connection between the *Coriolanus* scenes in question and the contemporaneous food-riots in the Midlands and the protests against enclosures. Shakespeare could portray on the stage the stance of the plebeian representatives like the 'great toe of the commonwealth' in *Coriolanus* in a telling manner giving them a strong voice. Their voice is accorded a certain legitimation, however qualified it may be, and whatever the ironies of Shakespeare at their expense. Making due allowances for the playwright's basic exploitation of the

---

5. Quoted from *The Riverside Shakespeare*, ed. G. Blakemore Evans (Boston, 1974), p. 1693 and p. 1691.

theatrical effect and value of the small and the powerless standing up to and speaking up against the great and the powerful, we can still sufficiently recognise the legitimacy which the playwright endows the popular voice with. This play of the popular voice in the theatre does not seem to have come to the adverse notice of the censor or the authorities.

It is instructive to consider certain features of the configuration of the well-known instance of the deletion of the episode of Richard II's abdication, a highlight of Shakespeare's *Richard II*, in the two quartos of the play printed in 1598 and 1604 and of the political use of the play by Essex's followers on the eve of the Essex rebellion in 1601, and, further, Queen Elizabeth's significant reaction to the play, albeit a second-hand one. Scruples either in anticipation of censorship or imposed by it on account of the sensitivity of the portrayal of the 'unkinging' of a monarch led to the excision of the major part of the scene (IV.i) in the printing of the first quarto (1598) and the subsequent one. But the episode came to be printed in the 1608 quarto of the play and also in the First Folio. The 'deposition scene,' theatrical highlight that it is, must have been staged in performances in the theatre all along. Otherwise, there would be little point in the use sought to be made of the play by the Essex faction by commissioning a special performance of it by the Lord Chamberlain's Men on 7 February 1601 as an inspiration and a morale booster for their design of conducting the Essex rebellion the next day and of ostensibly and eventually dethroning the reigning queen. The rebellion in the event failed and Essex was sent to the Tower and subsequently executed. Queen Elizabeth noted with displeasure the attempted exploitation of the play by her enemy who was her one-time protégé and favourite and the likeness sought to be suggested between Richard II and herself as monarchs. Indeed the provocation made her generalise what would seem to have been a once-off attempt at a particular political exploitation of the play. William Lambarde, the Kentish lawyer and historian, records the Queen's reaction in his account of his conversation with her:

> I am Richard II, know ye not that
> . . . this tragedy

> was played 40 times in open streets
> and houses.[6]

The historian Camden also testifies to the commissioning of the play for the rebellion eve performance as by Essex's steward Gilly Merrick. Yet, but for a questioning of the actor-shareholder Augustine Phillips, no action was taken against Shakespeare's company and they continued to perform at court, and performances of *Richard II* continued unhindered, while Sir John Hayward who published a prose history of King Henry IV dealing with Richard II had to suffer imprisonment and stand trial for the alleged analogies between Essex and Bolingbroke, Richard II and Queen Elizabeth. In Shakespeare's play for one thing, the chivalric model as something outdated and unsuitable is portrayed, not without a slight shade of nostalgia in *Richard II* whereas it was Essex who was emulating the chivalric-heroic ideal and it was his supporters who were trying to project it thus. For another, Shakespeare presents Richard II with a certain balance of imaginative sympathy and critical judgement which makes the play at once tragedy and history in a sense. So that it is difficult to see how the play was expected by the Essex faction to evoke an altogether adversarial reaction against the monarch.

In other words, the 'deposition scene' in *Richard II* for all its political sensitivity, had its fairly smooth stage life, barring the one event referred to of its single staging. If Queen Elizabeth had any real strong resentment against the play, she would not have waited till she counted as many as 'forty' performances, and even after reaching that count, evidently, she did not order action against the play or players or playwright. Similarly, even if the reference in *Hamlet* to the 'late innovation' in Rosencrantz's line with reference to the visiting players, 'the tragedians of the city',

> I think their inhibition comes by means of the
> late innovation.
>
> (*Hamlet*, II.ii.330)

is to be taken as to the Essex rebellion and not to the new vogue enjoyed by the two boy companies in London, St Paul's Children

---

6. Cited from the Arden edition of *Richard II* by Peter Ure, p. lix.

and the Children of the Chapel, the reference to the 'inhibition' is fictional rather than factual for there is no independent evidence of any ban on playing imposed by the court in the wake of the rebellion and of the commissioned staging of *Richard II* by the Essex faction. Also, the lines about 'an eyrie of children, little eyases' carrying the day at the expense of the popularity of the public playhouses (*Hamlet*, II.ii.335–58) were not printed in the generally reliable, 'good', second Quarto of the play published in 1604, though the indications are that the lines were spoken on the stage, and hence were included in the Folio text which omits several other Quarto passages. The omission of these lines of topical force cannot be put down to a fear about the risk of censorship. Nor can the omission in the same long scene (II.ii) of ll. 239–69 centring on the claustrophobic idea of 'Denmark's prison' developed by Hamet in the same second Quarto be attributed to fear of offending King James I's queen who was from Denmark. Uncomplimentary references to the Danes, their 'wassailing' (I.iv.8–22) for instance, are retained elsewhere. It is just as Shakespeare elsewhere in his plays makes uncomplimentary or satirical references to England and the English making them laugh at themselves.

Similarly, we are alerted to the double-edged or multipronged possibilities of the operation of the mere risk or actual action of censorship when we consider the omissions in the Quarto and the Folio texts of *King Lear*. There is now the near-orthodoxy of the current view that Shakespeare first wrote the play in the Quarto version and somewhere along the line after it had its stage life and textual existence for years himself revised and rewrote the play and left it in the Folio version. This view is partly based on one of its major assumptions that certain passages (I.i.40–5; I.ii.109–14; I.iv.322–33; II.iv.140–5; III.i.20–2; IV.i.6–9; IV.vi.165–70) and a whole scene (IV.iii) came to be omitted in the Folio version for the reason that these passages tended to offend patriotic sensibilities and hence the authorities. But these passages were printed in the First Quarto (1608) and also in the Second Quarto (1619). If the passages risked censorship these would have been deleted from the Quartos, as it happened in the case of the deposition scene in *Richard II* which was omitted in the first two Quartos of that play. Correspondingly the passages which happen to be omitted in the

Quartos do not exhibit signs of being politically provocative or sensitive. Viewed from the angle of the question of possible censorship, the omissions in the Quarto and in the Folio versions of the play as well as passages exclusively in the one or the other would seem to defy a clear-cut pattern and, thus, lacking a fully convincing rationale, would make one wary of accepting the revision theory or the two *King Lears* theory about the play which is perhaps the one and only *King Lear* in two versions. Nor were the authorities, ostensibly, provoked by the possible, oblique allusions in *King Lear* to King James I's known fondness for hunting or to his relationship with his court fool Archie Armstrong suggested through old Lear's engagement in hunting and his relationship to the Fool.

There is the notorious example of the boy company of the Children of the Chapel getting into trouble with the authorities in play after play almost in succession starting with Daniel's *Philotas* (1604) (this in spite of Daniel soon after becoming an official censor) through Chapman, Jonson and Marston's *Eastward Ho!* (1605) and Day's *Isle of Gulls* (1606) to one of Chapman's *Byron* plays (1608). What is striking is that despite repeated offences the company flourished as long as it did and the court-patronage was not denied them as they played at court in the 1608–9 Christmas season, by which time Shakespeare's company began making use of the Blackfriars theatre where the boy company was playing till then, as an alternate playhouse to the Globe. True, Jonson and Chapman landed in prison (while the third author Marston fled and escaped) for the gibes at the Scotsmen they had introduced into their play *Eastward Ho!* (III.iii.38–45) and also perhaps for the quips in the play about King James I's creation of a plethora of 'ten-pound' knights, that is, his selling of knighthoods. Not only did the author find deliverance soon enough but the play itself gained a popularity and not merely as a *success de scandale*, for the same play was presented at court in 1613 and 1614. Three quartos were printed in 1605 within months of the production of the play and, although in the press in the last moment, in the first of these the offensive gibe about the Scots (III.iii.38–45) was cancelled, other quips against them were left in as well as the several veiled references to King James I's indiscriminate conferring of knighthoods.

Another major example of a political play falling foul of the authorities is Middleton's *A Game at Chess* (1624). Here again,

Middleton, as has come to be increasingly recognised, had earlier been writing plays which were critical of the court and though he did not gloss over the drawbacks of the city he was on its side. For instance, the Duke in *Women Beware Women* was portrayed as exactly the same age as King James I and the play ends with a warning to the ruler on the need for sexual morals on his part. Middleton was the chronologer to the city, that is, the person in charge of civic pageants like the Lord Mayor's shows. Under the analogy of an elaborate chess game, Middleton was portraying in *A Game at Chess* (1624) the political relationship of Britain with Spain and especially the then impending marital alliance with Prince Charles the heir-apparent's wedding with the Spanish Infanta. The play effectively captured the general mood of fear and dismay over the country seeming to bend backwards to make friends with its traditional enemy and compromise its Protestant religion. The King's Men performed the play to crowded houses at the Globe for as many as nine days before the authorities came down on the play and suppressed it and that too only at the intervention of the Spanish ambassador. The point here is that the play was passed by the Master of the Revels and had a successful albeit brief run before the authority moved in with its action. Middleton subsequently resurfaced as chronologer to the city.

In this connection we may note the instance of Massinger's plays which could also, though from a conservative angle rather than from Middleton's questioning, ironical point of view, offer an oppositional standpoint as regards the court, especially his tragedy *The Roman Actor*. It is a play with three inset plays in which the characters of the main play are actors and which offers a defence of the drama and the stage in the face of the authority's prejudice and opposition in certain quarters, a defence which by itself turns out to be an ironical vindication of the power and value of the theatre. Paris the Roman actor speaks a lengthy defence of the theatre (I.iii) rehearsing the conventional arguments such as were put forward in Thomas Heywood's *An Apology for the Actors* (1612), and the arguments are proved true with a vengeance in part and, in an intended or unintended irony of the playwright, given the lie direct in part. Paris's, in effect Massinger's, main emphasis in the defence is that drama does not traduce the rulers. Only the first of the three inset plays illustrates the moral effect of drama; it is called 'The Cure of Avarice.' The miser is cured of his greed on witnessing the play. The other two inset plays in their curious intermixture of dramatic make-believe and real situations serve to expose the guilt and lack of moral scruples of Domitianus Caesar and Domitia his mistress and also the violence and ruthlessness in the court ambience in which the actor gets killed and immorality flourishes. In effect, the play, while claiming that drama does not traduce the rulers, actually exposes their moral weaknesses. The play with its critical portrayal in the court milieu was staged by the King's Men in the Blackfriars theatre in 1625 less than a year after Middleton's *A Game at Chess* and was printed in 1629.

Indeed, in the Stuart and the Caroline periods plays like Jonson's *The New Inn* and plays by Shirley and Brome could make their political points. Also in a kind of Elizabethan revival, in which old plays like Marlowe's *The Jew of Malta* were mounted, these could come to be viewed in a new political light alongside being seen in their old significance. Besides, several new plays could deal with contemporary political and politico-religious problems as Martin Butler shows in his *Theatre and Crisis* (1984).

Considering the large number of plays that were produced during the Renaissance period, very few were banned. Nashe and Jonson's *The Isle of Dogs* (1597) is one which gave such offence that it immediately resulted in the closing of the new Swan playhouse and a civil ban on all playing in London. But the fact that playing in the theatres was soon resumed would lead to the conclusion that the court intervened on behalf of the playhouses for it tacitly recognised the power of the theatrical institution and how the theatre could through the direct and indirect effects it could work, promote the power of the authority. *The Tragedy of Gowrie* (1604), a lost play of the King's Men, was suppressed after a considerable run by the Privy Council for the reason that it dealt with a very recent conspiracy in Scotland and portrayed on stage the living monarch King James as the character of James VI of Scotland.[7] Otherwise, allusions to the reigning monarch, compliments or tributes or

7. See W. Criezenach, *The English Drama in the Age of Shakespeare* (London: Sidgwick and Jackson, 1916), p. 182.

responses to her or him, as in *A Midsummer Night's Dream*, were taken by the audiences and the patrons of the plays in their stride.

In a brief consideration of certain aspects of the impact of censorship on Elizabethan and Jacobean drama such as the present one, the question of the playwrights either projecting characters as portraits of contemporary personages or implanting incidental suggestions of this kind in characters can only be glanced at. In many of these instances where there was room for 'decyphering' as Ben Jonson called the habit of identifying the real-life counterparts of characters in plays, a practice not uncommon in later interpretation, the plays in question would not seem to have created great problems for the playwrights or theatrical companies. Shakespeare, in the *Henriad*, changed the name of Oldcastle to Falstaff so that the descendants of the Lollard lord might not make too much of a grievance against him of the portrayal. If at all as Leslie Hotson thought, in *Twelfth Night*, the visiting Italian Duke Orsini was shadowed in Duke Orsino, Queen Elizabeth in Olivia, and above all the grumpy Comptroller of the Royal Household Sir William Knollys in Malvolio such a portrayal did not cause offence. If at all suggestions of King James I were seen in the Duke of *Measure for Measure* or if *Macbeth* was understood among other things as a tribute to the king, these did not attract adverse or favourable notice. Extant Quarto copies or Folios of the plays would not seem to bear any striking evidence of such marginalia as in the case of an extant copy of Spenser's *Faerie Queene* where the contemporary reader identified the topical allegory by noting the names of historical contemporaries against the names of the characters. This is however not to deny that topical analogies and contemporary resemblances were discovered in the plays. Indeed an apprehension of these would have been facilitated and encouraged by the traditional habit of perception of multiple levels of reality, in a way inherited from the late medieval theatre and culture and a capacity to move swiftly and with ease across these.

Such a consideration as the foregoing of certain ways in which censorship was a factor to reckon with in the English Renaissance theatre would lead one to wonder if it is not an exaggeration to portray the situation then obtaining in this respect as one of 'art tongue-tied by authority'. There were certainly occasions when playwrights were restrained from publishing material as Ben Jonson was from printing his Apologetic Argument in the Quarto edition of his War of the Theatres play *The Poetaster* (1602). The playwrights and printers had to adhere to the 1606 Act banning the invoking of God's name in profane fashion. Expressions which amounted to swearing had to be scrupulously avoided on the stage and in print after 1606. But certain acts restraining writers in general as the Bishop of London's 1599 ban on satirical writings led to satire coming to find an increasing place in drama. In sum, subject as it was to regulation, the art of the theatre with its ample resources of elusion and of ventriloquism found in possible or actual censorship action, an opportunity as well as a challenge and could hold its own against odds.

SECTION 2

On Particular Plays

12

Hamlet: The 'Curious Perspective' of 'Visuality'

Hamlet	My father, methinks I see my father.
Horatio	O! where, my lord?
Hamlet	In my mind's eye, Horatio.

(*Hamlet*, I.ii. 184–6)

and

Hamlet	I see a cherub that sees them.

(*Hamlet*, IV.ii. 51)

The expression 'visuality' is one of Carlyle's many coinages; he used it in several of his works to denote the idea of a mental picture or vision (see *OED*). The considerable figuring of the motif of 'visuality' in this sense of a visualisation in the mind's eye in *Hamlet*, together with the idea and action of looking, seeing and different kinds of observing and watching, not to mention the actual visual phenomena, all so dominant in the play, is well worth attending to in some detail. Indeed the motif of 'seeing' in its several forms occurs with nearly as much frequency in *Hamlet* as in *King Lear* where it has been accorded a great deal of interpretative attention,[1] and there is, moreover, a telling correlation in *Hamlet* between actual visualisation and 'visuality'. But except for two

1. For example, Robert B. Heilman, *This Great Stage* (Baton Rouge: Louisiana State University Press, 1948); Paul J. Alpers, '*King Lear* and the Theory of the "Sight Pattern"', in *In Defence of Reading*, ed. Reuben Brower

critics, R.A. Foakes and E.A.J. Honigmann, who have noted the dominance of the scenes and motif of observing and 'seeing' in the play and commented illuminatingly on it,[2] this feature of *Hamlet* has been neglected in criticism.

The interrelatedness of visualisation and 'visuality' as they function in the play sets, in a complex perspective, its crucial visual moments such as the Ghost's appearances, and the various confrontations between Hamlet and the others. In fact, through the employment of the visual technique in conjunction with that of 'visuality' Shakespeare provides guidelines not only for the viewer's eye but for his 'mind's eye', if the playwright does not manipulate audience response thus. The conjunction of 'visuality' and visualisation is a factor behind many of the rich theatrical effects and meanings and also the metatheatrical suggestions which emerge in the play. Moreover, the juxtaposition and, more interestingly, the fusion in the dramatic process of the play at times, of the idea of inner visualising and of the fact of seeing serve as a means of communication of some of the central themes of the play. Among

---

and Richard Poirier (New York: Dutton, 1962); and Stanley Cavell, 'The Avoidance of Love', *Must We Mean What We Say?* (Cambridge: Cambridge University Press, 1976). All quotations are from the text of *Hamlet* in the Oxford Shakespeare.

2. R.A. Foakes, 'Hamlet and the court of Elsinore', *Shakespeare Survey 9* (Cambridge: Cambridge University Press, 1956), pp. 35–43, esp. pp. 38–9. 'The words "watch" (eleven times), "eye" (ten times) and other words of seeing echo through the first two scenes of the play', n. 7, p. 43; and E.A.J. Honigmann, Chapter 5: 'Hamlet as observer and consciousness', *Shakespeare: Seven Tragedies: The Dramatist's Manipulation of Response* (London: Macmillan, 1976), pp. 54–76. Hamlet is alike 'the observed of all observers' and 'the prince of observers' (the latter phrase is Honigmann's, p. 58).

Recently Alan C. Dessen, *Elizabethan Stage Conventions and Modern Interpreters* (Cambridge: Cambridge University Press, 1984), pp. 150–4, has called attention to the importance of the issue of seeing and not-seeing in *Hamlet*. Professor Dessen blames Hamlet for failing to see Polonius behind the arras or Claudius's inability to pray or repent truly (p. 154), but in his unsympathetic reading of Hamlet's character he does not sufficiently recognise the uncanny kinds of seeing Hamlet is capable of.

other things, in and through the developing relationship in the play between Hamlet's 'inner vision' and what confront him as stark phenomena 'out there', we are led to contemplate the larger general relationship between the subjective and the objective, between 'inner' and 'outer', between appearance and reality and, above all, between dramatic or artistic illusion and the kinds of reality it can embody or create as well as represent or re-present. Such themes, as has been only too well recognised, are not only of mere psychological interest with reference to Hamlet as a character study, but of much wider philosophical and sociocultural, not to mention theatrical and metatheatrical, interest and also of interest in terms of the history of the idea if not the problem of perception—interests which are evoked in the play and give it its key place as a turning point in intellectual and cultural history.

We are alerted to what has appropriately been called Hamlet's 'address to the world'[3] and the 'engagement with the world' of 'a particular kind of consciousness' or 'the Hamlet consciousness',[4] in terms of the relation set up in the play between what his 'mind's eye' and his eyes see. We see through Hamlet's eyes, and, what is more, through his 'mind's eye', rather than seeing through Hamlet as the hypercritical attitudes to Hamlet would have us suppose. We watch others as Hamlet watches them, but we also watch the others as they keep their constant, prying watch over Hamlet, besides watching him examining himself and his consciousness. This is a major factor guiding our response to Hamlet and, surely, complicating it. The response is, ultimately, not one of hostility or inquisitorial judgement but one of imaginative sympathy qualified by an awareness of Hamlet's occasional distortions of vision and attitude and lapses of sensibility. Thus multiple perspectives accrue in the play through the complex interconnections between several kinds of inner and factual seeings, including the seeing of oneself by oneself, especially Hamlet's dialogue of the mind with itself which also takes the synaesthetic form of the dialogue of his mind's

3. Arthur Sewell, *Character and Society in Shakespeare* (Oxford: Oxford University Press, 1951), p. 27.
4. L.C. Knights, *An Approach to 'Hamlet'* (London: Chatto and Windus, 1960), p. 90, p. 43 and p. 50 respectively.

eye with itself. This complexity of perspectives makes for an immense enrichment of dramatic anticipation, foreboding and prolepsis, and an unlaboured communication of metatheatrical significances in and through the theatrical, and it makes a crucial contribution to the overall quality of *Hamlet* which relates the play to a shift in consciousness which Montaigne, for example, at once represented and probed in his writings, and to the scepticism and the epistemological problem of the 'labour of knowing', of perception, which D.G. James[5] found reflected in the play. At any rate, the 'mysteriousness' and the 'baffling appearances' which, according to Maynard Mack,[6] distinguish the play are in no small measure due to 'the curious perspective'[7] set up by varying kinds of 'seeing' in the play.

The remarkable evocation of an atmosphere of mysteriousness and keen expectation at the opening of *Hamlet*, so well brought out by Coleridge in his lectures, is counterpointed by the presence of Horatio who, against the testimony of 'this same strict and most observant watch' thinks that the dreaded sight of the Ghost 'twice seen of them' is but a fantasy ('Tush, tush! 'twill not appear', I.i. 30). As Bernardo and Marcellus start recounting how the Ghost came to be seen on the two previous nights, pointing towards the direction

---

5. D.G. James, *The Dream of Learning: An Essay on 'The Advancement of Learning', 'Hamlet' and 'King Lear'* (Oxford: Oxford University Press, 1951).
6. Maynard Mack, 'The World of *Hamlet*', *The Yale Review* 41 (1952), pp. 502–23. Rpt. in *Discussions of 'Hamlet'*, ed. J.C. Levenson (Boston: D.C. Heath, 1960), p. 93.
7. As Ernest B. Gilman, *The Curious Perspective: Literary and Pictorial Wit in the Seventeenth Century* (New Haven: Yale University Press, 1978) points out, the phrase 'the curious perspective' came to be used in seventeenth-century England to denote 'pictures or devices which manipulate the conventions of linear perspective to achieve ingenious effects' (p. 1), and also 'the anamorphic distortions, the double or reversible images, the unexpected concealments and clarifications made possible through the use of mirrors and lenses' (p. 50). Gilman provides an interpretation of Shakespeare's *Richard II* (centring on Busby's speech to the Queen [I.ii] in terms of the idea of 'the curious perspective' and also applies it to the comedies [chapters 4 and 5]).

of 'yond same star that's westward from the pole' where it was sighted, at that very moment the ghost makes its appearance there, its very first in the play. The effect is one of the sudden materialisation of what is being reported about. Unbeliever as he may be, Horatio cannot but believe the 'sensible and true avouch of mine own eyes', and takes most careful note of the facial expression, carriage and gestures of the Ghost, and later gives them out to Hamlet in answer to his questions. He reads the significance of its appearance as 'a mote it is to trouble the mind's eye', as something foreboding ill to the nation and a factor which would impinge upon the consciousness of individuals like Hamlet. The exact echoing in the next scene by Hamlet of Horatio's 'the mind's eye' will not escape the spectator's notice. Horatio's invoking towards the close of the opening scene of 'the morn walking over the dew of yon high eastern hill' is by way of the suggestion of a sharp visual image of a labourer in russet mantle climbing the hill as he goes to work at dawn, an image called up in the speaker's and the spectator's 'mind's eye'. Thus at the opening of the play a pattern of two-fold dialectics between what is seen, on the one hand, and between what is envisaged in the mind and what is told or heard, on the other, is fairly clearly felt.

Gertrude's consolatory injunction to Hamlet, the very first words of mother to son in the play, as he stands in genuine mourning, equally truly inward ('that within which passeth show') and outward with his suits of black and inky cloak, takes the ironical form of bidding him thus:

> And let thine eye look like a friend on Denmark.
> Do not forever with thy vailed lids
> Seek for thy noble father in the dust.
>
> (I.ii. 69–71)

Hamlet's preoccupation is in a sense with his image, nearly idolatrous, of his dead father. In his first soliloquy, and time and again in the course of the play, Hamlet has contrastive images of his dead father and Claudius – images he displays in the counterfeit (true) resemblance of pictures in his encounter with his mother in her chamber.

> So excellent a king; that was, to this,
> Hyperion to a satyr.
>
> (I.ii. 138–9)

> My father's brother, but no more like my father
> Than I to Hercules.
>
> (I.ii. 152–3)

No wonder then that in his meeting with Horatio, Hamlet as he makes withering reference to his mother's hasty wedding, comes out with what is equally uppermost in his mind in the words.

> . . . Horatio!
> My father, methinks I see my father
>
> (I.ii.183–4)

This proleptic anticipation by Hamlet of his coming face to face with the Ghost of his father is a forceful theatrical pointer which at once confirms the effect of the two sightings of the Ghost in the opening scene and prepares the audience as much as Hamlet for his crucial meeting with his father's Ghost. It is with a queer shock of recognition that Horatio responds with 'O! Where, my lord?' (I.ii. 185) to be reassured in a way by Hamlet's 'in my mind's eye, Horatio' and to go on to mention his seeing the 'goodly king' 'once', inconsistently with his remembrances elsewhere in the play of seeing him several times (I.i. 60–3; I.ii. 211). Horatio goes on to relate to Hamlet's 'attent ear' the marvel of the Ghost's appearances, with Hamlet eliciting from him particular details about the Ghost's mien, all of which would serve to prepare the audience for Hamlet's encounter with it.

The phenomenon of the Ghost in Hamlet takes on a kind of numinousness as Shakespeare portrays it. Quite contrary to the general run of ghosts in Elizabethan drama, especially revenge tragedies, the elder Hamlet's Ghost has an essential majesty, and dignity about it, although it also has its quota of routine albeit unusually dynamic stage-business as ghost with its *hic et ubique* movements on the stage and its shouts from the cellarage which in turn lead Hamlet to take off part of his hysterical tension by calling it 'boy', 'true penny', 'old mole' and 'worthy pioner'. It is certainly unlike its counterpart in the old play of *Hamlet* which, according to Nashe, cried 'Revenge' like an oyster-wife. The all-but-noumenal effect the Ghost's revelation – that Claudius killed the king to become king – has on Hamlet is by way of substantiating his inner hunches, as the exclamation, 'O my prophetic soul!' suggests. Just as Hamlet had anticipated the vision of his father's Ghost in what he saw in his mind's eye, his soul had in a fashion intuited Claudius's crime and sin; his sense of the corruption that had set in the world of Denmark and the court of Elsinore underlies his first soliloquy. Hamlet would imprint the Ghost's command for revenge in his memory and, ironically, at the same time, the wise saw 'That one may smile, and smile, and be a villain' (I.v. 108) in his commonplace book, thereby, more or less, announcing the preoccupation he is going to be engaged in with the ambivalences of illusion and reality. His first response to the Ghost is one of implicit faith in its status and revelation or at least one of reassuring himself of his faith in it.

> . . . Touching this vision here,
> It is an honest ghost, that let me tell you.
>
> (I.v. 137–8)

Hamlet immediately has Horatio and Marcellus sworn to silence about the 'vision' thrice over, signalling his command with the words, 'still your fingers on your lips', the familiar Harpocratic gesture.[8] He decides to put an antic disposition on, and to take advantage of 'such ambiguous giving out' perhaps as much because of an incipient sense already coming over him of the possible ambiguity of the Ghost and its revelation as because he wants to assume the antic disposition in order to penetrate the surface appearances of King, Queen and Court. Hardly any other Ghost in Elizabethan drama is imbued with the kind of ambiguity that accrues to the Ghost in *Hamlet* in the dramatic process of the play, even as it is the

---

8. Immediately after his meeting with the Ghost, there is an exaggerated display of gestures of several kinds by Hamlet in his tension-ridden state: 'arms encumber'd thus', 'this head-shake', and the series of meaningless fillers of phrases and words. See Arthur Girtsner-Hirzel, *The Economy of Action and Word in Shakespeare's Plays* (Bern: Francke Verlag, 1957), p. 92, on the encumbering of arms as an Old Saxon gesture signalling refusal to give evidence.

most dignified of stage ghosts. No wonder that the status of the elder Hamlet's ghost has been a subject of keen discussion among critics and scholars as well as in the play itself to a degree.[9] The Ghost, though seen as a reality by Hamlet, and as a reality confirming his imaginings at that, may still be an illusion. Though Hamlet formulates these fears of his much later in his second soliloquy, significantly, after his first meeting with the Players,

> The spirit that I have seen
> May be the devil: and the devil hath power
> To assume a pleasing shape
>
> (II.ii. 635–7)

he has perhaps instinctively felt them soon after his witnessing of the Ghost. He would have to test the Ghost's 'appearance' and test the witness of 'the very faculties of eyes and ears'. He would subsequently effect the testing through the play-within-the-play of the *Murder of Gonzago, the Mousetrap,* another kind of illusion, a visual reenactment with some telling modification of what the Ghost reveals, but an illusion which indeed holds the mirror up to nature twice over, once in the dumb-show and then in the main play-within. The dramatic re-presentation serves exactly to fulfil Hamlet's definition of drama. But, more interestingly, it exemplifies the curious correspondence in the play between 'visuality' and actual visualisation. The idea of his killing of his uncle, now the king, obsessively present in his mind as a mental phenomenon cannot be readily translated by him into action. It has to crystallise itself first as dramatic picture and dramatic action in the play-within-the-play in which it is Lucianus, Gonzago's nephew, who kills the player-king his uncle. Thus the idea concretises first as Hamlet's

---

9. Among the main contributions to the discussion are W.W. Greg, 'Hamlet's Hallucination', *Modern Language Review*, 12 (1917), pp. 393–421; J. Dover Wilson, *What Happens in 'Hamlet'* (Cambridge: Cambridge University Press, 1935), pp. 59–86; R.M. Battenhouse, 'The Ghost in *Hamlet*: A Catholic Lynchpin?' *Studies in Philology*, 48 (1951), pp. 161–92; Robert H. West, 'King Hamlet's Ambiguous Ghost', *PMLA*, 70 (1951), pp. 1107–17; Sister Miriam Joseph, 'Discerning the Ghost in *Hamlet*', *PMLA*, 76 (1961), pp. 493–502; and Eleanor Prosser, *Hamlet and Revenge* (Stanford: Stanford University Press, 1967), pp. 106–98.

killing of the reigning king in the curious mirror-image or surrogate figure of the king's nephew, the play thus truly looking before and after in its handling of past and future. Also, by channelling his twin impulses to kill for revenge and to put his mother to an inner shame into expression in the visual medium of dumb-show and drama, Hamlet may be said paradoxically to purge himself of the cruelty and blood-thirstiness of revenge and also by the same token to steel himself for the act while he makes sure of the guilt of Claudius and the truth of the Ghost's testimony by watching his reaction.[10]

The 'cunning of the scene' in the play in general owes itself considerably to the relentlessly ongoing duel-like rival mutual spyings, watchings and 'espials' of this kind between Hamlet on the one side and the others on the other. Many scenes in the play are cast in this form and movement. Hamlet is for the most part able to see the truth about the others (though not the whole truth about Ophelia and perhaps about Gertrude), and also about himself through his gifts of 'visuality' and keen observation. Polonius all too readily sees in Hamlet's 'madness' only what he seeks, evidence that Hamlet is mad on account of the pangs of disprised love for Ophelia. Hamlet indeed sees through the would-be investigators of his and is able to fob them off with suitable illusions by which they are taken in or sometimes with the reality disguised as mad illusion as in the case of his encounters with Rosencrantz and Guildenstern. The curious feature, however, of several of the scenes of observation which abound in the play is that the pictures called up in them are as often as not mental or verbal visualisation, not actual stage-pictures, and there is in some scenes of this kind a theatrically fruitful interaction between what is seen and what is evoked mentally or in words.

The scene in which Polonius after setting Reynolds to spy on Laertes, receives Ophelia rushing in with news about Lord Hamlet bursting into her room in his mad fit (II.i.) is an example. The inset picture of Hamlet's distracted appearance in Ophelia's closet (II.i. 77–84) and of how for a long while he made such a perusal of her face as he would draw it (II. i. 87–100) is verbal evocation; at least

---

10. R.A. Foakes, 'The art of cruelty: Hamlet and vindice', *Shakespeare Survey 26* (Cambridge; Cambridge University Press, 1973), pp. 21–31, esp. pp. 30–1.

some of these details such as his appearance in his shirt ('pale as his shirt', l. 81) were perhaps followed in Hamlet's actual mad appearance on the Shakespearian stage, as Antony Scoloker's contemporary reference would imply.[11] Part of what Ophelia saw Hamlet do was this:

> ... he lets me go,
> And, with his head over his shoulder turn'd,
> He seem'd to find his way without his eyes;
> For out o' doors he went without their help,
> And to the last bended their light on me.
>
> (II.i. 96–100)

This account of Hamlet seeing his way without his eyes and with his eyes fixed on Ophelia is another example of the two kinds of seeing, inner and outer, that Hamlet is capable of and the strange reversibility of the two kinds. In the decoy or nunnery scene of 'lawful espials' in which, *pace* Dover Wilson, there is no need to postulate Hamlet's overhearing of Polonius's plan, Hamlet exhibits a satirical and all but cynical severity and lack of sympathy towards Ophelia and for that matter towards humankind. Several times Hamlet prepares to go out of the stage and each time comes back to give Ophelia the refrain-like exhortation: 'Get thee to a nunnery' (in its literal meaning rather than any other). The 'steep tragic contrast' which Ophelia underscores in the picture she calls up of Hamlet after he leaves is one of her past memory of what was which she ruefully compares with what is.

> O! what a noble mind is here o'erthrown.
> The courtier's, soldier's, scholar's, eye, tongue, sword;
> The expectancy and rose of the fair state
> The glass of fashion and the mould of form,
> The observ'd of all observers, quite, quite down!
> . . . O! woe is me;
> To have seen what I have seen, see what I see!
>
> (III.i. 159–63; 169–70)

---

11. Anthony Scoloker refers to someone wearing his shirt only much like mad Hamlet in his *Diaphantus or the Passions of Love* (1604). The lines are reprinted in Gamini Salgado, ed. *Eyewitnesses of Shakespeare* (Brighton: Sussex University Press, 1975), p. 75.

We can see the predramatic Prince Hamlet in terms of description such as Ophelia's and, through whatever 'visuality' we are capable of, find something of him in what he actually is in the play.

Another striking instance of 'visuality' is to be found in the episode of the player's speech, an episode which has increasingly come to be recognised as a mirror episode. The momentary hesitation of Pyrrhus echoes Hamlet's momentous one and Hamlet and the whole company including Polonius who initially finds the speech too long are moved to tears by the recitative evocation of the destruction and mangling of Priam by Pyrrhus. The picture that is verbally evoked of Pyrrhus hesitating for a moment with his drawn and suspended sword over Priam (incidentally, a recurrent stage emblem this, in Shakespeare and Elizabethan drama, of a character's drawn sword remaining arrested or frozen in that posture) is visualised in our eye and perhaps also Hamlet's mind's eye.

> ... his sword,
> Which was declining on the milky head
> Of reverend Priam, seem'd in the air to stick.
> So, as a painted tyrant, Pyrrhus stood,
> And like a neutral to his will and maker,
> Did nothing.

It is a prefiguring of Hamlet's raised sword over Claudius at prayer arrested in that posture and subsequently put up. But, more significantly, it is an emblem of Hamlet's being halted in the execution of revenge.

The little phenomenological, 'duck/rabbit'-like game which Hamlet plays with Polonius is part of the pattern adopted by Hamlet of testing the reality about the others and himself with his gifts of illusion and 'visuality'.

> *Hamlet* Do you see yonder cloud that's almost in the shape of a camel?
> *Polonius* By the mass, and 'tis like a camel, indeed.
> *Hamlet* Methinks it is like a weasel.
> *Polonius* It is backed like a weasel.
> *Hamlet* Or like a whale?

Polonius Very like a whale.

(III.ii. 399–406)[12]

In addition to gleefully exposing the suggestibility of Polonius as something of a toady, Hamlet through imaginings such as these and those about drinking hot blood, prepares himself for the confrontation with his mother, and in terms of the theatrical rhythm and scenic connectiveness, pace and mood, for the opportunity which comes his way of dispatching King Claudius when he is in the vulnerable state of praying, an opportunity he rejects.

It is in the scene of Hamlet's confrontation with his mother in her chamber that the correspondence between 'visuality' and visualisation makes itself keenly felt. Hamlet starts with the announcement to his mother of his determination to

> ... set you up a glass
> Where you may see the inmost part of you.
>
> (III.iv. 19–20)

Before he proceeds to do this if anything too successfully, the Queen's fear that Hamlet may use rather than speak daggers to her makes her cry out for help and Polonius hiding behind the arras responds. Hamlet, unable to see the figure behind the arras and taking him to be King Claudius, in a sudden outburst of action decides to carry out what he has been contemplating and omitted to do when he saw the King at prayer—to plant his dagger into the spying, sneaky Claudius behind the arras. When he lifts up the arras to see, Hamlet finds the person whom he had envisaged to be King Claudius to be Polonius. Hamlet's admonition of his mother over her 'act' of remarriage, which is part of his technique of making her look in her heart, takes the form of a visual demonstration with pictures of the contrast between the two brothers, a contrasted pair of images constantly present in Hamlet's mind's eye now translating itself into either two miniatures or a pair of wall pictures. Hamlet drives home to his mother in sledge-hammer repetition that she does not have eyes to see, as otherwise she could not have

---

12. Compare Hamlet's teasing of Osric by alternately saying that it is hot and cold (V. ii. 97–105).

made her choice of Claudius as she did. Hamlet's impressions of the two brothers, though understandably against the Cain-like brother, cannot be taken entirely at face-value; nor can his statement to Rosencrantz and Guildenstern that the public made mows at his uncle when his father was King and that the same public give twenty, forty, fifty, a hundred ducats a-piece for Claudius's picture now that he is King (II.ii. 389–92). Yet Hamlet is in a fashion borne out by the 'ocular witness' of the two pictures he displays to his mother. Gertrude is deeply affected and convinced:

> O Hamlet! Speak no more:
> Thou turn'st mine eyes into my very soul;
>
> (II.ii. 88–9)

With Gertrude neither seeing nor hearing the Ghost who makes his appearance, she cannot know that the Ghost commands Hamlet:

> But, look! amazement on thy mother sits,
> O! step between her and her fighting soul
>
> (II.ii. 111–12)

She cannot see how pale the Ghost glares or how he looks upon Hamlet with 'piteous action'. She can only put it down to Hamlet's 'ecstacy', the diagnosis of Polonius. To the question of Hamlet who sees the Ghost, 'his father in his habit as he liv'd', stalk away, 'Do you see nothing here?' Gertrude can only say, 'Nothing at all; yet all that is I see'. It is Hamlet's capacity to see more than 'all that is' which enables him to 'foresee' in his 'prophetic soul' the fell design of Claudius on him to be worked through the agency of Rosencrantz and Guildenstern. He speaks about it to Gertrude towards the end of the chamber scene in his characteristic oblique manner before he takes leave of her (III. iv. 202–10). On the basis of this premonitory vision of his of the enginer hoist with his own petard, of two crafts directly meeting in one line, Hamlet tells Claudius when he announces his decision to send him to England:

> I see a cherub that sees them. But
> come, for England! Farewell, dear mother.
>
> (IV. ii. 51)

Hamlet's 'Farewell, dear mother' when she is not actually present there can be interpreted as a play of Hamlet's to make Claudius believe that he is in the confusion of madness (Claudius seeks to correct Hamlet) but also as Hamlet's utterance of a genuine farewell to his mother imagining her there.

By the image of his own cause, as Hamlet puts it, he could see the portraiture of the cause of Fortinbras, before his departure for England, and that of Laertes, after his return, as sons bent on revenge for their dead fathers. Hamlet's observation of the gravedigging for Ophelia and of her burial in which he comes to participate as chief mourner albeit obstreperously against Laertes is an experience of education and training for him in the *ars moriendi* or *memento mori* tradition though with a difference with its element of clowning. His meditations on the gravedigger's delving, the graves and the skulls are by way of an implicit giving of finishing touches to Hamlet's preparation of himself for death, and the observation and meditation lead him to an obscurely yet deeply felt perception of the relation between life and death, and, moreover, of the abiding, 'mythic' relation between death and love, especially at the moment of his leaping into the grave of Ophelia, a moment which perhaps did occur on the contemporary Shakespearian stage.[13] What Hamlet sees in the skulls he comes across or picks up, in Yorick's skull or, by analogy, the skulls of Alexander or Caesar, as he meditates on these, is the entire course of life and death along which the glories of the world end in the ingloriousness of dust. Conversely, Hamlet sees in a handful of dust the great designs and achievements of the Alexanders and Caesars, and also of the Yoricks, and what these come to, though, as is his wont, he 'consider(s) it too curiously to consider so'.

Hamlet has premonitions about the fencing match but he defies augury and goes to his fate, with the sense of a special providence governing it. His prophesy, at the point of his death, of the election of Fortinbras to the Danish throne anticipates and brings about, suitably for the play's closure, the advent of Fortinbras on the stage. Hamlet's particularly insistent dying wish is that Horatio should

---

13. As the evidence of the First Quarto stage direction and the reference of Burbage as Hamlet leaping into the grave in the 1619 elegy on Burbage (in that part of it known to be not a Collier forgery) would show.

report him and his cause aright and make the world see the truth about him by a full narration of the whole story from beginning to end. A special emphasis builds up in the closing lines of the play on the 'sight' of the final gathering of the dead bodies on the stage ('this sight', '(sight) of woe or wonder', 'the sight is dismal', 'give order that these bodies/High on a stage be placed to the view', 'such a sight as this'). Horatio promises to recount the entire story against the background of the body of Hamlet prominently staged, and thus vindicate Hamlet fully with the 'noblest to the audience'. What results is a sense of the ending of the play as another beginning.[14]

These intriguing anamorphic patterns of relationship between several kinds of inner and outer 'seeing' in the play carry implications for the problematic relation between the subjective and the objective, between the perceiving self and the world apprehended by it. Quite a few of Hamlet's subjective sensations and thoughts tend to become objective dramatic realities in the play world. It is not as if he simply imposes his subjective vision on realities. The realities have a way of turning out to be a materialisation of Hamlet's 'visuality'. Nor is it at all a matter of his subjective feeling being projected onto the Ghost; as W.C. Curry made clear with reference to *Macbeth* and *The Tempest,* [15] the Ghost had too much of objective existence, according to the thought of the period, for it to be regarded as a subjective projection. What the play, ultimately, suggests with regard to Hamlet is a keenness of the senses and sensibility on his part, notwithstanding his lapses of sensibility which are the other side of the coin, and a keenness of apprehension which enables him to sense, see, smell and feel the 'something' that is 'rotten in the state of Denmark'. Much as he is able to 'foresee' a future spectacle in a sort of Wordsworthian memory in

14. Other 'visualities' (to use the Carlylean expression as he does in the plural) are Gertrude's account of the drowning of Ophelia and Claudius's evocation of the Norman Lamord's horsemanship which looks forward to the spectacle of the Hamlet–Laertes fencing match in Lamord's expression of the idea 'it would be a sight indeed/If one could match (Laertes)', IV.vii. 98–9.

15. *Shakespeare's Philosophical Patterns* (Baton Rouge: Louisiana State University Press, 1937).

reverse, he is also able to detect and experience, antennae-like, the corruption around him in himself in a curious kind of sympathetic vibration.

> O this too, too [sullied] flesh would melt,
> Thaw and resolve itself into a dew
>
> (I.ii. 129–30)

This interiorisation by Hamlet in himself of the corruption in the exterior world is a factor to reckon with when we consider the phenomenon of Hamlet being touched and defiled by the corruption he crusades against. What the evocation in the play suggests – in its imagery and action, of the canker in the rose, of evil which undermines from within in Hamlet as elsewhere in Elsinore – is also something of an internalised apprehension and diagnosis as though by ingestion in advance of the evil outside him by Hamlet. The senses of smell and of touch and feeling are invoked in the course of the play in relation mainly to Hamlet but also sometimes to the other characters only slightly less significantly than the senses of sight and hearing.[16] If Hamlet then, smells the odour of mortality and seems to be ridden by what has been termed a death-consciousness, he also acquires towards the close of the play a keen engagement with the crowded life of the 'interim' which he calls his. The 'interim' is something like the fruit of his experience of killing Polonius, of a sense of the providential ordainment of his role as 'scourge and minister' and of an uncanny anticipation and escape of his death on the voyage to England, in addition to his meditations in the graveyard.

The Romantic shift in consciousness which could at any rate explore if not realise the possibility of the unity of the self and the world through an interpenetration of the subject and the object, the

---

16. For instance, I.i. 46 ('It harrows me with fear and wonder'); I.i. 56 ('You tremble and look pale'); I.v.16–20 ('Will harrow thy soul, freeze thy young blood/ Make thy two eyes, like stars, that from their spheres/ Thy knotted and combined locks to part,/ And each particular hair to stand on end,/ Like quills upon the fretful porpentine); II.i. 258–77 (Hamlet's claustrophobic sense of constraint); III. iv. 91–4 and 182–5 (sense of revulsion expressed through images of touch) and V.i. 220 ('And smell so? pah!').

perceiver and the perceived, was in the distant future at the time of the composition of *Hamlet*. Yet the address of Hamlet and his consciousness to the world around him has a similarity to the Romantic's address to the circumambient universe in terms of a desired unification of subject and object. Coleridge, at one point in his criticism, did say that in certain of the speeches and situations of Hamlet the excess of subjectivist reflection in him swamped the possibilities of an organic relationship (what he called 'Method') with the objective universe.[17] It is also important to note that Hamlet's habits of abstraction, reflection and generalisation coexist with a firm grasp on the actual, the particular and the concrete. One can understand why the charge of egoism has been laid at Hamlet's door as often as at the Romantics'. As Hamlet goes through the play-long process of observation of the world through subjective vision, meditation, objective seeing and testing, and through the use of the medium of drama as well as play-acting, his problem emerges as one of the perception of self and world in themselves and in their mutual relationship. The process can be seen as a search for, and a struggle on his part towards, a viable relationship between his self and the world. Though finally he arrives at the lesson, 'the readiness is all', his struggle at best only half-succeeds. In the process of his probing of the world around him and himself, Hamlet uses levels of reality and illusion in several degrees of intermingling among them in a manner which parallels the playwright's representation of reality through creation as well as imitation. Still the full recitative re-enactment of the whole Hamlet story which Horatio promises at the instance of the dying Hamlet will have to start again as a post-dramatic phenomenon. In that post-dramatic world the 'yet unknowing world' may get full knowledge of the story, and Hamlet may not leave a wounded name there, while the problem of knowledge and perception remains as an implicit yet forceful dramatic adumbration it finds in the world of *Hamlet*.

---

17. *Essay on the Principles of Method*, Essay IV in Barbara E. Rooke, ed. Coleridge's *The Friend,* Vol. 1 in the *Collected Coleridge* (London: Routledge and Kegan Paul, 1969), pp. 451–3. Also see p. 455.

13

Hamlet: A 'Necessary "Question" of the Play'

Easily one of the most questioned about of plays if not *the* most, *Hamlet* the play by itself all too often enters the question mode and invokes the interrogative mood besides evoking it. As it was well put by Harold Jenkins in his Arden 2 edition of the play, apart from 'the proliferation of . . . unanswerable questions' raised 'by its unrivalled imaginative power', 'Hamlet himself seems always to be asking questions much bigger and more searching than those we ask him'.[1] One may add, with the result that the critic's lot in respect of his or her scrutiny and surveillance of Hamlet, the prince or the play, is still more unenviable than that of Rosencrantz and Guildenstern in the play. Harry Levin and several other critics[2] have called attention to the frequency and dominance of questions and of the interrogative mood in the play. But what seems worth recognition at this hour of the day in *Hamlet* criticism, is Shakespeare's deployment, apart from the interrogative element, of the very word 'question', and sometimes its derivatives, with its then current manifold signification and its polysemous connotations at what may be called strategic loci across the play.

---

1. Harold Jenkins, ed. *Hamlet* (London: Methuen, 1982), p. 123, p.125. Quotations in this article from *Hamlet* are keyed to the Harold Jenkins edition of the play.

2. Harry Levin, *The Question of Hamlet* (New York: Oxford University Press, 1959); Maynard Mack, 'The World of *Hamlet*' in *Shakespeare: Modern Essays in Criticism*, ed. L.F. Dean (New York: OUP, 1961), pp. 239–40, essay reprinted from *The Yale Review* (1951).

Although the occurrences of the word are not numerous (they count no more than six), 'question' would seem to acquire in the play the status of a key word, through its placement and the subtle changes which Shakespeare unobtrusively rings on the word and its suggestions through a manipulation of its multiple meanings and of its tone and tenor. One can by no means claim that the key word would serve to unlock the mystery of the play or the heart of the prince's 'mystery'. Yet a study of the workings of the expression in the play at several levels of meaning and suggestion might serve to throw further light on quite a few of its aspects.

Besides its plain meaning of an interrogative statement which demands a reply the word 'question' in Shakespeare's English, had the senses of 'conversation or dialogue', the 'argument of a discourse', the 'subject of a debate', 'matter or idea', 'situation or occasion' in a general sense or one in the sense of its being fraught with doubts and problems to be resolved and 'serious and active consideration'. Most of these shades of meaning of the word in some contexts do survive to some extent in current English. And Shakespeare uses the word very occasionally in some of these several senses it carried then in plays prior to *Hamlet* and later.[3] But it is in *Hamlet* that he would appear to explore and exploit the manifold possibilities of the word by invoking it at I.i.49, I.iv.43, III.i.56, III.ii.43, IV.iv.26 and V.ii.80. As much in the general movement of the play as in the context of their occurrence, these uses of the word, in both direct and self-reflexive fashion, enforce suggestions and clues by way of a covert guidance and gentle manipulation of the spectator's or reader's response to the play and its issues if not its name and nature. The nuances of the word foregrounded in particular uses together seem to lead to such a cumulative effect. So much so that we may speculate if Shakespeare does not plant a clue to the overall importance of 'question' for the 'necessary questions of the play' to use that phrase of *Hamlet*'s (III.ii.43).

---

3. Samples from other works are: The Rape of Lucrece, l. 122: 'to talk, converse'; *The Merchant of Venice*, IV.i.73 and *As You Like It,* III.iv. 37: 'discussion', 'exchange of views'; *As You Like It*: V.iv.168: 'conversation', 'philosophical discourse'; *Measure for Measure*, I.i. 46: 'under consideration'; and *Macbeth*, I.iii. 43: to talk.

The first two occurrences of the word in the play are with reference to the Ghost and are related to its dramatic entry each of the two occasions. The play opens with questions by way of sentinel challenges. As Barnardo, Marcellus and Horatio sit down to listen to Barnado's report of the appearances of the Ghost on the previous two nights precisely at the hour of one, the Ghost makes his entry. The conversation as the Ghost approaches the spot where the three are stationed on the stage, traversing the distance on the platform stage, depicts the identification of the Ghost and the initial response to it by the three. Then follow the lines:

Barnardo It would be spoke to.
Marcellus Question it, Horatio.
Horatio What are thou that
usurp'st this time of night,
Together with that fair and warlike form
In which the majesty of Denmark
Did sometimes march? By heaven, I charge thee
speak.
Marcellus It is offended.
Barnardo See, it stalks away.
Horatio Stay, speak, speak. I charge thee speak. [*Exit Ghost*]
(*Hamlet* (I.i.48–54)

The Ghost approaches them as if it would like to be accosted and Barnardo notices this. Marcellus, who seems to be the most observant of the three and even more balanced than Horatio, suggests that Horatio, 'as a scholar', should engage in conversation with the Ghost in response to its desire to communicate. It is in the sense 'to converse or talk' that Marcellus asks Horatio to 'question' the Ghost. But Horatio, in the shock of surprise to his customary skepticism and in a kind of reflexive response, starts challenging, sentinel-like, the Ghost, understanding Marcellus's word to mean 'challenge'. Horatio unwittingly uses the expression 'usurp'st' to the elder Hamlet which is enough to give the Ghost offence as he considers himself victim of both murder and double usurpation by Claudius. That is Shakespeare's way with the word, 'question', in this context, letting, as it were, its two different senses share the word. Indeed the sense of conversation or talk in the expression is one in which Shakespeare employs it in several of his works, e.g. *As You Like It* (III.iv.37), (V.iv.168); *Lucrece* (1,122) and *Macbeth* (I.viii.43). The conversation mode is perhaps thus implicitly set in contrastive juxtaposition by Shakespeare with that of adversarial interrogativeness (a critical stance much canvassed, incidentally, in postmodern thought).

It may be suggested that the conversational stance or attitude is one which is at times invoked in *Hamlet* alongside and as a contrast to the confrontationist or duelling and spying and prying encounters in which characters in many instances face each other. When Hamlet meets his father's ghost for the first time, his exclamation is not only one of awe and wonder but one of a recognition of the genuine identity of the ghost as that of his father. Whatever be the antecedents and nature of the apparition with devilish affiliations or not, *Hamlet* is prepossessed and impressed in its favour mainly for the reason that the Ghost presents the look of someone earnestly inviting conversation and desirous of communication.

> Be thou a spirit of health or goblin damn'd,
> Bring with thee airs from heaven, or blasts from hell,
> By thy intents wicked or charitable,
> Thou com'st in such a questionable shape
> That I will speak to thee. I'll call thee
> King, father, royal Dane.
>
> (I.iv. 39–45)

What Hamlet calls the 'questionable shape' of the Ghost is what draws him to it, and Hamlet clearly means that the Ghost presents an address of readiness and eagerness to engage in communication. At this point and later generally, in the course of the play except for at one point, that too as a passing thought, Hamlet never mistrusts the Ghost's status and never associates it with hell and the devil. But the irony is that several twentieth century critics, for instance, Eleanor Prosser,[4] have argued their case precisely for that association. Hamlet who considers that possibility, rejects it, and to him it is no ambiguous ghost, and not at all 'questionable' in the modern sense if only because it is 'questionable' in the old sense.

4. Eleanor Prossr, *Hamlet and Revenge* (Stanford University Press, 1967), p. 140.

The question of Hamlet's 'To be, or not to be' soliloquy (III.i.88), perhaps the most famous of dramatic soliloquies, is one of the most controversial, and one of the most central, about the play. The question mainly is one relating to the thrust and tenor of 'the question' discussed as Hamlet opens his monologue with

> To be, or not to be: that is the question.

A major clue to an answer or something of it lies in the word 'question' itself. The word in the context carries the prime meaning of a 'topic for debate', 'a kind of theme for contemplation,' somewhat in the nature of an informal 'prolusion' or 'vacation exercise' set for university students in those days. Although the argument of Hamlet's meditation cannot be taken to be an abstract or much less purely academic debate, there is a preponderance of generality or universality alongside the particularities of Hamlet's predicament brought forward or suggested in the soliloquy. There is both a keen apprehension and sensitive expression of the human predicament in general, the 'miseries of the world' felt by him as misery which will not let him rest. To borrow Keatsian 'sensations' and phrases further, Hamlet feels it all 'on his pulses' and a relation to his circumstances establishes itself. All the same, for all Hamlet's contemplation of the idea of 'self-homicide', of action with 'arms' or 'a bare bodkin' against his enemy or himself, and of the idea of a resolve weakening before being put into action, the cast and orientation of Hamlet's utterance is one of a 'question' or general meditation.

In view of the word 'question' appearing in its different shades of suggestion as marks or milestones in the course of the play, Hamlet's penchant for 'question' in the signification of a 'meditation', only too well recognised in Hamlet criticism, has probably to be accepted as one of the givens of the play. At the same time, there is a good case for Hamlet as no less a man of action than a man of thought, canvassed by critics of the play, to cite, for example, not inappropriately for the father and son relationship as a strong motif of the play, Peter Alexander and Nigel Alexander.[5] The power of

5. Peter Alexander, *Hamlet: Father and Son* (Oxford: OUP, 1955); Nigel Alexander, *Poison, Play, and Duel: A Study in 'Hamlet'* (London: Routledge, 1971).

Hamlet as a play owes itself considerably to Hamlet's implicit grappling with the Renaissance ideal of a synthesis or fusion of the life of contemplation and the life of action as he and the play do with other antinomies.

When Shakespeare through Hamlet invokes the word 'question' in the very next scene (III.ii) in a very meaningful context, it is in a manner which brings into relief the relevance the expression might have to the ongoing play of *Hamlet* and our apprehension of it. Hamlet's advice to the First Player, before the start of 'the Mousetrap', 'The Murder of Gonzago', may legitimately be seen as reflecting Shakespeare's view on drama, acting and actors' ways and practices.[6] In his crowning injunction to the player Hamlet exhorts him:

> O reform it altogether. And let those that play your clowns speak no more than is set down for them – for there be of them that will themselves laugh, to set on some quantity of barren spectators to laugh too, though in the meantime some necessary question of the play be then to be considered. That's villainous, and shows a most pitiful ambition in the fool that uses it.
>
> (III.ii.38–45)

Here Hamlet–Shakespeare, as it were, registers his disapproval of the gags, intrusive improvisations and impromptu witticisms, deviation from their 'parts', traditionally indulged in by well-known actors of clown parts such as Tarlton, and Shakespeare's own Will Kempe who had by then left his company. And the warning acquires interest in view of the fact that Shakespeare and his company presumably accorded Robert Armin (a different kind of clown actor from Kempe) an all-too-brief single appearance in *Hamlet* and *Othello* after giving him a prominent enough role in *As You Like It* and *Twelfth Night*. Hamlet's objection is to irrelevant clowning which would distract attention from the main issues, matters or themes of the play in question, the 'necessary questions' under consideration in the play's progression.

6. It may not be valid to suggest that Shakespeare is being ironical at the expense of Hamlet and his exhortations on drama, actors and acting.

One might ask whether Hamlet's sustained advice to the player by itself is not one such digression from 'some necessary questions', and also whether Shakespeare's habit of introducing what used to be called 'comic relief' in his plays is not the same practice which he seems to object to here. The answer to the first problem may be sought in the implicit, informing conviction of the playwright that drama and the theatre matter and his commitment and concern towards these and in his adoption and delineation of the idea and practice itself as one of the 'necessary questions of the play' of *Hamlet*. The second query answers itself when we advert to Shakespeare's consistent use of 'comic relief' to the effect of tragic intensification and of thematic reinforcement. 'Questions' matter in plays in general and in *Hamlet* in particular. And in *Hamlet* the word and concept themselves in a way seem to demand attention.

In IV.iv. of the play, in the Q^2 version, though the better part of the scene is omitted from F, Hamlet in the company of Rosencrantz and Guildenstern who lead him to England, watches Fortinbras's army 'passing o'er the stage'. Hamlet, on learning from the captain that Fortinbras is leading his large army against the Poles to capture a worthless piece of barren land, which is already heavily garrisoned by Poland for its defence, is struck by the fact that so many so readily come forward to risk their lives for the sake of an 'eggshell' or 'straw'.

Hamlet Two thousand souls and twenty thousand ducats
Will not debate the question of this straw!

(IV.iv.25–6)

The 'issue' or 'matter' is the worthwhileness of the enterprise of fighting for a 'straw'. But, immediately after, we find Hamlet in his self-communing in the 'How all occasions do inform against me' soliloquy turning the 'occasion' into a debate of the 'question' of his revenge action against Claudius. The 'argument' crystallises thus:

Rightly to be great
Is not to stir without great argument
But greatly to find quarrel in a straw
When honour's at the stake.

(IV.iv. 53–6)

He painfully acknowledges that he has 'this great argument' of the duty of revenge to spur him to action, to put in the phrase which Milton in *Paradise Lost* perhaps echoed from Shakespeare. The 'question', the 'argument' of the play is 'this great argument' or revenge, an 'argument' conducted in most effective dramatic terms. The correspondence between Fortinbras and Hamlet as avengers, and as sons and as nephews in addition, is brought to the fore in the situation. The obvious contrast which works ultimately in Hamlet's favour is that Fortinbras despite Hamlet's reference to him as 'a delicate and tender prince', is one who would all too hastily 'stir' without any 'argument' at all. For all his self-reproach and self-condemnation here in this soliloquy and elsewhere Hamlet does conduct in the play's course the 'argument' of revenge in terms often generalised and universalised into agonising considerations of the human lot.

If Shakespeare brings up the word 'question' towards the close of the play, it is in a manner such as to alert the spectator or reader of the implications of the word and of its earlier occurrence in several senses in the play. Horatio undertakes the duty assigned to him by the dying Hamlet:

> Absent thee from felicity awhile,
> And in this harsh world draw thy breath in pain
> To tell my story.
>
> (V.ii. 352–4)

Fortinbras, who gets Hamlet's 'voice' for succession, and the English ambassador arrive on the scene of tragic carnage and are aghast at it; Horatio states in almost instant deference to Hamlet's wish:

> . . . since, so jump upon this bloody question,
> You from the Polack wars and you from England,
> Are here arriv'd, give order that these bodies
> High on a stage be placed to the view,
> And let me speak to th' yet unknowing world
> How these things came about. So shall you hear
> Of carnal, bloody, and unnatural acts,
> Of accidental judgements, casual slaughters,
> Of deaths put on by cunning, and forc'd cause,
> And, in this upshot, purposely mistook

> Fall'n on the investors' heads. All this can I
> Truly deliver.
>
> (V.ii. 380–91)

The immediate response of Fortinbras now in charge is

> Let us haste to hear it,
> And call the noblest to audience.
>
> (V.ii. 392–3)

And Horatio accords the vindicatory discourse he proposes the most urgent and highest priority.

> But let this same be presently perform'd
> Even while men's minds are wild, left more mischance
> On plots and errors happen.
>
> (V.ii. 398–400)

Such a recapitulatory and elucidatory discourse slated for the immediate post-dramatic stage of the play is often a feature of Shakespeare's endings, where the ending harks back to the beginning. In *Hamlet* the practice gets a particular emphasis of importance, and Horatio's elucidatory discourse is to take the form of an exposition (in Horatio's phrase) of 'this bloody question': what happened in *Hamlet*. It can almost be seen to have the effect of a sewing up, at the end, of the threads of suggestions of several ideational possibilities of the word 'question' running across the play.

In sum, it may not be an exaggeration to suggest that Shakespeare's implantation of the word 'question' in its multiple connotation in the play gives it the status of a minor clue or pointer to aspects of the dramatic and artistic design of *Hamlet*. The elements of 'dialogue or conversation', of 'discourse' of several kinds, of a 'debate, or discussion', of a 'topic for consideration and discussion', of 'a matter, theme or issue', and of 'a state of affairs which poses a challenge', all of which are connoted and sometimes denoted by the word, are, of course, all part of the rich abundance of the play which Johnson remarked on. The use of the word in its shifts of suggestion may alert us to the role of these factors in the play. The 'dialogue' in the play, sometimes considered to be 'full of soliloquies', may appear to be monologic; and the play itself and the Hamlet phenomenon can sometimes be regarded as the prime example of the Montaignean 'dialogue of the mind with itself' (in

Matthew Arnold's phrase). However, the self-communings of Hamlet for all their apparent self-analysis are really part of what Arthur Sewell designated as Hamlet's 'address to the world,'[7] that is, part of the adumbration in dramatic terms of Hamlet's apprehension of the moral world around him, of life and, more important, of death. Many an encounter in the play takes the form of a confrontation, either direct or oblique, it is true. But despite this, the element of discourse, meditative or expository, has its presence.

It is not for nothing that Gabriel Harvey whom we can credit with the chronological first in *Hamlet* criticism remarked that *Hamlet* 'please(d) the wiser sort'.[8] Thematic approaches to Shakespeare which had their day in the mid-twentieth century are at a discount now. But one may wonder if Shakespeare's signposting of *Hamlet* with 'question' in the manner outlined above is not meant to be an indirect signal that this play does carry strong and vital thematic concerns. After all, the primary root meaning of 'question' is 'seeking'. This feature of the play may be seen as a major factor behind the remarkable difference to the tradition of revenge tragedy the play makes; it is also one of the important areas in which Shakespeare's *Hamlet* may be seen to have its qualitative influence on his contemporary Chapman and his plays.

---

7. Arthur Sewell, *Character and Society in Shakespeare* (Oxford University Press, 1951), p. 27.
8. In his *Marginalia*. Quoted from *The Riverside Shakespeare* (1974), p. 1840.

14

Some Uses of *Topoi* in *Coriolanus*: An Approach to the Play

In the wake of the pioneering work of scholars like E.R. Curtius on the commonplaces of late medieval and Renaissance European literature, and of an increasing recognition of the place of rhetorical traditions and modes in literature and drama, later scholars such as Rosalie Colie have alerted us to the role of *topoi* as speculative instruments in Shakespearian drama and in Renaissance literature. Shakespeare's use of *topoi* or commonplaces in his early and middle plays, no less than in his late career, is often by way of a creative 'remaking'. Yet in his late Roman plays *Coriolanus* and *Antony and Cleopatra*, Shakespeare would seem to make not only a somewhat more extensive use of certain *topoi*, letting them serve as structural building units, but also a more deliberately self-conscious use of commonplaces, in consonance with the theatrical and rhetorical self-reflexivity that often marks Shakespeare's late dramatic mode. It is an exploratory–creative handling of commonplaces as much as of the other means and devices of theatrical communication, both verbal and other-than-verbal, that we witness in these plays: so much so that the commonplaces are no longer mere figures of speech but figures of thought and feeling, and modes of apprehension as well. In other words, the commonplace gets rethought and lifted far above the customary level of the cliché and the stock device.

In this chapter I shall consider some workings of three *topoi* in *Coriolanus*: the Fortune–Nature topos; the commonplace of the tongue and the heart; and the *topos* of the world-stage, the *theatrum mundi*, this last in certain particular aspects of it. Attention to the modes of operation of such commonplaces may help in our attempt to catch the rather problematic tonality of the play.

The Fortune–Nature antithesis figures at several places in the earlier plays: for example, in *As You Like It* and *King Henry V*. The antinomy, outlined by Boethius and widely applied in literature and drama, operated against a fairly rich background of the mythography and iconography of Goddess Natura and Goddess Fortuna. It served as a neat category for characterising the conflicting relationship between what a person is by birth and in his natural endowments on the one side, and what circumstances and environment do to that person on the other. The two concepts correlated respectively with the concepts of time and of grace – Fortune and time, Nature and grace. In *Coriolanus*, the antinomy, recurring in forms both direct and oblique, functions as a central factor in the characterisation of the protagonist, both in conception and in presentation.

Given the strong presence of the commentative element in this and several other late plays of Shakespeare, with many a crucial action or situation set in a framework of commentary, the categories of Nature and Fortune assume the status of foci of reference, or of coordinates helping to form and formulate the impressions of and response to Coriolanus on the part of the other characters as well as the spectator. In contexts where one of the two categories is involved, the other would seem to suggest itself implicitly as a matching point of reference. Especially in the light of a deliberately externalised, from-the-outside conception and presentation of the protagonist Coriolanus (exceptional individual and Herculean hero though he may be), and the sparseness of soliloquies or even asides in the play, *topoi* such as these perform an all-but-constitutive function in producing character impressions, given their nodal placing.

With regard to Coriolanus, the Fortune–Nature antithesis is sharply brought into focus at three crucial points of the play, which are central turning points in its movement. After the disastrous confrontation of Coriolanus with the tribunes and the plebeians, ranged in mutiny against him over the granting and the quick retraction of the plebs' 'voices', there occurs the comment on Coriolanus:

Patricians This man has marr'd his fortune.
Menenius His nature is too noble for the world . . .

(III.i.252–3)[1]

When Volumnia persuades Coriolanus to play-act courtesy towards the plebeians to win their 'voices' – with only slightly less catastrophic effect than when she prevails upon him to spare Rome towards the end of the play – she urges Coriolanus to dissimulate in these terms:

I would dissemble with my nature where
My fortunes and my friends at stake requir'd . . .

(III.ii.62–3)

Again, Aufidius in his important, longish discussion of Coriolanus (IV.vii) – an account almost like a 'character' in character-writing – is made to work out his estimation in terms of the two categories:

By sovereignty of nature.

(IV.vii.35)

Whether 'twas pride,
Which out of daily fortune ever taints
The happy man . . .

or whether nature,
Not to be other than one thing, not moving
From th'casque to th'cushion.

(IV.vii.37–43)

There are also as many as eight pointed references made to Coriolanus's 'nature' by a range of characters, including a few by Coriolanus himself (I.i.40; I.i.258; II.iii.185; II.iii.195; II.iii.256; III.i.135; IV.vii.10; V.vi.25). In several occurrences, the counter-category 'fortune' as a contrastive factor is suggested by implication. Similarly, the idea of fortune is invoked, apparently independently, in at least five places (I.iv.44; I.v.20; V.iii.119; V.iii.202; V.vi.117), either by or with reference to Coriolanus. Besides being in keeping

1. I cite the text of the New Arden edition of the play by Philip Brockbank (London, 1976).

with Shakespeare's habit of using the *topos* of the fortunes of war when depicting military scenes (as he often employs the *topos* of fortune and love), the references also suggest a contrast or conflict with the concept of nature in its topological significance.

Complementary to this topological shaping, as it were, of the emerging portrait of Coriolanus through the Nature–Fortune antinomy, is a much more pronounced and almost relentless deployment of the commonplace of the tongue and the heart, in the portrayal of Coriolanus as also of other characters and situations. The commonplace, extensively and often casually used in literature and drama, was memorably drawn upon by Roger Ascham in *The Schoolmaster* to condemn what he called the 'divorce between the tongue and the heart': the dichotomy, that is, between matter and expression, substance and form.[2] The *topos* develops inclusive suggestions of this and a whole series of allied polarities such as the inward and the external, reality and appearance, name and essence, action and speech, intention and effect, intrinsic honour and public opinion, dress and person etc. But what is interesting is that while the commonplace seems to emphasise the dichotomous pattern, in its effect it almost serves to deconstruct the bipolar opposition between the two items involved.

Even as the *topos* is multivalent in its meaning, it is 'multiform' in the sense that the commonplace appears in its variant, allotropically modified forms as well, such as heart and hand, heart and sword, heart and eye, heart and ear, 'voice' and tongue, feeling and breath, and several other such pairs of metonymic counters. There are over forty occurrences of the commonplace, ranging right across the play.[3] By their preponderance and proliferation in the play, these

2. 'Ye know not what hurt ye do to learning that are not for words but for matter, and so make a divorce between the tongue and the heart.' Roger Ascham, *The Schoolmaster*, ed. Lawrence V. Ryan (Ithaca, 1967), p. 115.

3. I.i.57–8, 59–60, I.i.73; I.i.114, 115, 116; I.iii.46–7; I.iv.24–5; I.iv.53; I.vi.26; I.vi.30; I.ix.37–8; II.i.52–3; II.i.233–4; II.ii.267–8; II.ii.29–31; II.ii.72; II.ii.80–1; II.iii.6–7; II.iii.46; II.iii.98; II.iii.150–1; II.iii.152–3; II.iii.201–3; III.i.22; III.i.33–4; III.i.75–6; III.i.131–2; III.i.155; III.i.255–6; III.i.270–1; III.ii.29–30; III.ii.54–6; III.ii.74–8; III.ii.100; III.ii.117–18, 122, III.ii.133–6; III.ii.28–9; IV.ii.19–20; IV.ii.21; IV.iii.8; IV.iv.13.

variants of the metonymic *topos* gain a particular valency against three key factors in it. These are: first, the background of Menenius's fable of the revolt of the members of the body against the stomach—itself a variant of the image of the body politic or the body of the commonwealth; secondly, the dominance in the play of the metonymic (or synecdochic) pole as contrasted with the metaphoric pole, to use the illuminating distinction made by Roman Jakobson. All the same, Shakespeare's choice and use of the metonymic mode in preference to the metaphoric would seem to result in effects which subsume rather than exclude the metaphoric. Thirdly, there is the dominant figuring, in the central part of the action, of the 'voices' which the plebeians give Coriolanus to elect him consul and at the same time take back all with their 'tongues'.

So iteratively is the tongue–heart *topos* pressed into service by Shakespeare in the characterisation of Coriolanus that its ramifications create a range of impressions that make up the image of the character. Coriolanus's quality of being 'too absolute', his 'stoutness' and his sense of his own inviolable integrity—all of which ultimately bring disaster on him—result from his faith in the absolute unity and identity of tongue and heart. That is to say, he is such a firm believer in, and assiduous cultivator of, the integrity of self and of being, that to him there is no distinction, indeed no question of any distinction, between inward and external, word and deed, name and essence; intrinsic worth and honour on one side and reputation and public opinion on the other.

To put it another way, binaries of this sort are to Coriolanus almost inconceivable, even as the two terms of such a binary are indistinguishable, so much so that for all his positive commitment to an impossible unity of being, Coriolanus turns out in effect to be an inveterate deconstructor. Here are some key utterances by and on Coriolanus which embody the conceit:

Martius I thank you, general,
But cannot make my heart consent to take
A bribe to pay my sword . . .

(I.ix.37–8)

Second officer . . . but he hath so planted his honours in their eyes
and his actions in their hearts, that for their tongues

to be silent and not confer so much were a kind of
ingrateful injury.
(II.ii.28–32)

Coriolanus When blows have made me stay, I fled from words.
(II.ii.72)

Menenius He had rather venture all his limbs for honour
Than one on's ears to hear it . . .
(II.ii.80–1)

Sicinus . . . and by his looks, methinks
'Tis warm at's heart.
(II.iii.150–1)

Coriolanus Must these have voices, that can yield them now
And straight disclaim their tongues? . . .
You being their mouths, why rule you not their
teeth?
(III.i.33–5)

Menenius His heart's his mouth:
What his breast forges, that his tongue must vent . . .
(III.i.255–6)

Volumnia Nor by th'matter which your heart prompts you,
But with such words that are but roted in
Your tongue . . .
(III.ii.54–6)

Coriolanus Must I
With my base tongue give to my noble heart
A lie that it must bear?
(III.ii.99–101)

It is this absolute and utterly single-minded idealism of a total integrity of personality and behaviour which at once lends the formidable warrior-hero awesome, Olympian or Herculean dimensions, yet leaves him insensitive to the practical realities of men and of life, and even more to the dire political realities of Rome or, for that matter, of Antium. This is what brings about his downfall and painful death. It is this personal make-up which lies behind his frequent states of rage and his outbursts, 'noble rage' though it may often be. His shunning of material rewards, of panegyric and public approbation of his victory over Aufidius and the

Volscians, and his unease (at least initially) over the assumption of his new cognomen 'Coriolanus', all spring from this basic factor of his personality.[4]

The episode in I.x.77–89, of Coriolanus wishing his host and benefactor in Corioles to be set free but forgetting the crucial detail of the man's name, is a tell-tale one in this regard. Rather than his forgetfulness being due to his war-weariness or to a haughty, aristocratic indifference to remembering names, it is a consequence of his instinctive dislike of, and refusal to recognise, the distinction of name and essence. His all but pathological hatred of the idea of standing as a candidate in an assumed vesture of humility, showing off his twenty-seven wounds to the plebeians and soliciting their 'voices', is in line with his—if anything too strong—conviction of his *integritas*, although the tribunes and the plebs take it as pride.

It is the refusal to acknowledge anything like a dichotomy between inner and outer that generates such loyalty in Coriolanus to the city of Rome and the state as institution, resulting in a tacit identification of himself with Rome—an idea of it rather—and of Rome with himself. Hence his fury at being labelled 'traitor' by the tribunes, and his retort 'I banish you' when the sentence of banishment is pronounced on him. Speaking as he does, at that point, of 'a world elsewhere', he implicitly assumes himself to be the real Rome, from which the actual Rome now so unjust and ingrateful to him, is banished by him. No wonder that he feels no compunctions about preparing to sack Rome, joining hands with Aufidius.

When the intervention of his mother and others of his family works a change of mind in Coriolanus, it is again because his assumed absorption of the ideal–real Rome into and within himself is displaced by a new or suddenly activated sense of an identity between his mother and nurse Volumnia—especially her womb—and Rome, wrought by Volumnia's words:

---

4. A contemporary play passage expresses the mundane, prudential understanding of the *topos*:

> He whose tongue and heart Run
> one self course, shall seldom find the way To a preferment.

(From *Distracted Emperor* in Dodsley's edition of *Old Plays*, vol. 3, p. 179.)

... thou shalt no sooner
March to assault thy country than to tread—
Trust to't, thou shalt not—on thy mother's womb
That brought thee to this world.

(V.iii.122–5)

Come, let us go:
This fellow had a Volscian to his mother;
His wife is in Corioles, and his child
Like him by chance.

(V.iii.177–80)

Yet on his final tragic return to the Volsces and Aufidius to die an ignominous death, he imagines that the identification he had also made between himself and the Volscian state continues unaffected; hence he is stung to fury when insulted as 'traitor' (and 'boy', 'boy of tears') by Aufidius.

Coriolanus's spontaneous drawing-back from the idea of play-acting or even role-playing, and his phenomenal failure to carry it out after most unwillingly undertaking it on the insistence of Volumnia and patrician friends like Menenius, are further consequences of his innate assurance of the inviolable unity of the self and its address to the world. Coriolanus's apprehension of the 'counterfeit', with its theatrical sense of effective acting, is very different: he would seem to understand it on the lines of the classical approximation in sense of 'actor' and 'hypocrite'. But the play-acting is thrust on him. The theatrical references in these parts of *Coriolanus* turn out to be an interesting variation on the ubiquitous *topos* of the world as stage. The political world of Rome as arena-stage, with Coriolanus as a glorious failure as actor upon it, tends to develop metatheatrical or subtheatrical resonances. It contributes in considerable measure to a certain dramatic self-consciousness which tinges the play. After all, a political drama is actively afoot in Coriolanus's Rome; the warrior-hero, great monolithic bastion of absolute integrity, is totally incapable of performing on that stage but is pitchforked into trying it.

Yet the player who played Coriolanus on the Shakespearian stage was the tragic actor *par excellence*: in all probability the great Burbage. Certainly he stood in no need of Volumnia's lessons in acting:

> Go to them, with this bonnet in thy hand,
> And thus far having stretch'd it—here be with them—
> Thy knees bussing the stones—for in such business
> Action is eloquence, and the eyes of th' ignorant
> More learned than the ears—waving the head . . .
>
> (III.ii.74–8)

Nor would Burbage have to expend much effort on what Coriolanus says he would do but just could not bring himself to:

> . . . I will practise the insinuating nod, and be off to them most counterfeitly; that is, sir, I will counterfeit the bewitchment of some popular man, and give it bountiful to the desirers.
>
> (II.iii.98–101)

With his virtuosic skills, Burbage as Coriolanus would indeed act out nearly to perfection Coriolanus's failure and inability to act. In terms of the stage dynamics of the world-stage *topos*, such double-take effects lend a piquancy and an extra dimension to the spectator's consciousness of the stage as stage, of drama as drama, and also at the same time of the stage as the world and of drama as mimesis.

Moreover, Shakespeare appears, as though of set purpose, to make the play an all-but-unbroken concatenation of fierce confrontation after confrontation, almost always between Coriolanus and a person or group of persons. It is as if through the deliberate underscoring of the confrontational, the playwright were presenting conflict, almost the central principle of drama with a vengeance. Again, features of the play such as Menenius's gestural enactment of the revolt of the members of the body; the frequent pointed presentation of gestures by actors as characters, as well as charaters as actors; the half-artificed, half-genuine rendering of ceremonious kneeling gestures by Volumnia and family towards the end of the play; a repeated use of the formal stage conventions of 'passing over the stage'—all these bring to the fore the element of self-conscious theatricality which runs through the play. Such dimensions to the deliberate, theatrical self-consciousness of the play tend cumulatively to produce a distancing effect in our response to the characters, especially the protagonist. This kind of distancing and disengagement has a double consequence; it makes us stop well short of empathising with the hero or with other characters, but by the same argument, it discourages our tendency to make moralistic, diagnostic or, worse, inquisitorial judgements. The detachment brought about, so to say, works both ways.

In the handling of *topoi*, Shakespeare in *Coriolanus* would seem to match elements of self-conscious theatricality in the play with a deliberate rhetorical self-consciousness. The intensive and extensive iteration of the *topos* of the tongue and the heart, and the much less frequent yet strong application of the Nature–Fortune commonplace, are perhaps meant to call attention to themselves and to the virtuoso effect created by employing the *topoi* as structural and formative elements. Again, this calls up a multiple effect. At one level, the persistent deployment of the *topos* creates an impression of at least slight parody of the commonplace as overworn cliché. But at another level it demonstrates convincingly the creative possibilities of commonplaces. In another direction, the implicit underscoring of rhetorical artifice brings about its own distancing effect, yet also brings home to the spectator the power of the artifice to embody and communicate reality.

Topicality in plays like *Coriolanus* has come to be much canvassed in recent New Historicist and cultural criticism, with a new interpretation being put on topicality. Tropes and images in this and other plays have had ample elucidation in the past. The topological element in the play, which informs its structure no less than its texture, would also seem to repay attention in some measure.

15

Antony and Cleopatra: The Functions of Theatricalism

Some of the distinctive features of the dramaturgy of the later Shakespeare and his Jacobean contemporaries may perhaps be identified as a pervasive quality of dramatic self-reflexivity; a self-consciously theatrical and at times ironic or even parodic use of theatrical modes and conventions and theatrical devices; an accentuation of the element of performance, play-acting and role-playing; the use of certain modes of detachment, aesthetic distancing and disengagement in the rendering of situation, character and action, the precedence of the societal over the individual in the playwright's interest; an externalised conception and presentation of character; *trompe l'oeil* effects of an intermingling of illusion and reality; and a kind of scene-for-the-scene opportunism. (Among the critics who pioneered an approach to Jacobean drama through its element of deliberate theatricality are R.A. Foakes[1] and Arthur Kirsch.[2] The tonalities and resonances of a play like *Antony and Cleopatra* can be better appreciated if we attend to the operativeness of some of these qualities springing from a deliberate dramatic self-consciousness in it. It would seem as though Shakespeare by design not so much manipulated his spectator's response by means of a self-consciously theatrical approach as he invited and encour-

1. *Shakespeare: From the Dark Comedies to the Final Plays* (London: Routledge & Kegan Paul, 1971).
2. *Jacobean Dramatic Perspectives* (Charlottesville: Univ. of Virginia Press, 1972).

aged his audience to identify and savour the artifice and art involved in a theatrically self-conscious manner of procedure, and thus to participate, though participate 'with a difference,' in the process of the play's theatrical realisation and communication. The spectator, especially in a play like *Antony and Cleopatra*, is called upon to maintain a delicate balance between engagement and detachment, between sympathy and judgement, thanks to a fruitful tension generated between the spectator's instinctive, natural tendency towards imaginative sympathy or empathy, on the one side, and the effects of distancing and disengagement (all but 'alienation effects'), on the other. The viewer, inheriting as he or she does, and participating in, a long and flourishing theatrical tradition, its history and recent legacy of a reaccentuated multiconsciousness about the stage, has every opportunity to take part in the process of deliberate theatricalisation at work in the play. At the same time, the multidimensionality which the stage and theatre gain through such theatricalisation does not in any sense nullify, or detract perceptibly from, the mimetic or verisimilar function and effect of the play. The great historical and also legendary figures of Antony, Cleopatra, and Caesar for that matter, for all the distanced and theatricalised mode in which they are conceived and presented and for all the viewers' engagement in this theatrical mode of disengagement, may be said to retain their Roman/Egyptian historicity, and also nonetheless their dimensions of the universal or the transcendent.

It was a good critical perception of Bradley's that the play in its final impression leaves us feeling sad that we are not left saddened enough by the tragedy of Antony and Cleopatra. The perception was born out of Bradley's insight into the essentially theatricalised and hence disengaged mode in which the play has been cast. Michael Shapiro, a foremost contemporary scholar and historian of the boy companies, especially the Children of the Chapel, and their plays, has, in a recent article[3] called attention to the probable affinities of *Antony and Cleopatra* with a considerable number of plays on Cleopatra (several of them not extant) in the children's theatre of the times and to the adoption by Shakespeare in his play of the self-

3. '"Boying her greatness": Shakespeare's use of coterie drama in *Antony and Cleopatra*', *Modern Language Review*, 77 (1982), 1–15.

conscious mode of playmaking taken over from the boy companies. This contextualisation of the self-reflexivity of Shakespeare's play in the boy companies' Cleopatra pieces, as much as the more general relating of the growing Jacobean dramatic self-consciousness to its first manifestation on the boy company stages, is a useful contribution of Michael Shapiro's. However, in his reading of the Shakespeare play, he sees a particularly sympathetic treatment of Cleopatra, and, more, accounts for this sympathetic view of the character as a carry-over from the children's indoor playhouse dramatists, tolerant if not admiring delineation of Cleopatra. This part of Professor Shapiro's argument does not quite square with one's general response either to the portrayal on the boy company stages, or to Shakespeare's conception and presentation, of Cleopatra. Shakespeare employs the mode of detachment and distancing through fairly consistent and deliberate theatricalisation to a greater degree in this play than perhaps he does in his other late plays.

Many scenes and situations, especially in the early parts of the play, are set in a framework of commentary by characters who are on-stage observers-cum-commentators. Not only does this device make the action which is often already in the nature of a performance appear all the more so as 'device' (in the Elizabethan sense of the term) but it also perspectivises the action further. It makes for a shifting of points of view, and brings about an effect of filtering of the audience's impressions and of anaesthetic distancing of the spectator. For example, Philo's opening condemnation of Antony's 'dotage' and of his captain's heart becoming 'the bellows and the fan/To cool a gipsy's lust', and his discussion of the enactment, the first in the play, of the love-relationship of the 'pair so famous' with his companion enclose the first of the performances of lovers' meetings, strange meetings, by Antony and Cleopatra in the play. Philo's use of the bellows and fan reference (Antony's 'captain's heart . . . becomes the bellows and the fan / To cool a gipsy's lust'), and his repeated calls to 'look', 'see' and 'behold', and 'see':

> The triple pillar of the world transform'd
> Into a strumpet's fool.[4]
>
> (I.i.11–21)

---

4. Quotations from the play in this chapter are from the new Arden *Antony and Cleopatra*, ed. M. R. Riddley.

are pointed enough visual clues but point as they do to the performance of Antony and Cleopatra.

The clues are as much proved to be inappropriate and inadequate to the witnessed actuality as the extravagance and cosmicising afflatus are made to suggest partly genuine grandeur and world-wide involvement, and partly grandiosity of gesturing. After all, it is the eunuchs who come fanning Cleopatra, according to the s.d., and not the most un-eunuch-like Antony. Added to this is the acting out by Cleopatra of her role as the teaser *par excellence* and as caprice itself in this as in other scenes. The discussions between Antony and Enobarbus of women in general and of Fulvia in particular (I.ii), of Antony by Caesar and Lepidus (I.iv), of Antony, again, by Pompey and Menas (II.i), and of Antony, yet again, by Enobarbus with Lepidus at the beginning of II.ii., the scene of the reconciliation of Antony and Caesar, and with Agrippa and Maecenas at the end of the same scene (as also Enobarbus's discussions of Antony with these in II.iv), are all commentaries which make for shifting perspectives on the action.

II.ii. starts almost as a quarrel scene and quickly changes gear in a sort of baroque manner into a scene of reconciliation and trothplight, and, further on, into the lyric evocations by Enobarbus in his account to Agrippa and Maecenas of Cleopatra's first meeting with Antony. In the central transactional part of the scene, after the politic Agrippa's proposal that Caesar should give his sister Octavia in marriage to Antony, lately widowed by Fulvia's death, finds all-too-ready acceptance with Caesar, Antony signifies agreement to the idea suggesting that the proposal be ratified with a handclasp betwen himself and Caesar and that the gesture be a true heraldry of hearts and hands together:

Ant May I never
To this good purpose, that so fairly shows,
Dream of impediment! Let me have thy hand
Further this act of grace; and from this hour
The heart of brothers govern in our loves
And sway our great designs!

Caes There is my hand.
A sister I bequeath you, whom no brother
Did love so dearly. Let her live

To join kingdoms, and our hearts; and never
Fly off our loves again!

(II.ii.148–57)

Sharing in the 'realist' choric perceptions of the on-stage observer Enobarbus, the spectator at this point will see that the marriage is a marriage of political convenience and that, for the same reason, the traditional gesture of handclasping emerges here suffused with irony. The emphasis on, and the implicit underscoring with irony of, the theatrical gesture of taking each other by the hand is matched by a similar, in effect, ironical deployment of the well-known commonplace of the hand and the heart (a variant from of the *topos* of 'tongue and heart').

A similar, at least half-ironic if also half-pathetic spotlighting of the stage gesture of the handclasp is in evidence in IV.ii., the scene on the eve of Antony's encounter in battle with Caesar, during the night when the mysterious music of Hercules leaving Antony's army is heard by the soldiers, and during which night Enobarbus crosses over to Caesar's side. Antony bids all his household servants to dinner that night, and shakes hands with everyone of them, ignoring class decorum and provoking both Cleopatra and Enobarbus to wonder what Antony means by it all:

Ant. Call forth my household servants; let's to-night
Be bounteous at our meal.

Enter three or four Servitors.

Give me thy hand.
Thou hast been rightly honest. So hast thou;
Thou, and thou, and thou. You have serv'd me well,
And kings have been your fellows.

Cleo. [*Aside to Eno.*] What means this?

Eno. [*Aside to Cleo.*] 'Tis one of those odd tricks which sorrow shoots
Out of the mind.

Ant. And thou art honest too.
I wish I could be made so many men,
And all of you clapp'd up together in
An Antony; that I might do you service
So good as you have done. . . . .

Cleo. [*Aside to Eno.*] What does he mean?

Eno. [*Aside to Cleo.*] To make his followers weep.

Ant. Tend me to-night;
May be it is the period of your duty.
Haply you shall not see me more; or if,
A mangled shadow . . .

Eno. What mean you, sir,
To give them this discomfort? Look, they weep;
And I, an ass, am onion-ey'd. For shame,
Transform us not to women.

Ant. Ho, ho, ho!
Now the witch take me if I meant it thus!
Grace grows where those drops fall! My hearty
friends,
You take me in too dolorous a sense;
For I spake to you for your comfort, did desire you
To burn this night with torches. Know, my hearts,
I hope well of to-morrow, and will lead you
Where rather I'll expect victorious life
Than death, and honour . . . .

(IV.ii.9–44)

The gesture of fellow-feeling, mutuality and hospitality very characteristic of Antony's 'bounty' and the sentiment of leave-taking with its sense of ending come through in the scene, no doubt. But the spectator's apprehension of these is complicated by his or her negotiation of the overt theatricalness of Antony's handclasping gesture and expressions, the underlining of it by the comments of Cleopatra and Enobarbus, and also by the sudden, near-baroque swing of Antony's stance into cheery bonhomie. There is a further inlaid possibility of a bit of theatricalism in the weeping of the servants which Enobarbus calls attention to twice. The no-nonsense Enobarbus almost blames himself for the moistening of his eyes: 'And I, an ass, am onion-ey'd'. There is a genuine 'sense of tears in (these) things mortal'. But the shadows or supernumerary actors of the servitors' roles may have possibly had a problem in working up the tears, and it is possible that they had to have recourse to onions for the purpose, and hence the expression 'onion-eyed' (which Enobarbus uses also in an earlier, fairly serious context of Antony's breaking of the news of Fulvia's death to him (I.ii.167).

The scene of the strange encounter between Antony and his attendants on the one side and Cleopatra and her maids on the other (III.xi), after Antony tastes his first ever defeat in battle as a result of Cleopatra's flagship fleeing is another scene in which the theatrical gestures and utterances of extreme sorrow and disappointment predominate. Antony's long bewailment of his predicament (IV.iv.8–24) in which he almost announces his abdication of captainship and adjures his men to disperse with his ship and treasure comes to a close with his staging of the old theatrical gesture (used by the early Shakespeare prominently and in straight fashion in *Richard III, King John* and *Richard II*) of sitting down on the ground or floor as a mark of overwhelming grief. If all this happens stage-left or stage-right, on the other side appears at this point Cleopatra led by Charmian and Eros, a Cleopatra most hesitant to face Antony and being almost dragged and pushed by her maids.

Eros Nay, gentle madam, to him! Comfort him.
Iras Do, most dear Queen.
Char. Do? Why, what else?
Cleo. Let me sit down. O Juno!
Ant. No, no, no, no, no.
Eros See you here, sir?
Ant. O fie, fie, fie!
Char. Madam!
Iras Madam, O good Empress!
Eros Sir, sir!

(III.xi.25–34)

Apart from the comicality which intermingles with the seriousness of the situation and which arises out of the two of them, Antony and Cleopatra, having to be prodded and egged on to meet each other, there is a particular highlighting of an effect of staginess in the matching use of the stage-gesture of 'sitting down' in the scene by Antony and by Cleopatra on two opposite sides of the stage, and in Cleopatra's adoption of the gesture with the words

Let me sit down, O Juno!

being unattended yet responded to by Antony with his moaning

No, no, no, no, no . . .

the two short lines thus giving rise to a deliberate jingle.

The entrances and exits of the messengers in the play are a strong recurrent visual phenomenon which have a way of adding to the pronouncedly theatrical mode of existence and of operation. Contrasted to the formal, measured utterances of the messengers in general are the violence and indecorousness (stagy in its actual manifestation in the theatre) of the treatment meted out to the messenger in two instances. To match Cleopatra's haling up and down of the Messenger who brings her news of Antony's marriage in Rome to Octavia (II.v.) and her making him run for very life as she draws her knife on him, there is Antony's ordering of the whipping of Caesar's ambassador to him and to Cleopatra (III.xiii). (Though the actual whipping is carried out off stage, the soundly whipped Thidias is brought on stage before he exits.)

The scene of the death of Enobarbus (IV.ix) is so ordered that the theatrical is very much to the fore alongside and in spite of the pathos of Enobarbus's dying of a broken heart feeling guilty of ingratitude to Antony coming through as well. There is something comic and theatrical in the discovery by improbably slow stages by the sentry and his watches, first, of the presence of Enobarbus and, finally, of the fact that Enobarbus is dead, together with their inability or incapacity to make anything out of Enobarbus's speeches in spite of carefully cupping their ears to listen. The watches mistake Enobarbus who drops dead after his last speech (ll.12–23) to be asleep and try to wake him up. Only a few lines later, the sentry discovers that he is dead. As they remove the body at the end of the scene, the watch says:

> Come on then, he may recover yet

so much so that it in effect turns out to be yet another stage exploitation in Shakespeare of the old similitude of sleep and death, and furthermore, an exploitation of the sameness of sleep and death as stage reality and of the idea that the actor, once he is removed off stage, will get up and go.

A vein of self-conscious theatricalism is to be traced in the crucial monument scenes (IV.xv.) and (V.ii). The scene of the lingering and painful process of the death of Antony is, among other things, a *tour de force* of staging. The exploitation of the acting area of the 'above' in relation to the platform stage below takes place, as Richard Hosley has shown, as a standing example of the interconnected and interdependent use of the two theatrical spaces. Without damage to the purport and import of seriousness governing the last parting of Antony and Cleopatra, the stage dynamics of the rendering gives rise to certain effects of theatricalism in the details of the presentation. The frantic desire and effort of Cleopatra to pull Antony, wounded and dying as he is, to her at the top of the monument.

O Antony,
Antony, Antony! Help, Charmian; help, Iras, help;
Help, friends below! Let's draw him hither.

(IV.xv.11–13)

are curiously complemented by Antony's longing for the long farewell of a last kiss on Cleopatra's lips.[5] Cleopatra dare not leave the monument for fear of being caught by Caesar's men and she calls, once again upon her women

Help me, my women—we must draw thee up;
Assist, good friends.

(IV.xv.29–30)

They heave Antony aloft to Cleopatra, as she vocally accompanies the operation with the words

Here's sport indeed! How heavy weighs my lord!
Our strength is all gone into heaviness;
That makes the weight . . .
. . . Yet come a little.
Wishers were ever fools. O, come, come, come,
(*They heave Antony aloft to Cleopatra.*)
And welcome, welcome! Die when thou hast liv'd.
Quicken with kissing. Had my lips that power

---

5. No wonder that Fletcher in his comedy *The Wild-Goose Chase* (c.1620) makes a character allude, parodically, to the scene and situation. A mischievous and libidinous servant eyeing a woman standing on the upper gallery, fantasises the idea of a kiss from her to him on the lower stage. His words are set in quotation, 'Come, Anthony, and kiss me' (Cf. Cleopatra's 'Come, come, Antony', l. 29). Quoted from *Drama of the English Renaissance II: The Stuart Period*, ed. Russell A. Fraser and Norman Rabkin (New York, 1976).

Thus would I wear them out.
All A heavy sight!
(IV.xv.33–40)

Even if Burbage who played Antony were not to have been of such large and massive build as his predecessor Alleyn, heaving the figure aloft is likely to have been a fairly strenuous operation for the combined physical powers of the 'boy-actresses' who played Cleopatra and her maids although the 'boy-actress' playing Cleopatra (perhaps it was John Rice) could earlier hale the Messenger up and down with aplomb. It would have been a strenuous operation even if a suspension gear were used with Antony seated in a chair. The physical pain besides the mental agony of the dramatic character Antony after his somewhat bungled killing of himself and after the late revelation made to him about Cleopatra being alive and not dead, is a factor which gets further complicated in its acquisition of another stage dimension in the process of enactment of the difficult haul. After pronouncing her epitaph on the moving death of Antony, Cleopatra falls in a faint which in that particular stage moment has all the appearance of her death, as her women take it to be (half lines 68–70).

The 'one scene of excellent dissembling' (to quote her own words, [I.iii.78–9] which Cleopatra plays before Caesar when he comes to see her in the monument (V.ii.) is followed by Cleopatra's anticipation and contemplation of what would happen to her and her maids after they are taken as war trophies and exhibited in Rome by the Romans. After imagining herself and her companions as undergoing the fate of being shown as Egyptian puppets, she envisages future stage representations of herself and Antony as a certainty thus:

. . . the quick comedians
Extemporally will stage us, and present
Our Alexandrian revels; Antony
Shall be brought drunken forth, and I shall see
Some squeaking Cleopatra boy my greatness
I' th' posture of a whore.
(V.ii.215–19)

The multiple layers of theatrical consciousness and self-consciousness the passage involves in its stage realisation, on the part of actor, audience and playwright, need hardly be laboriously sorted out. But we could see that it is no mere give-away gesture on the part of playwright or actor. Shakespeare was sure of his 'boy-actress' of Cleopatra speaking and acting the lines with the deftness and confidence which would self-reflexively return upon the actor in just the adequate measure of disjunction and would also at the same time show *this* Cleopatra to be no squeaking Cleopatra boying her greatness in the posture of a whore. It would also serve as an appropriately and slightly derisive hit at the presentation of Cleopatra in the several Cleopatra plays on the children's theatre stages.

While such self-referentiality in the passage and the situation enacted has applicability to performances of the Cleopatra legend and history including the ongoing Shakespearian performance in its part negative and part oblique relevance, the contextual factor in Cleopatra's speech is that the Roman dramatic representation (misrepresentation or *sub*-representation) which she fears will take place in her very presence. This suggests something of anti-masque or antic masque which will entail a travesty or demeaning of the customary Presence on a masque occasion. In addition, it turns out to be allusive, in the context of theatrical history and environment, to plays which represented or sought to represent living monarchs, as Peele's *The Arraignment of Paris* introduced Queen Elizabeth as a 'guest' character or as a play of Shakespeare's company *The Tragedy of Gowry* during its short run (it was soon aborted) in 1604 portrayed the new king in his old status as King James VI of Scotland. Middleton and Dekker portrayed the living phenomenon of Marion Firth or Moll Cutpurse in their Admiral's Men play *The Roaring Girl* for which perhaps Marion Firth was present among the audience in the Fortune playhouse.

Cleopatra's elaborate designing and acting out of her death by the ruse of the application of the asps have all the elements of drama and staging, what with her costuming of herself with queenly robes and crown and what with the drama of her dream of Antony which amounts to a pantocratic vision of him on her part. The last service which Charmian performs for her queen is indicated in her

> Your crown's awry;
> I'll mend it, and then play—
>
> (V.ii.317–18)

Then, after momentarily holding the Guard who 'rustles in' at bay, she plays the same part or ruse as her mistress and dies by applying an asp to her bosom.

At the close of the play, Caesar in his final speech pays his tribute to the dead in fairly self-reflexive terms:

> No grave upon the earth shall clip in it
> A pair so famous. High events as these
> Strike those that make them; and their story is
> No less in pity than his glory which
> Brought them to be lamented.
>
> (V.ii.356–60)

Leaving on one side the self-gratulation indulged in by Octavius that is implanted in the speech, the lines may also be seen as containing a tribute in an epilogue-like manner, to the play, in an adaptation of the formula of Minturno's for the response to tragedy, the twin response of 'admiration and commiseration' (in modification of Aristotle's 'pity and terror'), the 'admiration', in Minturno's interpretation, being particularly for the art and design, the skill and execution, of the poet-playwright. The passage is a highly deserved tribute.

Such an 'admiration', especially in the sense of a response of marvelling at the design and creativity behind the work, is indeed due to *Antony and Cleopatra* on several grounds, not the least of which is that the artifice of 'theatrics' would seem to make for the life and vitality of the play by virtue of rather than in spite of the theatrical virtuosity. The apprehension and communication of realities in and through the theatrical and the theatricalist not only enhances and sharpens one's sense of reality at many levels but serves to bring home the truth that life and the world may confront one with surprises and ironies and intricacies as theatrical, romance-like or dream-like as these may be.

16

Theatricality and Mimesis in *The Winter's Tale*: The Instance of 'Taking one by the Hand'

A significant feature of the dramaturgy of the later Shakespeare which has come in for a good deal of fruitful attention in recent years is the quality of deliberate dramatic self-consciousness or 'self-conscious theatricality' that marks the late tragedies and the last plays, if not some of the problem comedies also. It may be described as a new flowering and pronounced manifestation of, and a further refinement on, the quality of 'multi-consciousness' inherent in the English dramatic tradition and this is in ample evidence in the earlier Shakespeare; this trend perhaps first arose in the boy companies at the turn of the century and came to be adopted in the public playhouses also, sooner or later. This quality of dramatic self-consciousness may be regarded as the basis for certain other characteristics which seem distinctive of the Jacobean dramatic mode. These characteristics may be listed thus—a self-reflexive and parodic use of dramatic conventions and devices, or sometimes rhetorical *topoi*, the use of certain 'modes of detachment' by which an 'aesthetic distancing' of characters and action is often-enough effected; the presentation of characters, especially the protagonists, in a less inward and more societal or general perspective, with 'give-away' asides mostly replacing the older soliloquies; the framework of commentary serving as a means of the dramatist's manipulation of response; scenic impact or a scene-for-the-scene opportunism taking precedence over the sequential or cumulative impression; the other *trompe l'oeil* habit of collapsing illusion and reality together; the sudden contrasts or baroque clashes of mood and tone, if not sudden changes of scene, and, lastly, the strong element of play-acting and role-playing. These general characteristics of dramatic conception and technique are in evidence in the later plays of Shakespeare in varying degrees of magnitude and importance from play to play; but they are to a greater or less extent shared by the later Shakespeare and his colleagues in the theatre of the times, both public and private, such as Marston, Jonson, Chapman, Beaumont, Tourneur, Middleton and Webster. This latter fact only confirms that Shakespeare as a Jacobean playwright, for all his being like a star, did not dwell apart from his fellow-playwrights, and was, in the ultimate sense, engaged in a collaboration, a common pursuit of true dramatic endeavour, with them.

We will do well thus to recognise the abundant experimental vigour of the later as well as the earlier Shakespeare and his remarkable response to, as well as full participation in his theatrical milieu (neither was he bored with things nor was there a decline in his powers). But perhaps it is equally, if not more important, for us to note the qualitative differences between Shakespeare's use of the modes of self-conscious theatre and of disengagement, and the use of the same modes by Marston (in *Antonio's Revenge* and *The Malcontent*) or by Beaumont (in *The Knight of the Burning Pestle* or *The Maid's Tragedy*) or by the trio of Marston, Chapman and Jonson (in *Eastward Ho!*) or Tourneur (or Middleton) (in *The Revenger's Tragedy* or *A Chaste Mind in Cheapside*). The difference, baldly stated, is simply that Shakespeare in his later plays often achieves a simultaneous effect of self-conscious theatricality and convincing verisimilitude or lifelikeness, to both of which the spectator can fully respond at the same time. The self-reflexive use of dramatic conceptions and devices in the other playwrights can often detract from the essential mimesis of drama. But in Shakespeare's late plays the virtuoso-like prestidigitation of the 'dyer's hand' of the playwright, with all the sophistication of a certain theatrical *tour de force* and the juxtaposition or fusion of the naive and the 'marvellous'—or of the realistic and the idealistic—has a way of evoking at once an attention to (and admiration for) the art of the playwright and a feeling for the human reality of the drama. I shall now go on to illustrate this co-presence of theatrical virtuosity and truth-to-life with an analysis of a recurring example from *The Winter's Tale*.

Shakespeare's stylised conception and rendering of the crucial second scene of the play, the scene of the sudden onset of Leontes's jealousy, have been noted by critics though not the distancing effect of the conventionalisation. The part it plays in the dramatist's manipulation of our response to Leontes's jealousy has perhaps not been given its due in commentary. But a curious phenomenon of this scene, and as a matter of fact of *The Winter's Tale* as a whole, is the figuring in the scene and in the play of an all-too-commonplace stage gesture, the gesture of handclasping. More curious perhaps than the extensive and highly effective use of this gesture in the play is the critics' neglect of this visual gesture, which occurs prominently in this scene and at several other key points in the play, serving as a powerful visual punctuation or rhythm. The double impression of a self-reflexive and a mimetic use of a dramatic convention is well instanced in Shakespeare's deployment of the gesture of the handclasp in the play, and in this scene.

The note of graceful idealism and of the Arcadian idyllic sounded in the opening scene, and carried on into the second scene upto a point, registers its sudden and apparently disastrous change the moment Hermione 'gives her hand to Polixenes' (I.ii.107), signalling the pact of his acceptance of her plea to him to extend his visit. The dramatically self-conscious technique of the whole scene is such that the rise of the jealous fit on Leontes's part as set out in his utterances (I.ii.108–18; 125–6) has for its visual correlative in the stage picture the figures of Hermione and Polixenes holding each other's hands, the two as it were remaining arrested in that posture, albeit in interesting inset, silent (their mimed words if any are not to be heard), for the space of the long outburst of Leontes. It is in many ways a stage underlining of an obvious gesture. Much like the emphasising and repetition of the Biblical word, 'verily,' first spoken in the opening scene by Archidamus (I.i.11) and in the second scene by Hermione (I.ii.46–55), the bizarre verbal motif of Camillo's 'though absent, (the two kings) shook hands, as over a vast, and embrac'd as it were from the ends of oppos'd winds' is picked up in Leontes's congratulation of Hermione on her successful persuasion of Polixenes to stay on:

that was when
Three crabbed months had sour'd themselves to death,
ErеI could make thee open thy white hand,
(And) clap thyself my love . . .

(I.ii.101–4)

However, we need not assume that at this point the action of Leontes now putting his hand into Hermione ought to suit the words. Incidentally, the rhythms of the alternating spells of silence and speech on the part of Hermione, Leontes, Polixenes and Mamilius contribute to the dynamics of the scene through an alternation of stage presence and utterance. Added to this is the stage reality of the visibly pregnant condition of Hermione. It is the sight of Hermione and Polixenes sitting hand in hand that whips up Leontes's feelings. The deliberate calling of attention to the onstage tableau

. . . to be paddling palms and pinching fingers,
As now they are,

(I.ii.115–16)

and

Still virginalling
Upon his palm?

(I.ii.125–6)

(this latter for the moment breaking off his by-play with Mamilius) in the context of the cumulation of references to handshaking does serve to theatricalise Leontes's jealousy. So do the rhetorical excesses of his speeches and their overplus of dislocated energy, as well as the extravagant concern he shows with the all too down-to-earth details of Mamilius's personal hygiene, which contrasts with the 'fury' in the words and the situation. Out of the 'nothing' of a single detail of the handclasp Leontes's mind could soon call up a chain of hallucinatory evidence for his jealousy in his indictment of Hermione addressed to Camillo:

Is whispering nothing?
Is leaning cheek to cheek? is meeting noses?
Kissing with inside lip? stopping the career
Of laughter with a sigh (a note infallible

Of breaking honesty?) horsing foot on foot?
Skulking in corners? Wishing clocks more swift?

(I.ii.284–90)

. . . he, that wears her like her medal hanging
About his neck, Bohemia . . .

(I.ii.307–8)

In terms of theatrical impact the situation does get aesthetically distanced among other factors though the use of the handclasp. We see Leontes as in a condition or a fit of disease. Yet as its victim he does undergo real throes and pangs. For all their ultimate tragicomic happy resolution the events that are the outcome of this jealousy involve the sad death of the prince (as sad as that of Prince Henry in the view of some scholars), the loss—though perhaps not so sad—of the boldly commonsensical Antigonus with his fitting ripostes, and the privations of the Queen. The 'unreality' of Leontes's jealousy and its real, existential force are simultaneously brought home to us. The visual rhythm of the handclasp punctuates the close of the long scene when Polixenes takes Camillo's advice that he should flee from Sicily taking him by the hand.

Give me thy hand,
Be pilot to me, and thy places shall
Still neighbour mine . . .

(I.ii.447–9)

This in turn in to be the beginning or anticipation of Camillo's role in the play of 'piloting' and of joining hands.

When Leontes, now far gone in his state of jealousy—which to him is confirmed by Camillo's flight—banishes the Queen from his company, Antigonus speaks up and speaks out most vocally among the lords on behalf of the Queen. In answer Leontes employs a gesture to convince Antigonus of the materiality of his 'cause' in a manner not dissimilar to the Johnsonian, anti-Berkelean stamp. Saying,

I do see't, and feel't,
As you feel doing thus

(II.i.152–3)

he *grasps his arm* (s.d.).

The use of the handclasping gesture in the second, Bohemian half of the play matches its counterpart in the Sicilian, first half in its revealing nature, particularly in its double effect of reality and theatricality, and the motif is easily one of the most outstanding of the many correspondences between the two parts of the diptych that the play is.

In the scene of the sheep-shearing feast, masque-like structure and details are employed to bring us a sense of the paradoxical interweave of 'performance' and genuineness, of art and nature, and nature and grace, the popular and the courtly. The artifice of the dramatic action of the taking of hands, simple as it is, forms an important part of the natural beauty of the art and life of the scene. To start with, the festival dance entails a joining of hands between Florizel and Perdita. The dance is referred to first by the Shepherd in terms of no more than a domestic, true-hostess-like efficiency and nimbleness (*hic et ubique*) (IV.iv.58–60), and later by Florizel in terms of an ideal cosmic dance (like the dance of Siva) apprehended as a warm, felt, living reality in Perdita.

> When you do dance, I wish you
> A wave o'th'sea, that you might ever do
> Nothing but that; move still, still so,
> And own no other function.
>
> (IV.iii.140–3)

Florizel takes Perdita's hand, and as they 'dance featly' a dance of shepherds and shepherdesses it turns out to be a sort of masque-dance in a sort of courtly-pastoral masque, to be followed later by the antimasque of the dance of the Twelve Saltyrs or Saltiers. The multifacetedness of the illusion–reality intercommunication in the dance and the situation as a whole are something which resemble the unified-field awareness and simultaneity of pattern recognition characteristic of 'electronic circuitry' indeed.

But Florizel's handclasping with Perdita, interrupted as it is by Polixenes, is the centrepiece of the action of the scene. Here again there is a theatrical underscoring of the holding of hands, as in the second scene of the play, as well as a sudden manifestation of anger on Polixenes's part, involving a sudden, masque-like change of tone and mood in the scene, answering to the sudden outbreak of Leontes's jealousy. Florizel makes, rightly, a ceremony of it.

I take thy hand, this hand,
As soft as dove's down and as white as it,
Or Ethiopian tooth, or the fann'd snow that's bolted
By th' northern blasts twice o'er.

(IV.iii.361–4)

The mutual clasping of hands is, again, called attention to in the not unadmiring words of the soon-to-be angry Polixenes:

How prettily th'young swain seems to wash
The hand was fair before!. . .

(IV.iii.366–7)

But when the Shepherd is about to solemnise the 'handfast', with

Come, your hand,
And, daughter, yours.

(IV.iii.390–1)

Polixenes makes an interruption, first raising the question of the father's consent to the son's choice and subsequently by all but parting their hands, 'discovering himself' with his 'mark your divorce' in answer to Florizel's 'mark our contract'. Yet in spite of its turning out to be a broken ceremony (and the sheep-shearing feast a broken feast also, as most Shakespearean feasts are) the two are united till '. . . death do (them) part', though 'the heavens will not have their contract celebrated', as Perdita puts it later (V.i.202–3).

It is in the 'marvellous' final scene of the play that the stage device of handclasping is employed by Shakespeare to the finest, most characteristically subtle double effect of a *coup de theatre* and a moving communication of reality in the play. The paradoxical interfusion of art and nature and of nature and grace suggested throughout the play crystallises itself into an impressive stage-reality in the scene, with the 'figures-in-words' so far materialising themselves into the 'figures-in-action'. But in the preceding mood-setting scene of reporting (V.ii), a number of gestures are enthusiastically reported by the three Gentlemen who vie with one another in their effort to communicate the vividness of their impressions of the events witnessed. Yet the handclasping gesture is referred to and indulged in by the Clown in his stocktaking of the recently passed incredible developments with his father the Shepherd. His 'preposterous' declaration to his father is

> But I was a gentleman born before my father; for the King's son took me by the hand, and call'd me brother; and then the two kings call'd my father brother . . .
>
> (IV.ii.139–42)

In what one may call in this context an antimasque-like or, better still, an antimasque-like use of giving somebody one's hand, the Clown on getting an 'ay' in reply to his question to Autolycus if he would amend his life gives him his hand in his new-fangled gentlemanliness, and agrees to commend Autolycus to the Prince. In this comic use of the gesture it is its overt staginess which is to the fore; yet it should be noted that all this immediately precedes the great final scene, and the Clown announces at the end of his scene that they all like 'the king and the princes, our kindred' should go to see 'the Queen's picture'.

As with Hermione's 'wrinkles-and-all' statue, the art of 'taking one by the hand,' as it is in evidence in the finale of the play, is 'an art which does mend Nature but the art itself is Nature'. Perdita's response to the statue of the Queen is to kneel (another gesture used meaningfully at various points in the play, incidentally) and 'to implore her blessing'. Shakespeare does prepare his audience, though, through half-hints and faint-enough suggestions for the final surprise (which he exceptionally holds for them in this play), but it is a preparation which takes the form of Paulina-the-stage-manager's provision of hints of possibilities of the Queen's coming back from the dead to Leontes and the others (as early as the opening of Act V). An important stage in the course of this process in the final scene occurs when Perdita, taken in by the 'life' of the statue in one sense, but rightly grasping it in another more important sense, is about to take the statuesque Queen by the hand.

> Lady,
> Dear queen, that ended when I began
> Give me that hand of yours to kiss
>
> (V.iii.44–6)

and Paulina in effect warns her of 'wet paint'. A still more important stage in the movement of the scene is reached when Paulina promises the onlookers the magic of art, rather art as magic, the *trompe l'oeil* phenomenon by which

> I'll make the statue move indeed, descend
> And take you by the hand . . .
>
> (V.iii.88–9)

(Paulina's or rather Shakespeare's *trompe l'oeil* here far outdoes whatever the artist Julian Romano was capable of.) Leontes is 'content' to submit himself and to consider it legitimate magic. As in *The Tempest*, at this point in *The Winter's Tale* music does it as much as magic, and it is to music as well as to Paulina's command that Hermione awakes and starts moving. As Paulina exhorts the spellbound Leontes, 'Nay, present your hand' (V.iii.107), he readily takes Hermione by the hand, a second hand-fasting echoing the echo in I.ii of the pre-dramatic first; the handfasting now makes the reunion a true re-marriage. The quiet but deeply felt energies of drama, released in the moment of the handclasp, as Leontes says:

> O, she's warm!
> If this be magic, let it be an art
> Lawful as eating
>
> (V.iii.109–11)

are limitless. As Camillo's running commentary indicates, 'she hangs about his neck', a transformed stage-realisation of the gesture attributed to Hermione and Polixenes by Leontes in his jealous fit—

> he, that wears her like her medal hanging
> About his neck, Bohemia
>
> (I.ii.307–8)

And Hermione, finding her tongue for the first time, takes by her hand the kneeling Perdita after pronouncing the best blessings on her head.

The mellowest of the instances of the handclasp is reserved to the very end. For Paulina who has rediscovered and restored his Queen to him Leontes finds a husband in Camillo by way of fitting repayment. There is the further 'fit' of the two stage-managers who have in the play been 'fitting' others (in Elizabethan theatre terminology) taking each other's hand in marriage, as King Leontes with his newly-gained masterfulness over the situation commands:

> Come, Camillo
> And take her by the hand . . .
>
> (V.iii.143–4)

The repetition and underscoring of the gesture do make for the gesture showing itself up in all its obviousness; yet the old turtle (as she calls herself) and the old dove join hands in marriage, which is a marriage of true minds. Coming in the wake of the reunion, as good as a new or second marriage, of Leontes and Hermione, the idea (and the fact) of the wedding of Paulina and Camillo evokes the same kind of response as the golden wedding of a happily married elderly couple would evoke. There is a reunion of Hermione and Polixenes, 'my brother' too. Florizel, as the King reminds Hermione (and us), is, 'heavens directing troth-plight to your daughter'. The reader or spectator with a good memory will not forget at this point the three daughters of himself and Paulina that Antigonus mentions earlier; the eldest at the end of the play is twenty-seven years old. But Shakespeare can afford to forget them.

Metadramatic as Shakespeare's complex manipulation of the simple dramatic gesture of handclasping may be, it is in his hands one of the means of representing reality. Similarly, Shakespeare seems to use in this play the scenic form of the Mystery-cycle plays of the Slaughter of the Innocents (with Herod at the centre) in ironic or palimpsest form in the scene (II.ii) in which Leontes rages like Herod as Paulina brings his newborn infant, reprimands him and, at the end of a slanging match, leaves the child, only to be ordered by Leontes that it be killed or abandoned. But while the scenic reminiscence of Mystery drama, and the implicit supersession of the mode suggested in its ironic use, make for a disengagement or disorientation of the spectator, the analogy lends the scene, at the same time, an extra-dimensionality and an impact which strangely combine disturbance and reassurance. The suggestions of the Mystery-cycle play on Herod's Massacre of the Innocents in the configuration of the scene are confirmed by the verbal echo in the scene (II.iii.110) of the Middle-English term of abuse, 'lozel', which occurs in the Mystery plays but whose sole occurrence in Shakespeare is to be found in this scene. Similar to Shakespeare's use of the tableau of the handclasp in this play is his use of the kneeling tableaux in it. Also, as he exploits the scenic form of a Mystery-cycle play in II.iii, and also perhaps in the scene of Hermione's trial (echoing the trial scenes of the Mystery plays, especially those of Christ's trial), so he employs the masque structure and masque elements in the scenic configuration of the scene of the sheep-shearing feast as well as the final scene to double effect. These latter instances of scenic motifs and dramatic devices in the play, of course, will have to be considered separately. Our brief study of the dramatic functions of the device of 'taking one by the hand' in *The Winter's Tale* should serve to reassure us that Shakespeare's later plays, as his middle and early ones, more than most of the plays of his Jacobean colleagues, are for all their self-reflexive qualities no 'self-consuming artifacts'. They are not solipsistic contrivances, nor entirely or mainly plays about playmaking and playmaking devices; there is 'an appeal always open (in them) from art to nature', and, again in Johnson's words, 'they are just representations of general nature'.

17

Mucedorus and Shakespeare: and his Company

It has come to be increasingly recognised that Shakespeare did not dwell apart like a star from his playwright and theatre colleagues and predecessors; considerable attention has now been accorded to the probable and possible interactive, reactive and intertextual relationships between the Shakespeare plays and plays by other dramatists of the period.[1] For longer than this, old scholarly traditions have traced the influence of Shakespeare's predecessors and earlier dramatic modes on him, as also his influence on his contemporaries and immediate successors. More recent trends in this have been to identify the impact of his immediate predecessors in the theatre like Marlowe and Kyd, Lyly and Greene, and Peele, as providing a stimulus to him to go and do perceptibly otherwise rather than imitating them. In this area Shakespeare's possible response to the anonymous play *Mucedorus* which could arguably be regarded as the 'most popular Elizabethan play'[2] still awaits anything like sustained consideration. True, in incidental references in critical and editorial commentary, Shakespeare's likely

1. M.C. Bradbrook, 'Shakespeare and his contemporaries: other poets and playwrights,' J.F. Andrews ed. *William Shakespeare: His World, His Work, His Influence, Vol. 2. His Work* (New York: Charles Scribner's Sons, 1985), pp. 331–42, provides a conspectus of the mutual impact of Shakespeare, and his immediate predecessors and contemporaries.
2. G.F. Reynolds, '*Mucedorus*, most popular Elizabethan play?' J.W. Bennett, *et. al.*, eds. *Studies in the English Renaissance Drama* (New York: Columbia University Press, 1959), pp. 248–68.

reminiscences of *Mucedorus* have been pointed out.[3] But certain aspects of Shakespeare's relationship to the play, and some important implications of the use by way of revival of this play in 1610 by Shakespeare's company with additions put in by them, would seem to deserve attention.

The play which originated in the popular London theatre circa 1590 not only held the stage for long but turned out to be the Elizabethan–Jacobean play to go through the largest number of quarto printings, starting with the first 1598 quarto, for the better part of the seventeenth-century with *The Spanish Tragedy* making only a second in this respect. For all its look of a gallimaufry or hodgepodge in typical Elizabethan fashion and for all its appearance of a naive 'tragical-comical-historical-pastoral' of a play, in the Polonian taxonomy, the extravaganza-like play in its uneven course of quality presents also evidence of sophistication and skill in places. Shakespeare mocked plays of this sort in the plays-within-plays in his early drama, *Love's Labour's Lost* and *A Midsummer Night's Dream* and the Induction frame in *The Taming of the Shrew*. Yet in his final phase of tragicomic romances Shakespeare would seem to have remembered features of *Mucedorus* and incorporated these in his characteristically individual and masterly manner in the series *Cymbeline, The Winter's Tale* and *The Tempest*. What is more, among the scenes added to the play (the new Prologue, scenes i, ii, xiii and the concluding section of xviii) when the play was mounted in the King James I's banqueting hall on Shrove Sunday in 1610, evidently on royal command, there is one scene, scene xiii, which carries a striking conflation of echoes and of iterations and approximations to Shakespeare's *Twelfth Night*. The reminiscences are verbal, situational and scenic, thus raising a strong possibility of Shakespeare's hand being traced in this particular scene among the

3. In the new Arden editions of *Cymbeline*, *The Winter's Tale* and *The Tempest*, for instance: Patricia Russell, 'Romantic narrative plays: 1570–84', *The Elizabethan Theatre*, Stratford-on Avon Studies No. 9, eds. J.R. Brown and B. Harris (London: Edward Arnold, 1966), 127–9 and A.R. Braunmuller and M. Hattaway, eds. *The Cambridge Companion to English Renaissance Drama* (Cambridge: Cambridge University Press, 1950), p. 65, p. 67 and pp. 216–17, among other instances.

four added scenes which were all written by the playwrights of the King's Men.[4]

Furthermore, the Epilogue scene in the play featuring Comedy and Envy and serving as the induction frame at the play's close, which was an addition by the King's Men's playwrights and which ends with an enacted tribute to King James I as the prime spectator in the audience, makes certain highly revealing topical references to the boy companies, especially to the Children of the Chapel, who had recently been restrained from playing, for their compulsive habit of thinly coded satirical attacks in their plays on the king and the court. The nature of this topical reference in the Epilogue of *Mucedorus* might offer further insight than that which we have about the relation and interaction between Shakespeare's men and the Chapel boys, the public playhouse and the private playhouse, especially at a time when the boys had practically ceased playing and Shakespeare's company had started using the Chapel boys' venue, the Blackfriars' indoor playhouse, as their winter theatre. Also, by the time Shakespeare's company expanded and revived *Mucedorus*, the dramatic self-consciousness and 'multiconsciousness' inherent in the original play had perhaps come to acquire further dimensions in the self-conscious artistry and theatricality of Jacobean, as distinct from Elizabethan drama. Besides, the tragicomic generic cast of *Mucedorus*, old hat as the play was, would acquire a new relevance in the vogue for tragicomedy circa 1610. In addition, the crude comments of the 'natural' clown Mouse in the play on class, rank, status and name including those on the king might take on certain originally unanticipated sociopolitical and sociological resonances in the Jacobean context.

There is near-synchrony in the Shakespeare's men's revision and revival of the old play which was mounted by them in very early 1610, and in Shakespeare's full launching of himself into the phase of tragicomedy, but for the considerably exceptional case of the earlier play *Pericles*, and his writing of *Cymbeline* which is to be assigned to late 1609 and early 1610. If the chronologically prior *Pericles* is a

4. Citations from *Mucedorus* are from the text of the play in R.A. Fraser and N. Rabkin, eds. *Drama of the English Renaissance I. The Tudor Period* (New York: Macmillan Publishing Company, 1976), pp. 463–80.

romance and tragicomedy, it is more the former than the latter, and it is in *Cymbeline* that Shakespeare introduces an extensive pastoral component into tragic-comic romance – the element of prince or princess adopting the guise of shepherd, life in the woods and dangerous encounters, motifs which are common to *Mucedorus* and *Cymbeline*. The kind of structural looseness which seems to mark *Cymbeline* may well have to do with Shakespeare's deliberately adopting and working out differently the limp structural movement of the old play. The scene-by-scene, frame-by-frame rather than the sequential kind of progression which Cymbeline has may be an experimental taking over of the *trompe l'oeil*-like scene-for-scene, moment-for-the-moment opportunism and near-sensationalism of *Mucedorus* and certain plays of the early 1590s such as Marlowe's, although such a relative disregard of sequence is also a feature of Jacobean dramaturgy such as Beaumont and Fletcher's and that of others. The basic source of the framework of action of *Cymbeline* is Holinshed, and the wager plot may owe itself to a story or stories in Boccacio's *Decameron* with other motifs in the play coming from several romances including Greek ones in translation. But the central action of the princess Imogen's experiences in the woods near Milford Haven together with the princes Guiderius's and Arviragus's resembles in its cast the experiences of Amadine and Mucedorus in disguise in the woods in *Mucedorus*.

The killings in *Mucedorus*, of the bear, Tremelio, and Bremo the wild man, all three committed by the hero Mucedorus, are a bold introduction of deaths, not only dangers, into a comedy and tragicomedy. If Shakespeare found sanction in the old play for his introduction of deaths (he had done it in oblique fashion at the end of *Love's Labour's Lost* very early in his career) in *Cymbeline* and *The Winter's Tale* immediately after, Shakespeare goes about it in a different way in his plays. But for the behind-the-scene dispatching of the bear by Mucedorus in his play, the other two killings take place luridly onstage. The killing of Tremelio by Mucedorus takes place with such an abrupt suddenness that it produces an effect of near-comic shock, for once making the customary uncomprehending bewilderment and befuddlement of the 'natural' clown, Mouse, an onstage witness, not unjustified. Mucedorus's braining of Bremo the wild man is represented on the stage with more than the violent sensationalism of the braining of Bajazet by himself in his cage in Marlowe's *Tamburlaine*. Whereas Shakespeare would make the actual killing of Cloten occur as reported offstage action, as he does with the death of Mamilius, the reported 'death' of Hermione, and the dining of the bear on Antigonus in *The Winter's Tale*. At the same time, the theatrical play with Cloten's head in *Cymbeline* (IV.ii) is not dissimilar to the display in *Mucedorus* of the bear's head as a trophy by Mucedorus after he encounters and kills the animal and thus rescues Amadine to win her love, and also subsequently in the play. It is, of course, the use of a stock item of stage property, the severed head (Henslowe's property inventory mentions quite a few heads), of which Shakespeare makes striking use in *Measure for Measure* and *Macbeth*. In *Cymbeline* the theatricality of Guiderius's display of Cloten's head (IV.ii.113–23)[5] which he later calls 'clotpoll' (IV.ii.184), suggesting that it is a wooden artifact of a stage property, is followed by Imogen-Fidele mistaken for dead and laid by the side of Cloten's headless trunk which is dressed in Posthumus's clothes; she wakes up from her stupor, and in the half-confusion of her awakening takes the headless man by her side to be Posthumus alive, and starting on a foot-to-head Petrarchan blazoning in reverse, she discovers as though by slow degrees that it is a dead man, and blames the killing on Pisanio and Cloten (IV.ii.306–32). The germ of the confusion of Imogen, the rendering of which is a master-stroke of self-conscious theatricality of Shakespeare's, could have been suggested by the confused manner in which the clown Mouse only half-realises that Tremelio is dead and the uncomprehending way he deals with the dead body (scene vi). Also, the romance motif of the true prince with his worth and valour and his royal culture and qualities of noble nurture showing even in the circumstances of a state of nature, occurs both in *Mucedorus* and in *Cymbeline*. The old play in its conception and portrayal of Bremo the wild man, while drawing on the literary and cultural type of the wild man figure, and also perhaps on instances in Spenser's *Faerie Queene* of similar figures, also raises, though it does not quite broach, the question of the relationship between na-

5. Citations from Shakespeare are keyed to the old Oxford *Shakespeare: Complete Works*, ed. W.J. Craig, 1974.

ture and nurture, nature and art, a question which Shakespeare brings forward and discusses in *Cymbeline*, *The Winter's Tale* and *The Tempest.*

The figuring of the bear in *Mucedorus* has often been seen as an analogue to Shakespeare's strange use in *The Winter's Tale* of this animal character, the only one other than Launce's dog in *The Two Gentlemen of Verona* to be used in a play of Shakespeare's.[6] The bear in *The Winter's Tale* kills instead of getting killed as in *Mucedorus*. The deliberate, theatricalist play with the bear which Shakespeare refines upon and exploits to a greater degree is already there in germ in *Mucedorus*. The bear makes its appearance very early in that play. The clown Mouse carrying a bottle of hay on his head enters expressing his dread of the bear only to be surprised by it from behind. He makes his exit dropping the protective buffer of the hay bundle. In the very next scene (scene iii), the bear re-enters pursuing Amadine and Segasto who have to take flight from the animal. Mouse's comment here in particular and his comments on the bear elsewhere in general are revealing.

> *Mouse* . . . A bear, Nay, sure it cannot be a bear, but some devil in a bear's doublet, for a bear never have had that agility to have frighted me.
>
> (scene II.ll.2–4)
>
> [See also his comments in scene iv, ll.34–60.]

It is theatrically 'multiconscious', calling attention to the fact that the bear part was enacted by a human actor. Two factors about the remark of Mouse are worth noting. First, the lines figure in scene ii, an addition by Shakespeare's company to the play, and are in the vein of the self-conscious theatricality of Jacobean drama. Second, there is evidence that for the Whitehall performance of the play on the Shrove-Sunday night of 1610 a live bear (evidently tame) was

6. There are the horses and the dogs invoked verbally in the dialogue in the plays and their presence must have been suggested aurally through off-stage noises. Besides Launce's dog in *The Two Gentlemen of Verona*, and the cock-crowing in *Hamlet*, there is the rehearsal attempt of Snug and Bottom to get the part of the lion in 'Pyramus and Thisbe' in *A Midsummer Night's Dream* and Snug's playing of the part in the play-within-the-play at the end.

pressed into service. Such occasions must have been exceptional. In *The Winter's Tale*, whether in the Globe performances, or the Blackfriar ones, a human actor would have made do for the bear. The piquant theatricalism of Antigonus's 'exit pursued by a bear', and of the elaborate account of the slaying and eating of Antigonus by the bear given by the clownish younger shepherd to the father shepherd in *The Winter's Tale* (III.iii.86–105) would seem to be in a way Shakespeare's development of hints from *Mucedorus* with its clown's response to and remarks on the bear. The account which Shakespeare puts into the mouth of the clown with its description of the destruction and consumption of the ship by the sea storm and of Antigonus by the bear running tandem also exploits the traditional tropical and imagistic association between storms and wild animals.

More particularly, the introduction of a live bear in place of a man 'in a bear's doublet' in the court performance of *Mucedorus* came at a point of time, in the year 1610, when the kind of 'illusionism' that the masque stage (then beginning to flourish in the court and in noble households had introduced) started to interact in some fashion with the patchy realism of the Elizabethan theatre with its 'impure art'. The live bear in the *Mucedorus* performance is a precursor of, say, the live rabbits in the Henry Irving *Midsummer Night's Dreams* of the late nineteenth century. Perhaps around 1610, the traditional 'multiconsciousness' of the English dramatic tradition which had in the Jacobean era acquired further extension and new dimensions of theatrical self-consciousness, was also tending to give room to a confusion, however slight it might be, between dramatic illusion and reality. Symptoms of such a shift in theatrical 'multiconsciousness' would seem to be captured in such a play as Beaumont's *The Knight of the Burning Pestle* (circa 1607). Shakespeare who makes excellent capital of the illusion of reality and the reality of illusion in baroque fashion, especially in *The Winter's Tale*, would seem deliberately to have brought in the bear into the play and to have the role deliberately assigned to a human actor playing the animal character. Could he have anticipated what risks (in several senses) illusionism could lead to in what happened a few years later in 1613 when cannons were fired for real in the performance, perhaps the first, of his *King Henry VIII*, the fire accident in which the Globe theatre burned down?

Bremo, the instance of the wild man character-type figuring in *Mucedorus*, must have been one of the factors going to make Shakespeare's Caliban the complexity of whose genesis and function is getting to be more and more expatiated on in interpretative comment. In at least a place or two in the play, Bremo's sensitiveness of perception suggesting something of a poetic sensibility is in evidence (scene xi.ll.37–54; scene xv.ll.23–55). This side to Bremo as a character, and the relationship he attempts to forge with the heroine Amadine in the play after taking her prisoner, serve as forerunners of the sensitiveness of perception and of poetic apprehension which Shakespeare endows Caliban with and Caliban's ambitions of a relationship with Miranda. Moreover, the question of the nature–nurture binary which is no more than vaguely implicit in *Mucedorus* is given the poetic–dramatic role of a 'necessary question of the play' in *The Tempest.*

Certain lines and passages in *Mucedorus*, originally introduced mainly or merely as dramatic repartee and stichomythia-like exchange or just clowning, would in the context of Jacobean sociological and sociopolitical development resound with significances of new questions and debates about class and status and also kingship. In scene vi, when Mouse asks Segasto of what occupation he is, Segasto replies:

> No occupation; I live upon my lands

which elicits the reply from the clown:

> Your lands? Away, you are no master for me. Why, do you think that I am so mad to go seek my living in the lands amongst the stones, briers, and bushes, and tear my holiday apparel? Not I, by your leave.

And Segasto assures the clown that he would serve him staying in the court, not in his lands. The words acquire the tone of a double satirical reference to living off the fat of the land and at the same time to the problems of making a living out of the lands in the Jacobean context of farmers' problems, the enclosures and the polarity between the court and the country arising in the Jacobean age and growing to greater proportions in the course of the century. Mouse in the next few lines asks:

> What's that same king, a man or woman?

Segasto replies:

> A man as thou art.

There is another similar exchange in scene ix.

Mouse	What should shepherds do amongst us? Have we not lords enough on us in the court?
Mucedorus	Why, shepherds are men, and kings are no more.

Such utterances, though in the generalised vein of the sentiment, 'A man is a man for all that,' suggest a particular trend of questioning the status and inherent authority of the king, a trend which had started making itself felt in the early Stuart era and finally led to the rebellion and regicide in a few decades. One might wonder how King James I with his strong views on the monarch's supreme authority sitting in the audience of the play in Whitehall in 1610 would have taken the lines. Or could they have been tactfully cut?

It is in scene xiii of *Mucedorus*, one of the additions made by Shakespeare's company to the play for the court performance, that there are indications of Shakespeare's hand or finger. The scene begins thus:

Sound music

Enter the King of Valencia, Anselmo
Roderigo, Lord Borachus, *with others.*

King of Valencia Enough of music, it but adds to torment;
Delights to vex'ed spirits are as dates
Set to a sickly man, which rather cloy than comfort.
Let me entreat you to entreat no more.

Rod. Let your strings sleep; have done these,
Let the music cease.

The scene starts to the sound of music, with the king in a state of melancholy over the separation of his son Mucedorus much like Duke Orsino at the start of *Twelfth Night* in his luxuriance in love melancholy. And the music is ordered closed, as by Orsino in

Twelfth Night, only to be ordered to resume at the end of the short scene by Valencia:

Valencia Music, speak loudly now, the season's apt,
For former dolors are in pleasure wrapped.

And Valencia is made to use the term 'surfeit', the term used by Shakespeare for Orsino in his opening speech of the play (I.ii).

Anselmo The prince, your son, is safe.

Valencia Oh, where, Anselmo? Surfeit me with that.

Also, Valencia's 'let me entreat you to entreat no more' echoes Orsino's 'Give me now leave to leave thee' in *Twelfth Night* (II.iv.73). However, it is the collocation in the *Mucedorus* scene in question:

Anselmo Whether report gilded a worthless trunk
Or Amadine deserved her high extolment
(II.34–5)

which is more strongly reminiscent of a corresponding one of an equally highly individual stamp in *Twelfth Night*:

Antonio Virtue is beauty, but the beauteous evil
Are empty trunks o'er flourished by the devil.
(II.iv.405–6)

The use of the metaphor of the 'worthless trunk' 'gilded' or the 'empty trunk' 'o'er flourished' is unusual, though the sentiment of a Platonic appearance–reality contrast or the idealist Platonic equation between inner and outer (which would seem to be the ideal of an inveterate platonist that Shakespeare makes Antonio to be) may be a great commonplace. Editors of *Twelfth Night* have so far failed to note and cite this parallel in *Mucedorus* to Antonio's somewhat intriguing expression. All this would point to the possibility that it could have been Shakespeare who wrote this scene among the additional scenes in *Mucedorus* supplied by his company.

The Epilogue in *Mucedorus*, one among the additions put in by Shakespeare's company, whichever of their dramatists might have composed it, consists of a 'flying' between the figures of Comedy and Envy, with Envy making a bid to get the better of Comedy by way of satire overrunning comedy, and with Comedy putting Envy in its place and humbling it through a vindication of comedy sans satire, and, finally with Envy falling down and quaking in submission and joining comedy in the kneeling obeisance it offers to the Presence, the monarch King James I. A crucial part of the exchange between Comedy and Envy is a pregnantly topical-theatrical reference to the boy company of the Children of the Chapel and their troubles with the authorities and the court over the satirical allusions to the monarch and the court figures in their plays.

Envy This scrambling raven, with his needy beard,
Will I whet on to write a comedy
Wherein shall be composed dark sentences,
Pleasing to factious brains;
. . . .
Then I myself, quicker than lighting,
Will fly to a puissant magistrate,
. . . .
. . . rehearse those galls
With some additions,
So lately vented in your theatre.
He, upon this, cannot but make complaint
To your great danger, or at least restraint.

Comedy Ha, ha, ha! I laugh to hear thy folly;
This is a trap for boys, not men, nor such,
Especially desertful in their doings,
Whose staid discretion rules their purposes.
I and my faction do eschew those vices.
(Epilogue, ll.38–56)

The playwright who put in these lines for the performance by Shakespeare's company as almost meant for the ear of the ruling monarch and the court was trying to show how the adult company of the King's Men, though now playing in the private playhouse of the Blackfriars as well as in the public Globe playhouse, would never commit the indiscretions of repeated indulgence in satirical attacks for which the playwrights of the Chapel Children had to face arrest and prosecution in instances following year after year with regularity since 1604. The 'new university wits' or the 'new intellectuals' among playwrights, the ones who wrote for the Children of the Chapel such as Marston, Chapman, Ben Jonson, and John Day provoked the wrath of the authorities in successive years with the result that by about 1608 the company disbanded. By the end of 1608 or the beginning of 1609 the Blackfriars indoor playhouse where they were playing, came to be taken over for the King's Men's use. The lines quoted are the adult company of the King's Men's boast that they have always kept themselves on the right side of the law and of the court's, and the King's favour. The topical vaunt has another significance too. The adult public playhouses' fear and dismay over the rivalry and the real challenge offered by the beginning of the century by the two boy companies, the Children of St Paul's and the Children of the Chapel, expressed, for example, in the reference to the 'principal public audience . . . turn(ing) to private plays and to the humour of children' in the First Quarto of *Hamlet* and to the 'little eyases' carrying the day in the Folio *Hamlet*, gave place in a few years' time to the public playhouses responding to the challenge by themselves absorbing the modes and techniques of the relatively 'coterie' private playhouse dramaturgy, and with plays like *The Malcontent*, an original boy company play, being taken over for performance by them. But this near-collaborative give-and-take relationship could, by the closing years of the first decade of the seventeenth century, lead to a confident stance on the part of the public theatre ensuing from its total absorption of the once-competing private theatre into itself as it were and from the circumstance of the real rival private boy companies having had to close down. The passage in the *Mucedorus* epilogue, added as it was in and around 1610, thus offers crucial evidence about the concluding phase of the theatrical history of what Alfred Harbage not very accurately called the 'rival traditions' of the public and private theatres or what was by earlier scholars called the 'war of the theatres.'

Attention to the implications of what Shakespeare and his company did to a hardy perennial of an ace popular Elizabethan play in his time like *Mucedorus* offers some such opportunities for an understanding of certain modes of procedure and of some workings of mind of the playwright in interaction with the theatrical traditions and environment he operated in.

SECTION 3

Intercultural Perspectives

18

Some Principles of Sanskrit Dramaturgy with Application to Shakespeare

A student of English literature and drama born and bred in the Indian tradition, of whatever varying degrees his or her exposure to Sanskrit and Indian popular theatrical traditions may be, has opportunities of garnering several kinds of insights relating to dramatic theory and practice, insights relevant for his response to English drama, from different Sanskrit texts and from various Sanskrit stage traditions and from features and points of Sanskrit stagecraft. The monumental codification of dramatic theory and theatrical practices that is Bharata's *Natyasastra* constitutes an all-but-unparallelled instance in world literature of comprehensiveness of treatment of all aspects of drama, for all the element of occasional lack of clarity and inconsistency the treatise contains. Bharata's *Natyasastra*, taken together with texts like Abhinavagupta's *Abhinavabharati* (an elaborate commentary on *Natyasastra*), Dhananjaya's *Dasarupa*, Ramachandra and Gunachandra's *Natyadarpana* and Nadikeswara's *Abhinayadarpana*, offers a most forceful presentation of the principles and practices of non-illusionism and conventionalism in drama and the theatre. The tone of prescriptivism which seems to mark Bharata's treatise has partly led Western scholars to regard it as a rigid formularisation which more or less dictated as holy writ the practice of playwrights great and small. Whereas Bharata's treatise, despite its exhortatory tone, embodies experience and establishes current practice in dramatic art, and hence is really to be regarded as descriptive rather than merely prescriptive. This holds if anything more true of the later codifications such as those of Abhinava and Nandikeswara. These and similar works, together with commentaries on actual plays like Raghavabhatta's on *Sakuntalam*, with their exposition of actual staging details and theatrical conventions and practices, would bring us not only theoretical knowledge about the nature of Sanskrit drama and theatre but suggestions for a reconstruction of the modes and sometimes minutiae of the actual practices of the Sanskrit stage. Such theoretical and practical findings as we may glean thus will serve as a source of cross-cultural cross-illumination between English drama and Indian. No wonder that knowledge of Sanskrit theatrical principles and stagecraft inspired a theatre producer like William Poel in the late nineteenth century, whose innovations by way of a historicisation of the production of late medieval, Elizabethan and particularly Shakespearian drama in turn inspired a scholar-producer like Harley Granville-Barker of the early twentieth century. By the same argument, it was, in good measure, his knowledge of the staging principles of conventionalism and stylisation behind a play like *Sakuntalam* which suggested to a truly path-making theatre historian and historical scholar of the Shakespearian stage like G.F. Reynolds of America fruitful insights, besides methods of investigation, into the staging of plays in Shakespeare's times and their theatres such as the Globe and the Red Bull.

Furthermore, in addition to the assumptions and indications available in Bharata and other treatise writers as regards the name and nature of dramatic illusion, the conception of the theatre, and theatrical communication, the Sanskrit rasa theorists who, in a sense, take up again from Bharata like Lollata, Sankuka, Bhattanayaka and above all, Abhinavagupta, have in the process of their expanding of their theories about rasa and rasas, between them, offered a searching and many-sided discussion of dramatic illusion, and theatrical presentation and communication. This discussion affords an illuminating parallel to, and an emphatic confirmation of, the views of Johnson and Coleridge, for example, on dramatic illusion.

In addition, there is an important imaginative point of contact between the Indian Sanskrit and popular dramatic traditions on the one side and the English late medieval and Renaissance drama and theatre on the other in what one may call the shared context of both these two dramatic traditions, divided in space and time, each functioning in an ethos of a cultural homogeneity (at least, relatively speaking) and of a community of values and sensibility linking playwright, actor, the stage as an institution and the various sections of audience, whatever the stratifications of class and taste that might have governed this last.

The large as well as minute attention which Bharata pays to the architecture of the theatre—the erection of the theatre, the setting up of the stage with its tiring house, the waiting room in the wing and the stage proper, and the arrangement of the auditorium—may not have much of relevance for a study of the English theatre, but is an indication of the abiding importance of a consideration of the physical conditions of the theatre and the stage for an appreciation of drama. The Sanskrit theatre may originally have been a temporary structure put up for the occasion, just as the play performance itself may have been to mark a festival or a king's birthday, victory or coronation, etc. The use of the permanent curtain (*javanika*) and the absence of the drop curtain in the Sanskrit theatre together with the adoption of conventionalistic scenography render the Sanskrit stage a timeless and spaceless one, much like the medieval or Shakespearian stage, with little need or use for illusionistic localisation with the help of scenery. As in Elizabethan drama, in the Sanskrit theatre the sense of *locus* is evoked in terms of words and poetry, but at the same time, again as in the Shakespearian theatre, not without the deployment of some stage-properties and hand-properties as part of the visual, scenic idiom of the theatre. The use of a traverse or curtain, called *tiraskarini*, spoken of by Bharata and others, a curtain like the Kathakali *tirraseela*, to reveal and mark the entry of a character on stage, which parallels the use of a similar curtain on the Tudor interlude stage (see Richard Southern, *The Staging of Plays before Shakespeare*, p. 271) is in line with the non-naturalistic spirit and mode alike of the conception and presentation of Sanskrit drama.

So are the stage conventions adumbrated by Bharata and later codifiers, which also are either identical with or resemble in good part the conventions of the Shakespearian stage. In the absence of elaborate or realistic sets the change of locale is indicated on the Sanskrit stage by the characters walking a few or many steps on the stage to suggest a short or somewhat long distance covered by them in moving to a different place. This is much like characters going out through one door and re-entering through another on the stage in the Elizabethan theatre to signify a journey made. The basic principle of conventionalism, as evident in the use of 'primitive conventions' (in the best sense of the phrase), which governs the Sanskrit and the early English stages alike, particularly manifests itself in the fascinating exploitation of the several different acting areas on both these stages, and especially in the form of 'simultaneous settings' or the *decor simultane* of which we find striking examples in the plays of Shakespeare and his contemporaries and in the drama of Bhasa, Kalidasa and Sudraka. In terms of this specific convention of multiple staging, the characters and stage properties which participate in a scene or situation of a play may be left on stage and may remain as visual presences, if apparently, inactive presences, after the stage action moves to the next or a later scene or situation. Some instances in Shakespeare are the sleeping pairs of lovers, and Titania asleep ('They sleep thro' the act') in *A Midsummer Night's Dream*, Orlando and Adam of *As You Like It*, both famished, entering in II.vi. frantically searching for food while the banquet is already set on the table onstage for the exiled Duke and company in the course of II.v.31–2 and the figure of Kent set in the stocks in front of Gloucester's Castle in II.ii. still onstage when Edgar enters and utters his speech in II.iii. Remarkable instances of 'simultaneous settings' of this kind are to be found in Bhasa's *Pratimanataka* (Acts IV and V), his *Svapnavasavadatta* (Act IV), Sri Harsha's *Ratnavali* (Act I), Kalidasa's *Sakuntala* (Act V), and still more striking, Sudraka's *Mrichakatika* (Act I and Act IV). (There is a detailed discussion of 'multiple setting', as the author calls the phenomenon, in Sanskrit plays in E.W. Marasinghe's *The Sanskrit Theatre and Stagecraft* (Delhi: Sri Satguru Publications, 1989, pp. 328–36). William Poel mounted productions of *Sakuntalam*, and plays like *Romeo and Juliet* and Thomas Kyd's *Spanish Tragedy*, towards the end of the nineteenth century in England in order to highlight early dramatic conventions and specially the use of 'simultaneous settings'. G.F. Reynolds, the American theatre historian and scholar who emphasised the significance of multiple staging, developed his insights in this regard and applied them to his study of the early English theatre at least partly on the basis of his knowledge of the staging of *Sakuntalam*.

While the formal, stylised gestures of acting described by Bharata and his successors may not have much similarity to conventions of Elizabethan acting, even granting possibilities of a dominantly formalised acting style obtaining on the Shakespearian stage, the exploitation of the imaginative resources of certain semi-formal gestural action in concert with verbal evocation would seem to be another point of contact between the Sanskrit and early English stages. The kind of gesticulatory movements and actions practised, for example, to re-present (rather than to represent) Sakuntala's watering of the plants in her ashram or her state of fear and annoyance as she is chased by a bee, or Dushyanta's chariot or his mounting, riding or dismounting of it, are basically formalised enactments. These gestural enactments, with their accompanying verbal utterances, communicate the effect of their presence in the absence of water pots or plants or a bee or a chariot on the stage in the name of sets or properties. It is such gestural enactment and verbal evocation as are called for in the staging of the 'airy dagger' scene in *Macbeth*.

The *rasa* theorists of the few centuries around the tenth century in their elaboration of Bharata's cryptic dicta on *rasa*, especially with reference to dramatic and theatrical experience, have several insights to offer on the nature of the experience of the *rasas*, the moods, feelings and sentiments and the kind of relish, generated and communicated on the stage and from the stage to the spectators. These inquiries in effect amount to an exploration of the nature of drama as mimetic re-presentation of feelings and experience and of stage illusion and communication. Lollata's *utpatti-vada* theory of *rasa* puts the emphasis on the basic emotions the *sthayis* roused and intensified by *vibhavas* and *anubhavas* turning into *rasas*; these *rasas*, according to Lollata, are there in the characters and are transferred to the actors who identify themselves with the characters. That is how the *rasas* are generated.

Since Lollata's theory of the production of *rasas* fails to take into account the spectator's realisation of *rasa* in its exclusive association of *rasa* with the characters or actors, Sankuka the Nyaya-oriented theorist propounds the *anumanavada* of *rasa*. In Sankuka's view, the spectator comes to perceive and realise the *rasa* by a process of inference from the actor's imitation of, which is not quite an identification with, the character and his actions. Bhattanayaka, who in a sense prefigures his important successor in the exposition of the *rasa* theory by identifying the key factor of suggestion and suggestiveness (*vyanjana*), lays particular stress on the pre-dominant element of illusion in drama in which it is all illusion that is produced and not reality. Bhattanayaka analyses the poetic or dramatic experience into the three constituents of *abhidha* (rendering or enactment), *bhavakatva* (the generalisation of sentiment) and *bhojakatva* (the enjoyment which is the spectator's). If Sankuka considers the actor's impersonation of the character as falling short of identification with the character, and Bhattanayaka underscores the illusion of drama, Abhinavagupta with his *vyakti-vada* gives central importance to the element of suggestion; the *rasa* is not actual mundane feeling or emotion; it is not felt as personally belonging either to the spectator or the actor or the character, and hence it is not 'worldly'. Yet Abhinava accords the spectator the greatest place and role in the theatrico–aesthetic transaction. The spectator should be a person of keen sensibility, and in Abhinava's reckoning of true *vasana*. Only then can he be a true *sahrudaya* or 'kindred spirit' of drama and literature.

While not every playgoer in the old Sanskrit theatre or in Shakespeare's theatre could have been an ideal *sahrudaya*, the audiences and the respective societies of these periods had a similar cultural situation in which a shared community of sensibility and a common scale of values that obtained in each respective society linked the spectators among themselves and these with the actors and playwrights and made a *rapport* possible. This was a potent factor which could enable dramatists like Bhasa, Kalidasa, Sri Harsha and Sudraka, though not a playwright like Bhavabhuti, to harmonise the learned and the popular elements in their drama and to combine sophistication with a certain kind of spontaneity of appeal. The theatre as an institution in its heyday, fully participating in the social structure and process of the times, could enjoy the advantage of the prevalent general cultural homogeneousness. The decline of the Sanskrit theatre which seems to have set in with the allegorisation of drama and its use for religious, denominational controversy and propaganda from the eleventh and twelfth centuries onwards is mostly due to the split one could trace in the drama and theatre between the learned and the popular. All the same, the 'multiconsciouness', the double awareness that what takes place on the stage is an illusion while it brings a sense of reality, which the *rasa* theorists point to in their terminology, endured in the Indian popular dramatic tradition even after the decline of what may be called the classical Sanskrit tradition of drama. It could endure till very recently, perhaps well into the twentieth century in the traditional popular theatre in some of the regional languages, thanks to the survival of a homogeneity of culture and values in the country. This example of cultural unity should help us to understand a similar cultural milieu and ethos of drama in England till the middle of the seventeenth century.

As may be clear from this brief outline of a survey, there are about three relatively unexplored areas of common ground and of fruitful cross-illumination between the early English and Sanskrit dramaturgy. Firstly, the findings one may gather from Bharata and subsequent commentators on the essential non-illusionistic basis and orientation of Sanskrit theatrical tradition, and on the conventions and techniques of stage, corroborated by what we know to have possibly happened in the actual performance of the plays lend themselves to an illuminating application to our response to the stage dynamics of Shakespeare, and earlier and related drama. The Sanskrit example does seem to have helped certain Western scholars and producers to gain insights into the modes of conception and of stage presentation of early English drama. Second, the implications which the *rasa* theorists' examination of the process of poetic-dramatic and theatrical rendering and communication have for our understanding of dramatic make-believe, the mimesis which drama is, are considerable, and these remind us forcefully of the paradoxical intermixture of reality and illusion in drama, the reality of illusion as well as the illusion of reality which we get to experience in the theatre. At least, the discussion makes clear that dramatic illusion is not to be equated with delusion. Thirdly, the relatively free and easy cultural intercommunication between the courtly and the common, the learned and the popular, which may be traced in classical Sanskrit drama suggests a sociocultural paradigm which is quite applicable in the contextualisation of Shakespearian drama in its culture and society. It is possible, though, that the kind of cultural uniformity in the sociocultural ethos of Renaissance England postulated by Leavis and the *Scrutiny* critics will be regarded as too much of univocalisation of culture. Yet, making due allowances for certain inevitable sociocultural stratification, the kind of 'Bakhtinian' interchange and intercommunication which probably took place between high and low (and middle) in Renaissance England made for a fruitful concert of 'voices', a creative *heteroglossia*, alongside if also in spite of an overall unity of cultural structure. It is a similar durability of the total cultural fabric accommodating a multiple play of 'voices' and stances, which we may find in classical Sanskrit and early English drama and theatre.

19
The Application of *Dhvani* to *Macbeth*

Among Shakespeare's plays, *Macbeth* is perhaps one most amenable to an approach through the Sanskrit literary–critical category of *dhvani*, a critical concept formulated and instituted as a leading principle of literary and dramatic interpretation by Anandavardhana (9th century) and by Abhinavagupta (10th century) with his *Dhvanyalokalochana*, a classic commentary on Anandavardhana's *Dhvanyaloka*. Though the concept can be distinctly recognised and perceived for what it is, it has a comprehensive sweep of significance which covers almost the whole gamut of the range of viable imaginative response to drama and poetry. In other words, it includes almost all legitimate modes of response to imaginative literature. Thus the critical category of *dhvani* is not in any real conflict with other Sanskrit literary–critical principles such as *guna-dosha* (quality or its violation); *riti* (style in the organic, holistic sense); *aucitya* (decorum); and, above all, *vakrokti* (strikingness through deviation in expression), but subsumes these categories. No wonder *dhvani* is a cardinal principle of Indian criticism. It is also in close association with the other major principle of Sanskrit criticism, *rasa* (sentiment, its relish), and the two go together, *rasa* making itself felt through *dhvani* and *dhvani* justifying itself through *rasa*, so much so that it is termed *rasadhvani*. Generally translated as suggestion, suggestivity or suggestiveness as *dhvani* is, its definition or description is not perhaps so relevant for an attempt to apply it to *Macbeth*[1] as the connotations of the

---

1. I cite in this essay the text of the play in *The Riverside Shakespeare*, ed.

principle of suggestivity or rather the suggestiveness of suggestion. Some ways and modes of operation of *dhvani* in our response to *Macbeth* are our present concern.

Abhinavagupta was the classic exponent of the critical category after its discovery and formulation by Anandavardhana; both of them are outstanding and masterful in their grasp of and insight into the nature of literary and dramatic experience in its essentials. Abhinava laid the utmost stress on the imaginative response of the *sahrudaya*, the kindred-spirited reader or spectator. Such a one will be able to tune in properly and develop a rapport with the work before him and savour its effects of many-dimensioned suggestiveness. Abhinava offers a vigorous vindication of the status and reality of *dhvani* as a critical entity and a major one in literary discourse against the logician-like arguments of those who might and did question its *locus standi* and tried to apply Occam's razor on it. As he amply establishes the point, it is the 'logic of the imagination' and not the logicians' logic that is to be followed in literary response, and that alone will enable one to recognise and receive the *dhvani* effect. (It is a different matter, though, if Abhinava in his rhetorical defence of *dhvani* against the logicians employs the logicians' logic to refute them.)

Otto Jespersen the linguistician pointed out in *The Philosophy of Grammar* (p. 390), that suggestion is 'impression through suppression'. We may also remember that Maurice Morgann in the late eighteenth century in his *tour de force* of *An Essay on the Dramatic Character of Sir John Falstaff* presented the insight that 'Shakespeare contrives to make *secret* impressions upon us' in his drama. It is such secret impressions that make for the quality of *dhvani*. More important, it is the 'fit' audience (though not always or necessarily 'few') of the *sahrudayas* who can be most receptive to *dhvani* in the dynamic of the artistic transaction.

G. Blakemore Evans (Boston, 1974). Accessible editions with translation are there by K. Krishnamoorthy both of Anandavardhana's *Dhvanyaloka* (Dharwar: Karnatak University Press) and of Abhinavagupta's *Dhvanyalokalochana* (New Delhi: Meherchand Lechhmandas Publications). V. S. Seturaman, ed. *Indian Aesthetics: An Introduction* (Macmillan, India, 1992) is a valuable compendium of essays by various hands and excerpts, with translation, from the original texts.

Although it is true of other Shakespeare plays also, the poetry and the total theatre language of *Macbeth* would in particular seem to specialise in a sensational or at times even visceral or subliminal mode of communication and impact. So it abounds in qualities, many of which would seem readily to yield to a response in terms of *dhvani*. Put another way, it is the predominant suggestivity of the play, not so much its plain meaning or character or action by themselves, which lends it its dimensions of greatness as tragic drama. The opening scene and its stage effects set the mood. Indeed, the play opens with 'thunder and lightning', that is, with *dhvani* in its literal sense of the sounding of rolled drums by way of off-stage noise to suggest thunder on the Shakespearian stage, accompanied by the visual suggestion of lightning with fireworks of some kind and also perhaps stage-smoke for 'fog and filthy air' through which the Witches hover. All these together with the cryptic utterances of the Witches suggest equivocation and a reversal of values:

> Fair is foul, and foul is fair.
>
> (I.i.11)

In the very next scene (I.ii.), the stage image of the 'bleeding sergeant' and his rhetorical narration of Macbeth's valour followed by Rosse's report of Macbeth's feats of loyalty to King Duncan, and Duncan's response of ready and warm appreciation and reward for Macbeth are rich with ambivalence and irony in hindsight of what Macbeth subsequently is to do. The stage blood on the 'bleeding sergeant' figure starts the considerably significant strain of blood imagery, verbal and visual, in the play. Importantly, the blood imagery has a duality of significance as the blood references or instances of stage blood across the play communicate at subtler levels than that of a drama of blood and thunder and evoke the sense as much of the positive associations of blood such as a giver of life, creativity, nobility and curativeness (through bloodletting) as those of horror, cruelty and crime.

Similarly, the ironies which underlie the utterances of Duncan and his approbation of Macbeth as his saviour are ultimately to be recognised to be not merely verbal or situational ironies, but ironies which build up towards the central tragic irony of the play. This is brought home in the oblique mode of suggestion, that Macbeth in the very process of his strenuous if not agonising desensitisation of himself for the murder of Duncan and the ones to follow is made to reveal his essential sensitivities of mind and conscience in that very process. It is not simply that Macbeth is poetic in his sensibility or, as Bernard Shaw put it, he is a 'nervous gentleman in galligaskins'. Even as he might assert

> 'twere best not know myself
>
> (II.ii.70)

all along he fully knows himself despite himself. Deep within he is aware enough of what he goes in for; yet he proceeds in the name of ambition, which is, again ironically, shattered a moment sooner than it is achieved, coupled with the inspiration from Lady Macbeth who goes almost into a sustained state of possession by spirits in the 'great business' as well as from the equivocating Witches' prophecies. Macbeth may also be seen as trying to perform the murder of Duncan and the subsequent acts as though he were an actor playing a role as much assigned to him by the script and stage-management, between the two, of the Witches and Lady Macbeth as consciously chosen and adopted by him. He puts on appearances to conceal in one sense and in another, enact the all-too-stark and dire realities as if these were semitheatricalised, detached action and acting. The suggestions are there, among other things particularly in the recurrent motif of a deliberately willed divorce of 'the heart' and 'the eye' on the one side and 'the hand' on the other on Macbeth's part.

Yet, amidst all this, Macbeth has a nagging sense that the 'borrowed robes' of power and kingship, actor's costumes in the theatrical and stage context do not sit well on him. The choric observer characters in the play also express this opinion almost in tune with a now-not-sufficiently recognised Renaissance convention of belief and thought in relation to the idea of clothes. The convention finds expression in Renaissance courtesy books such as Sir Thomas Elyot's *The Governor* (1541) which Shakespeare and his audience were familiar with. The formulation by Elyot runs like this:

> If he (a king or 'magistrate') have an ancient robe left by 'his ancestor . . . it diminisheth his praise to them which know . . . the virtue of him that first owned it. If he that weareth it be vicious, it

> more detecteth how he is unworthy to wear it, the remembrance of his noble ancestor making men to abhor the reproach given by an evil successor.
>
> S.E. Lehmberg, ed. Sir Thomas Elyot's *The Governor* (1541), (London, 1962), p. 105

Such nuances in the question of the 'fit' of Macbeth's kingly robes[2] are more complex than Caroline Spurgeon's linear interpretation of the clothes imagery which she was first to isolate. Her reading is that the off-size garments idea suggests that Macbeth is to be taken as a 'dwarf in giant's robes'. Indeed the nuances of suggestions, noted so far, could all be regarded as instances of sustained effects of *dhvani* in the play. Such intimations are precisely the ones that, far from letting us view Macbeth simply as 'dead butcher' or for that matter as degenerate sinner going to his damnation, bring upon the reader or spectator who is a *sahrudaya* a sense of Macbeth's dimensions of tragic value and tragic greatness and evoke the imaginative apprehension and response which would preclude a reductionist understanding or uncritical sentimentalism.

In other words, Macbeth's aliveness to what his deeds involve by way of a violation of nature, natural order and the sanctities and pieties of life and of a total upset of values, comes through in terms of suggestivity in the dramatic rendering of the hero-villain's deliberately wrought commitment to evil. The truly responsive *sahrudaya* is enabled to perceive this central feature of the play through the underlying suggestions, the operations of which can be apprehended as the function and effect of *dhvani*. Often, such oblique connotations function as a counterpoint to the more obvious denotation. The emphasis laid by the great exponent of the *dhvani* theory on the *sahrudaya* response, based on kindred-spirited receptivity tuned in on the right wavelength as the essential requisite, is relevant. It is especially so when we recognise how necessary, yet how hard it is to avoid the fallacy of reductionist or partisan reading, none too uncommon in critical interpretation now as then.

2. I develop these and related suggestions of the imagery in greater detail in 'Macbeth in the tiring-house: the actor and clothes motifs in the play', *Anglia,* 100 (1982), pp. 18–35 and in my *On Shakespeare's Dramaturgy* (New Delhi: Spantech, 1993), ch. 6: 'Use of costume', pp. 134–6.

The question does pose itself whether the concept of the *sahrudaya* is not too elitist for one's consumption. Some of the terms Abhinava employs to characterise his idea of the *sahrudaya* do give the suspicion that exclusivity or being one of the elect few, let alone the select few, is a mark of such a one. But the concept in its basic significance is not essentially elitist when set in its true context of cultural life, that is, in a context where cultural unity can coexist with social stratification without a dichotomy between 'high culture' and 'low culture'. More important, we should be mindful enough to take Abhinava's concept of the *sahrudaya* with his other central concept of *sadharanikarana*. The two are in his reckoning the twin key factors in the process of dramatic and literary response, and the complementary relationship between the two in their implications needs underscoring. By *sadharanikarana*, Abhinava meant to indicate the psychological-cum-experiential transmission and reception of the impressions and effects, individually and collectively, which brings about a vicarious participation on the reader's or spectator's part in the poem or play. Customarily, the term is rendered as 'universalisation', but it has been usefully and valuably glossed as 'transpersonalisation' (Mohan Thampi) and as the process of 'raising the emotional complex to the aesthetic level of common enjoyability' (K. Krishnamoorthy). Presumably, it was Bhatta Tauta, Abhinava's teacher, who conceived the idea and broached it and offered valuable insights into the theatrico-dramatic transaction on its basis in his treatise *Kavyakautuka* which, unfortunately, survives only in a few fragments. Abhinava develops the idea, and offers insights on the lines of his teacher, in his *Lochana* and his commentary on Bharata's seminal *Natyasastra* called *Abhinavabharati*. Whatever the exact meaning of the term used to denote the concept, the first factor to note is that it points to sharing in common of feeling and experience at once between the play event or poetry utterance on the one hand, and the spectator or reader on the other, *and* among the spectators or readers themselves in like fashion. The experience thus is intersubjective, say between spectator and character and, to a great or less extent, among the spectators. Such implications of universalisation in *sadharanikarana* will sufficiently offset whatever exclusivist bias that the *sahrudaya* idea may seem to suggest. Moreover, the process in Abhinava's envisionment would lend support to the phenomenon of collective audience response guided often by a community of basic values and basic sensibility.

The two other immediate factors to note about the basic artistic transaction, as Abhinava emphasises these, are as follows. First, it is an entirely present-oriented process, however beneficial the results of the experience may be for the future. In this sense, though not in the Paterian aesthetic sense, it is the experience itself, not the fruit of experience, which counts. Abhinava uses the metaphor of a 'magic flower' which appears and disappears, implying thereby the existentiality of the experience. Second, a common enjoyability, a joyfulness, and also 'joy in widest commonalty' though this last in a limited sense, distinguishes the experience. Although Bhatta Tauta in the *Kavyakautuka* fragment, philosopher that he was, seems to err on the extreme of etherealising drama by denying that the staging is a physical occurrence or phenomenon at all, he would seem to have well recognised something such as what a critic like S.L. Bethell identified as the 'multiconsciousness' of the audience of the actor on stage as character and the actor as actor at one and the same time. On the basis of this feature, Bhatta Tauta places a play and its happenings in a kind of midway 'third realm' between pure actuality and pure ideality, which factor provides fruitful imaginative access to it. This middle location of drama or, for that matter, literature in general somewhere between the ideal and the actual, brings about its virtual or non-ontological status and invests it with what Susanne Langer, in the twentieth century, called 'virtual life' or virtual reality well before the advent of the cyber age.

An even more relevant implication of this finding is that drama, as Bhatta Tauta and Abhinava seem to have insisted, is 'representation' (*sadrsya*) rather than 'imitation' (*anukarana*), that is, more of a re-presentation than an impersonation. In terms of spectator reaction, it amounts to, as Viswanatha, a later theorist, well pointed out in his *Sahityadarpana* (*The Mirror of Literature*), the feeling that as the character engages his or her imaginative sympathy, the experience of the character is the character's, but not entirely only the character's and that the experience closely touches the spectator himself or herself, though not altogether. It is what makes for a right balance of simultaneous engagement and detachment or of sympathy and judgment.

The foregoing longish intervention on Sanskrit dramaturgical theories entailed in the central idea of *dhvani* or *rasadhvani* will help particularly in clarifying our response to a play like *Macbeth.* On such critical premises as sketched above, we should be able to perceive the limitations which the old historicist or the new historicist and cultural political readings of *Macbeth* because of their 'local' orientation may be prone to, though we should not discount the perceptions on the play which such readings bring us. We may be able to see for example the limits of the relevance of King James I to the play, and refrain from offering a King James version of it, sometimes with the Gunpowder Plot foregrounded. We may also remember not to bring the Witches and the contemporary ideas of witchcraft and of the supernatural quite centre-stage while we should by all means accord these their due place.

What is centrestage is Shakespeare's presentation of both the 'night's great business' (though the murder of Duncan itself is an offstage one), of Macbeth and Lady Macbeth and the further deeds of Macbeth on the one side and the repercussions, personal as well as interpersonal, national as well as cosmic, and the reaction phase which Macbeth provokes. The ramifications of the sort of suggestiveness, *dhvani* one can call it, through which Shakespeare effects the communication may be felt to have the overall consequence of an evocation of the *rasa* or sentiment of an 'unknown fear'. It is a 'fear' which comes to pervade the individual characters, the protagonists Macbeth and Lady Macbeth and others including the choric figures, and finally gets communicated to the viewer as *rasa.* In the case of the protagonists it leads to a 'see-sawing' between fear and security which when false is 'mortals' chief enemy'. It pervades the whole nation once it gets under Macbeth's regime in the form of the atmosphere of mistrust, and is carried into England by the exiles. Whether it is the poetic–dramatic evocation of the 'airy dagger' envisioned by Macbeth in phantasmagoric fashion or the mysterious voice crying out 'sleep no more' to Macbeth or the nine-times-repeated 'knocking', all these in the theatre language of verbal, aural and visual force communicate a sense of 'fear'. So do, at a more subtle and more generalised level, the active poetic–verbal and visual stage suggestions and associations of hell in the scene of the porter 'at Hell gate' and in some of Lady Macbeth's sleepwalking utterances. A suggested semblance to the souls in Hell and Purgatory rising to the trumpet call on the Judgment Day emerges in the disposition of characters onstage immediately after the discovery of Duncan's murder when all of them crowd around in their nightgowns, in their 'naked frailties'. Not that one should in the manner of Lily B. Campbell play it solely by the books of Elizabethan psychology and the pathological symptoms of fear described in these, it is 'fear' in an aesthetic and also moral rather than in a psychological sense.[3] Yet the irony that 'Bellona's bridegroom', the great warrior-hero who has ideas of 'manliness', should subject himself to such 'fear' as also that with his keen feeling into the enormity of his violation of the basic pieties Macbeth should commit himself to evil is what E.E. Stoll called the 'steep tragic contrast' that makes for tragic effect.

In the immediate prelude to Banquo's murder and to his son Fleance's great escape, a murder which he plots without taking Lady Macbeth into confidence as part of his swift retreat into isolation from her too and into loneliness, because

> Our fears in Banquo
> Stick deep
>
> (III.i. 48–9)

Macbeth speaks to his wife in dark hints and guesses about what he has planned.

Macbeth

> . . . . ere the bat hath flown
> His cloister'd flight, ere black Hecat's summons
> The shard-borne beetle with his drowsy hums
> Hath rung night's yawning peal, there shall be done
> A deed of dreadful note.

Lady Macbeth What's to be done?

Macbeth Be innocent of the knowledge, dearest chuck,
Till thou applaud the deed. Come, seeling night

3. Wilbur Sanders, *The Dramatist and the Received Idea,* Cambridge, 1968, Ch. 13, has a penetrating if intriguing account of this quality of 'an unknown fear' in the play.

> Scarf up the tender eye of pitiful day,
> And with thy bloody and invisible hand
> Cancel and tear to pieces that great bond
> Which keeps me pale! Light thickens, and the crow
> Makes wing to th' rooky wood
> Good things of day begin to droop and drowse,
> While night's black agents to their preys do rouse.
> Thou marvel'st at my words, but hold thee still;
> Things bad begun make strong themselves by ill.
> (III.ii. 40–55)

Shakespeare so ordains the evocative afflatus of these lines that the deliberately mystifying, all but, but not quite or really, poeticising theatricality of Macbeth's utterance is called attention to in the indicated response of his onstage listener. 'What's to be done?', 'Thou marvell'st at my words, but hold thee still'. The drift of Macbeth's vaunt is that as the 'secret'st man of blood' he would have Banquo's elimination smoothly accomplished in the secrecy of night; such suggestions of a 'nocturnal' genre for the play recur across it. Here again, through the undertones of the utterance there emerges the speaker's keen aliveness, despite the overt hints of cruelty, to the positives implied in the very items he conjures up as a catalogue, replete with sensuous auditory and visual suggestion, of the horrors of the night. These very natural phenomena are representative of the regular natural order and rhythms which Macbeth recognises in his subconscious, though all he does is in violation of the spirit of these. And he knows it only too well.

The multiple force of suggestion in the apparent statement

> Light thickens, and the crow
> Makes wing to th'rooky wood

has been the subject of intricate and detailed comment, as witness those of Empson in his *tour de force, Seven Types of Ambiguity*. There is no need to rehearse these, except perhaps to remind oneself of the fund of associations of the bird on its flight to its tree home, of the associations of gregarious and chattering (rooky) togetherness, secure, restorative rest in the protection of the rookery though in misty surroundings, all conveying the idea of sleep and peace which Macbeth fully recognises as what he misses. It is interesting that the Sanskrit literary theorist Bhamaha (7th century) (*Kavyalankara*) who propounded the idea of oblique expression in poetry which was later developed into the theory of *vakrokti* (deviated, striking expression) being the hallmark of poetry by Kumtaka (10th century), cited as a hypothetical example of direct descriptive verse which does not at all qualify as poetry the lines:

> The sun has set, the moon has risen
> and the birds fly to their nests.

Bhamaha's contemporary Dandin (*Kavyadarsa*) took issue with him. He maintained that such a collocation of words could take on rich poetic power if used in a context and a manner in which they produce effects. Shakespeare's lines for Macbeth uncannily testify to Dandin's point and, as Sigurd Burckhardt, an original critic, stated with reference to Shakespeare, many meanings have a single word in such instances rather than a single word having many meanings. This last perception was expressed long ago by Bhavabhuti the ancient Sanskrit dramatist, often paired with Kalidasa, in a verse to the effect that if in the case of the wise of the world word runs after sense, with the seers (the great poets in that reckoning being synonymous) sense rushes after word.

Again, Macbeth's much-discussed speech soon after hearing of Lady Macbeth's death is remarkable for the positive impression the utterance of stark nihilism conveys in its overtones alongside and in spite of our recognition of the fearfulness of this 'full look at the worst' and of our moral bearings on the situation, on the wages of sin and crime which Macbeth for all his tragic stature, is seen to have brought upon himself.

> *Macbeth* Tomorrow, and tomorrow, and tomorrow,
> Creeps in this petty pace from day to day,
> To the last syllable of recorded time.
> And all our yesterdays have lighted fools
> The way to dusty death. Out, out, brief candle!
> Life is but a walking shadow, a poor player,
> That struts and frets his hour upon the stage,
> And then is heard no more. It is a tale
> Told by an idiot, full of sound and fury,
> Signifying nothing.
>
> (V.v. 19–28)

We may not share the celebratory, romanticising tone and attitude of Lascelles Abercrombie[4] to the passage. In his classic comment indicating the positive thrust of the speech, Abercrombie said that because of Macbeth's mastering of his terrible awareness of the meaninglessness of life, acquired by generalisation from his case,

> Macbeth's personality towers into its loftiest grandeur . . . we see not only what he feels, but the personality that feels it; and in the very fact of proclaiming that life is a tale told by an idiot signifying nothing, personal life announces its virtue, and superbly signifies itself.

The point however, is well taken that the effective poetico-dramatic conception-cum-communication of the deep-felt awareness of the hollowness of life achieves the irony of bringing home that feeling and at the same time a vindication, if not an affirmation of life, through the sense it conveys of the dimensions of greatness of Macbeth's tragic awareness beside that of the moral values which should govern our balance of imaginative sympathy and judgment. It is Shakespeare's mastery over the power of poetic-dramatic suggestivity that brings about impressions where apparent opposites are harmonised. It is accomplished by the poet–playwright's subtle manipulation of diction, rhythm and movement and his superb exploitation of a flurry of three-stranded imagery and imagistic associations and their implications in their live theatrical context. It should suffice to consider in brief one or two of these. The emblematic image of the candle reinforcing the brevity of life shades off into a particular form of the then ubiquitous world-as-stage metaphor. It takes the form of life being a 'walking shadow'. It is not so much the light-candle-shadow train of associations as the synecdoche of an insignificant actor, a 'shadow' who has only an all-too-brief speechless and walk-on-and-walk-out part to play on the stage that draws our attention, an actor who is nothing, representing the very nihilism of life. But on the live stage as the lines were spoken by Burbage the leading tragic actor in Shakespeare's theatre, the actor's stage-presence, performance and delivery would

4. *The Idea of Great Poetry,* 1925, pp. 176–7.

give the lie direct to the insignificance of the actor. The awareness that clumsy walk-on parts apart, there are actors like Burbage who played Macbeth will not fail to work on the minds of the audience. Similarly, the story that the playwright tells in and through the on-going and now-about-to-end play of *Macbeth* has been anything but a 'tale told by an idiot / signifying nothing' to the responsive spectator or reader. The point is worth noting for our purpose that in a play like *Macbeth* the *dhvani* effects are carried conjointly by the verse and the theatrical dynamic.

This point together with the idea that an attentive and responsive *sahrudaya*-like apprehension is a requisite in order to savour the *dhvani* effect will receive further corroboration from a brief look at the sleepwalking scene in *Macbeth* (V.i). Shakespeare, indeed, calls up and subtly guides or manipulates the spectator's or reader's response to the scene in many ways, great and small. He designs the scene as a scene-within-the-scene. It is a framed scene with the Doctor of Physic and the Waiting Gentlewoman introducing it, preparing us for Lady Macbeth's somnambulistic performance and providing an illuminating running commentary on its nature, details and import. Our response is all the keener and if anything gets further heightened for its coming through the mediation of such a filter. The marvel is that such mediation renders the immediacy of the total impact on us closer. T.S. Eliot, one may remember, in his early revisionist review-essay on *Hamlet* spoke of what he called the 'artistic failure' of that play (though he later more or less recanted) to find an adequate 'objective correlative' for Hamlet's emotion, and thus introduced a critical term which had its currency for long. This critical term corresponds to the combination of factors required for the realisation of *rasa*, the imaginative experience of sentiment, such as the two *vibhāvas* (characters and setting), *anubhāvas* (the physical symptoms of gestural expression of emotions of character) and *vyabhicharibhāvas* (adjunct emotions of the primary feelings of characters) which together almost alchemise the *sthayibhāvas* (the primary feelings of characters) into the *rasa* experience on the part of the spectator. Eliot in the *Hamlet* essay cited as an example of the successful communication of feeling and emotion through the right 'objective correlative', the sleepwalking scene in *Macbeth*. It is easy to see why Eliot chose the scene.

Every movement, gesture and utterance of Lady Macbeth in her sleepwalking state is underscored through the comments of the Doctor and the Gentlewoman who turn the spotlight of attention on the actions and gestures. Incidentally, this would facilitate the audience in the Globe of Shakespeare's day where the large dimensions did not quite make for ideal sight lines. The fearfulness of the pangs of guilt-stricken conscience and of the state of sinfulness and proleptic damnation and hell is carried with force into the spectator's heart. The recurrent stress on the sticking blood on Lady Macbeth's hand which would not go, make as if to wash however hard she might, links with her initial cavalier belief that a little water would do the trick and also with the strand of blood references in the play. (Incidentally, few Shakespearians would seem to note a grisly parallel in recent world history. After the atom bomb attacks on Hiroshima and Nagasaki, a contrite Robert Oppenheimer told President Truman, 'I have blood on my hands.' Truman replied, 'Don't worry. It'll come out in the wash.'). The sighs and starts, and all other sensory impressions besides the obsessive, making as if to rub and wash her hands and the confessional blurting out about the serial murders are expressions of the depths of her consciousness in spite of herself. The communication is poetic-dramatic though the scene is all in prose except for the concluding speech of the Doctor, and the poet-playwright demands and obtains attunement from the spectator or reader.

In general, it requires a reader or viewer rightly attuned to the literary text, play-performance or an art object for a rapport, a successful artistic encounter and transaction, to be brought about between the two. Eric Gombrich, the art critic and historian, used the term 'resonance' to denote such a relationship of rapport between a work of art and its viewer.[5] Also, Abhinavagupta himself traces back the word *dhvani* to Bhartruhari's use of it in a seminal statement in his *Vakyapadiya* that speech emerges as *dhvani* or the resonance as that of a ringing bell led up to by the concatenation of sounds, the process of conception behind these being called *sphota* (the plosion of sound). Abhinava terms the suggested sense in poetry which is resonant like the ringing of a bell *dhvani*. He calls

5. *Meditations on a Hobbyhorse,* London, 1963, p. 56.

dhvani by other alternative names among which are *dhvanana* (resounding), *dyotana* (flash of illumination), to indicate the workings of the *vyangya* (suggestion) of *dhvani*. Given Abhinava's desideratum of the kindred-souled reader/viewer establishing a true dialogue with the work for *dhvani* to make itself felt, we could say that the phenomenon of the 'resonance' in Gombrich's sense is what Abhinava envisages. For this reason, it may be more appropriate to render *dhvani* as 'resonance' than 'suggestion' as we generally do. For it is not 'suggestion' in any too liberal a sense. It is not any irrelevant or wayward 'suggestion' entertained either subjectively or as a result of critical bandwagonism, but such 'suggestiveness' as can be recognised and absorbed by the *sahrudaya,* a culturally equipped and attentive spectator/reader, who is capable of establishing a rapport with the work in and through her or his real, steady and whole, experience of it.

That leads us to consider how *dhvani* may relate to the critical term and concept of 'resonance' as twinned with the term 'wonder' as 'resonance and wonder' by the leading new historicist critic Stephen Greenblatt and highlighted by him as the twin poles of response to significant art or literature. Greenblatt identifies 'resonance' as 'the power of the object displayed to reach out beyond its formal frontiers to a larger world, to evoke in the viewer the complex, dynamic cultural forces from which it has emerged'.[6] In the same breath he proceeds to describe 'wonder' in terms such as the power '. . . to stop the viewer in his tracks, to convey an arresting sense of uniqueness, to evoke exalted attention', and above all, 'to generate in the spectator surprise, delight, admiration and intimations of genius' (p. 170). Now, *dhvani* for all its *alaukika* or non-ordinary or not merely worldly or practical quality, does reach beyond mere formalism or the purely aesthetic. It does so if only in its awakening of moral values. It awakens a sense of not only the cultural forces behind the work but also, beyond these, the cultural-cum-moral (the two being inseparable) values that govern the cultural energies. In other words, *dhvani* as it could subsume the 'local', much canvassed in cultural political criticism would go beyond the 'local' in emphasis and could save us the distortions that

6. 'Resonance and Wonder', *Learning to Curse,* 1990, p. 170.

preoccupation with the 'local' may produce. However, *dhvani* could answer eminently well to 'wonder' in Greenblatt's outline. He takes the useful term from the classical critic Minturno who had the term 'admiratio' for it but in the sense of 'looking upon something in wonder'. Minturno's formula 'commiseration and admiration' was a modification of the Aristotelian 'pity and terror' to mark the response to tragedy, which meant to suggest that the spectator/reader feels for the sufferings of the protagonist and, importantly, responds with wonder not only to him but to the playwright's artistry in presentation. Such a formula has its relevant application to Shakespeare's tragedies like *Macbeth*.

An attempt like the present one to apply as a speculative instrument a central principle of Sanskrit poetics like *dhvani* to the interpretation of an English drama classic like *Macbeth* and to some of its problems will help clarify certain issues. The value of *dhvani* as a critical principle and tool lies in the fact that the *dhvani* effects are 'something understood' (in George Herbert's phrase from 'Prayer I') in the sense of being immediately and almost intuitively felt in and through the total experience of the work. The proper *dhvani* response saves us from the predicament of getting the meaning or rather whatever of it one sees, but missing the experience of a play or poem. We justifiably quote in studies by way of application of Sanskrit aesthetic criteria to the Shakespeare plays statements such as that of Susanne Langer:[7]

> Some of the Hindu critics . . . understand much better than their Western colleagues the various aspects of emotion in the theatre . . . the vital feelings of the piece. This last they call *rasa*; it is a state of emotional knowledge, which comes only to those who have long studied and contemplated poetry.

or the statement of Ananda Coomaraswamy (*The Dance of Siva*, p. 137) that 'the works of Shakespeare are in close accordance with Indian canons of dramatic art'. But it would be very relevant here to quote another utterance by Ananda Coomaraswamy as cited by L.C. Knights together with Knights's important comments.[8]

---

7. *Feeling and Form*, New York, 1953, p. 323.

8. 'King Lear as Metaphor,' *Hamlet and Other Shakespearean Essays*, 1979, pp. 252–3.

> In *The Transformation of Nature in Art* Ananda Coomaraswamy glosses the term *yun* as used by a Chinese writer on aesthetics: 'The idea *yun*, of operation or reverberation, is strictly comparable to what is meant by the *dhvani* of Indian rhetoricians, it being only as it were by an echoing in the heart of the hearer that the full meaning of a word (or any other symbol) can be realised' (p. 187). *Dhvani*, he adds, 'is literally "sound", especially sound like that of thunder or a drum, hence "resonance" or "overtone" of meaning'—i.e. the verbal noun 'sounding', rather than the noun 'sound' (p. 198). I am ignorant of Chinese and Indian aesthetics, but it seems to me that this comment throws light on the metaphoric process we have been considering . . . . it is only through the reader's imagination responding to the imagination of the poet (bringing 'the whole soul of man into activity') that the work becomes alive . . . the imagination thus conceived is an instrument of knowledge—not 'knowledge of' something fixed and definite, but knowledge as a 'sounding', 'an echoing in the heart of the hearer'.

An approach to a play like *Macbeth* in terms of *dhvani* does bring its reward or rather, it is its own reward. We may not claim that the method has the advantage of uniqueness, granting that there is at all anything like a unique method. But it serves to bring us clearly closer to what we may call the 'feel' and quality of the play.

20

Dramatic Illusion as 'Dream': The 'Dream' Plays of Shakespeare and Bhasa

In dramatic and aesthetic theory, the likening of dramatic illusion to the experience of dream has been made by critics – by Lord Kames and A.W. Schlegel in the eighteenth century and, most memorably, by Coleridge in the nineteenth. The dream analogy thus adduced in discussions of the name and nature of illusion in drama is a revealing and valuable metaphor, considerably helpful in our address to the question of the mode of existence and mode of operation of a play, a poem or a text of literature. This question of the quiddity or reality of a play-text has perhaps acquired a particular relevance in its ontological and hermeneutic implications in the current climate of postmodern 'theory' which generally tends to cast doubt on the identity, let alone the integrity, of the text as an entity. In such a context, the dream analogy for the experience of drama will provide a convenient speculative instrument to probe the question.[1] In this chapter, a brief attempt will be made to explore how the idea of dream is exploited to telling effects

1. The historical dream analogy has been used recently by R.A. Foakes in his discussion of the question. See his *Hamlet vs. King Lear: Cultural Politics and Shakespeare's Art* (Cambridge University Press, 1993), pp. 130–5. J.I. Cope, *The Theatre and the Dream: From Metaphor to Form in Renaissance Drama* (Baltimore: John Hopkins University Press, 1973) treats the analogy from a different point of view, that of the ideas of Florentine Neoplatonism. From yet other points of view dreams in Shakespeare are dealt with in Marjorie

with an interweaving if not a blend of illusion and reality almost throughout, in a Shakespeare play such as *A Midsummer Night's Dream* and in a famous dream scene by Bhasa in his well-known, ancient Sanskrit play, *Svapnavasavadatta*.

Lord Kames and Schlegel initially formulated the idea of drama or for that matter poetry as a 'waking dream' suggesting the voluntary element in the viewer's or reader's participation in dramatic or literary experience, and Erasmus Darwin confirmed the view in the prose interchapters in his poem *The Botanic Garden* (1789). But it was Coleridge who critically developed the idea and its implications in his Shakespeare lectures, especially his lecture on *The Tempest*, pursued its implications and applied it to actual plays by Shakespeare. His resultant theory[2] of a 'willing illusion', 'an inward illusion', 'negative belief', 'temporary half-faith', and 'willing suspension of disbelief' provided not only a corrective to Dr Johnson's rather patronising view of theatrical illusion as tantamount to a kind of delusion though a willing one in its way, but also a basis for a theoretical and practical understanding of literary or theatrical response. Coleridge's emphasis is on the active engagement of the will and choice of the spectator ('We *choose* to be deceived'), similar and parallel to the critic's emphasis on the role of the voluntary exertion of the moral will in an act of true imagination. Coleridge also stresses the essential ultimate inwardness of the experience of the illusion of drama or literature. His reaction against the spectacular staging of the Shakespeare plays in his contemporary theatre with a preoccupation with scenic illusion in the name of stage

---

B. Garber, *Dream in Shakespeare: From Metaphor to Metamorphosis* (New Haven: Yale U.P., 1974), and John Arthos, *Shakespeare's Use of Dream and Vision* (London: Bowes and Bowes, 1977). The aesthetician and hermeneutist Freidrich Schleiermacher also proffered the similitude between dream and art/poetry/drama, making the important distinction between the ordered nature of art and the lack of order in dream. See Benedetto Croce, *Aesthetic* (London: Vision Press and Peter Owen, 1953), p. 318.

2. Terence Hawkes, ed. *Coleridge on Shakespeare* (Harmondsworth: Penguin, 1969), pp. 53–4, pp. 94–5 and pp. 222–4. See also the well-known passage in Coleridge's *Biographia Literaria*, ed. James Engell and W.J. Bate, *Collected Works of S.T. Coleridge* vii (two volumes, Princeton University Press, 1983), vol. 2, p. 6.

illusion led him to point out the importance of the viewer's inner realisation of the 'semblance of reality' in drama. The vividness of the impression of reality, Coleridge argued, was like the unreal reality of dream of the psychology of which he and De Quincey, at once his disciple and rival, made subtle and penetrating investigation. In his view, it amounted to a 'mythic' sense of reality which was neither true nor false. He saw such a 'virtual reality' (in Susanne Langer's phrase) to be the essential quality of drama and its illusion producing as they did an imitation, not a copy of life.

In his marginalia on *A Midsummer Night's Dream* Coleridge wrote, 'I am convinced that Shakespeare availed himself of the title of the play in his own mind as a dream throughout.'[3] Jonathan Bate in his definitive study of the impact of Shakespeare on Coleridge and the other major Romantics[4] appears to be convinced that Coleridge's theory of dramatic illusion with its critical development and application of the idea of drama as dream but 'with a difference' is partly inspired by the motifs of dream and of imagination as a sort of dream as these figure in Shakespeare's 'dream' play. The play starts with the suggestion to 'dream away the time' (Hippolyta, I i.8)[5] and the command of Duke Theseus to his Master of the Revels to commission festive revels to mark the royal wedding, even as it ends with Puck as the Epilogue offering the conventional apologetic request to consider the play 'but a dream.' This is not to mention that Bottom's discourse on his 'dream' as 'Bottom's Dream' (IV.i.206–26) is, among other things, Shakespeare's ironical way of putting the whole play in the perspective of 'Bottom's Dream'.[6] However, Shakespeare in the course of the play, activates the 'multiconsciousness' inherent in the popular dramatic tradition of his times and plays on level after level of dramatic illusion and reality, indeed on different layers of the spectator's consciousness. So much so that the play has actions and

3. Terence Hawkes, ed. *Coleridge on Shakespeare*, p. 275.

4. Jonathan Bate, *Shakespeare and the English Romantic Imagination* (Oxford: Clarendon Press, 1989 edn. orig. pub. 1986), pp. 57–8.

5. I cite from the old Oxford Shakespeare, ed. W.J. Craig.

6. Also Oberon's comment earlier on in the play: 'When they next awake, all this derision/shall seem a dream and fruitless vision' (III.ii.370–1).

situations set in plays-within in plays-within-the-play in Chinese-box-like intricacy of inlaid structuration. The final effect that emerges is one of a fascinating and piquant if implicit underscoring no less of the reality of illusion than of the illusion of reality. The mode and process of representation in the play, at one level, raises the question of dramatic and theatrical representation. At the other levels, the world-within-world structure of the play with its web of interconnection among these worlds, those of the court, the citizens, the artisans and the fairies, besides complicating levels of illusion and reality, serves to bring out an impression of the complex lines of imaginative intercommunication between the stage-world and the world-stage. If the potent 'theatre of the world' metaphor was an active presence in the imaginative climate of the drama and literature of Shakespeare's period, if 'all the world is but a stage,' the playwright in the last phase of his career also came to put the idea into Prospero's mouth in *The Tempest*, 'we are such stuff as dreams are made on,' even as Calderon the Spanish dramatist almost contemporaneously called one of his plays *Life is a Dream*. (Calderon, we may remember, entitles another play of his *The Grand Theatre of the World*.) In the process, the close linkages, if not a merging or shading into one another, would seem to establish themselves between the world and its reality and illusion, on the one hand, and drama and dream and their 'virtual realities' and illusions, on the other.

The 'green world' of the 'Duke's wood' near Athens, the chief venue of action is the dream world of this comedy; it is a pastoral make-believe world, the bewildering maze of multiple illusions at play of which locale leads and resolves itself into the triple weddings of the lovers, into the right sympathetic response of Hippolyta and then also of Theseus to the 'device' of the play of 'Pyramus and Thisbe' presented by Quince, Bottom and company as wedding revels, and, finally, into the protective auspices of the now reunited Fairy King Oberon and Fairy Queen Titania at the royal wedding. Sleep figures in the play as much as a 'figure-in-action', as a prominent and persistent visual stage phenomenon, as it is a dominant 'figure-in-word,' a verbal reference. The experiences of cross-wooing, corrected by the same instrumentality of the magical juice and the agency of Puck as produced these into right wooing, occur in the play, as though these are undergone in dream fashion. No wonder the lovers try to form their impressions of these experiences on recall in such terms as these.

Lysander My lord, I shall reply amazedly,
Half asleep, half waking
(IV.i.152–3)

Demetrius . . . .
These things seem small and indistinguishable
Like far-off mountains turned into clouds

Hermia Methinks I see these things with parted eye,
When everything seems double.

Helena So methinks.
. . . .

Demetrius Are you sure?
That we are awake? It seems to me
That yet we sleep, we dream. Do you not think
The Duke was here, and bid us follow him.

Hermia Yea; and my father.
. . . .

Demetrius Why then, we are awake. Let's follow him.
And by the way let us recount our dreams.
(IV.1.193–205)

Bottom and company exhibit an amateur albeit amateurish enthusiasm for matters histrionic and, more particularly theatric. Bottom is, if anything, stage-struck. Hence his avid desire to don as many roles as could be in a versatile manner (I.ii.27–44, 53–7, 73–6, 81–7 and 93–9). No wonder among the dreamer-characters in the play Bottom is the dreamer par excellence. In their own way, his speculations about the illusion of their play 'Pyramus and Thisbe' transforming itself into too much of reality such as Snout, the lion frightening the ladies, raise the question of the nature of stage illusion. Shakespeare thus prompts our thinking (in metatheatrical fashion) about the question, while he may also be making gentle ridicule of the old gild theatricals' amateurishness and the mechanics of stage representation as he would seem to take occasion to do often in inset dramatic performances in his plays. Within the fairy-world in the play-world, Oberon, with Puck as stage-manager, sets the script and scenario of Titania's wooing of Bottom with the ass's head on his. The 'translation' and the wooing go to make 'Bottom's Dream' which comes through as an inset play-within in the play-within-the-play, something of a dream-within-a-dream Shelley spoke of in a poem.

A kind of final response and summative estimation is provided by Shakespeare as if these emerge in the exchanges between Theseus and Hippolyta and also in those between the royal couple and the Athenian genry of Lysander and Demetrius (V.i). There is an estimation of the lover's dream-like experiences of the wood, the 'story of the night', and there is also a generous sympathetic and participative reaction to Bottom's play expressing the inadequacy of the captious and unsympathetic response of the Athenian youth. Hippolyta offers a prompt corrective to Theseus's rationalising mistrust of visions and of 'strange things' such as the lovers had experienced in the world. It is worth noting, all the same, that Shakespeare makes Theseus associate the poet, the lunatic and the lover as a trio who

> Are of imagination all compact:

and suggests in the process that the trio could become a quartet with the addition of the clown Bottom (played by the Fool Will Kemp). If Hippolyta it is who puts Theseus right by pointing out that the dream experiences in their imaginative reach exceed beyond 'fancy's images',

> And grow to something of great constancy

thus vindicating the imagination, it is Theseus who later corrects her saying

> The best in this kind are but
> shadows, and the worst no worse,
> if imagination amend them
>
> (V.i.214–17)

It must be, as Hippolyta interposes (l. 218), the spectator's imagination also, though. Theseus's reference to 'shadows' connotes the theatrical sense the word had in Shakespeare's times of 'actors', especially actors who take minor or supernumerary walk-on parts or bit parts with hardly any lines to speak.

The self-reflexive suggestion would emerge that if it comes to carping criticism even the best of players in the theatre, including the present ones in the main play performance, would appear really no better than 'shadow' actors or actors like the artisans who presented the 'Pyramus and Thisbe' play. Oberon is called, earlier in the play, 'king of shadows' (III.ii.347), suggesting of course the 'fairy king' but also a main player. In the epilogue Puck says,

> If we shadows have offended,
> Think but this, and all is mended,
> That you have but slumber'd here
> While these visions did appear
>
> (V.ii.54–7)

The boy-actor speaks for fairies and actors alike and suggests that the whole play-experience can be regarded as a dream or vision. The upshot of all this is a sense communicated of the validity and reality, in the final reckoning, of dream and drama and of the active in one respect and passive (in another respect) role of the spectator's imagination and judgement. Indeed, the changes which Shakespeare rings in the course of the scene on the term 'imagination' run the whole gamut of the shift in the significance of the expression from the Augustan–Johnsonian mistrust to the Romantic apotheosis of it.[7]

There is an instance of a memorable use of the device of the dream and the dream motif in what is perhaps the best play of

---

7. There are other instances of the use of the dream/vision device in Shakespeare; besides the narration of his dream by Clarence (*King Richard III*, I.iv. 9–63), there are the enacted dream-visions experienced by Posthumus in *Cymbeline* (V.iv.29–151) and Katherine in *King Henry VIII* (IV.ii.83 and long s.d.). The 'tablet' left behind by Jupiter on Posthumus's breast in the course of the dream enactment remains with him as a concrete reality and subsequently figures in the play. Also the Induction to *The Taming of the Shrew* carries the overall suggestions that life, after all, could be a dream. See James L. Calderwood, *Shakespearean Metadrama* (Minneapolis: Minnesota University Press, 1971), for a different reading of the metadramatic element in *A Midsummer Night's Dream* and other plays.

Bhasa, the father of drama in Sanskrit, his *Svapnavasavadatta*. Indeed the play bears the alternative title, *Svapnanatakam* ('the dream play'). The playwright entitles his play thus in relation to its central scene, the famous dream scene (Act V).[8] There takes place in this scene a prefiguration of the final reunion and restoration between the protagonist king Udayana and the heroine Vasavadatta with which the play ends in Act VI. The play is about the separated queen Vasava living incognito, at the instance of Udayana's minister Yougundarayana who deliberately gives it out that Vasava has been killed in a fire accident, as part of an elaborate stratagem he adopts to accomplish the end, which he eventually does, of getting Udayana married to Padmavati the Magadha princess as his second queen and investing him with new power to regain his lost territories. Vasava joins Padmavati as her favourite maid and confidant, adopting the name Avantika, and has to be an accessory to the love between her husband and the princess, and, to the two getting wedded, giving rise to a number of piquant moments of drama. And she is portrayed as playing such a delicate role with phenomenal self-effacement and empathic understanding.

The dream scene (Act V) opens with the maids searching for Vasavadatta–Avantika who would be the best person to attend to the newly wedded Padmavati who is lying in the Sea-House (evidently a palace apartment kept cool by surrounding water currents, afflicted with a headache). They inform King Udayana's companion, the jester who immediately intimates his master about the new queen's fit of headache. Udayana, who under the impression that his beloved first wife is dead, has married Padmavathi but could hardly get over his constantly lingering thoughts about Vasava, feels sorry for the suffering of Padmavati and decides to go into the Sea-House to be of comfort to her. By then Padmavati had changed plans and is not there in that place. Udayana enters to find the prepared bed vacant, and waits hoping that Padmavati might arrive. The jester's attempt to beguile the time with story-telling only puts Udayana to sleep, and the jester leaves him well covered and fast asleep. Vasavadatta-Avantika enters and takes the sleeping figure to

8. Citations and translations are from M.R. Kale's edition of the play (Delhi: Motilal Banarsidas, 1982, orig. edn. 1929).

be Padmavati and lies down by 'her' side on the bed, clasping 'her' in a gesture of intimacy. Udayana, as ever, dreams about Vasava and in the dream meets that real dream-girl of his. He starts talking aloud addressing her. Vasava who is there for real, albeit in her concealed identity, has to meet the situation with exemplary presence of mind and also takes right advantage of it to the proper degree as it were. The intercommunication between the dream world and the real world, between the dreaming Udayana and the awake Vasavadatta could last only for a short while. Vasava has to cut it short by leaving before Udayana awakes. But she rushes out only after offering the affectionately solicitous gesture of lifting the dangling arm of her sleeping husband and placing on the bed. The action rouses him from his sleep, and catching a fleeting glimpse of Vasava going out of the door he rushes out only to strike against the door panel in his haste and lose momentum. The jester who arrives back then dismisses the King's reposrt of his encountering Vasava alive as a dream experience or, worse, an elf-smitten state.

This bare outline of the action of the scene can hardly convey the uncanny force of the theatrically effective poetic–dramatic rendering of the scene by Bhasa. The dramatist brings about a remarkably piquant blend of illusion and reality and captures the sense and feel of the meeting place between dream and dramatic make-believe on the one hand, and reality and dire hard facts, on the other, by a process of actualisation through the suggestions of the dream device. Such an effect is well prepared for in the scene when the jester encounters, as he enters the Sea-House with the King, a loose hanging jasmine garland dangling on the floor from the decorative arch and takes it to be a snake in the soft light of a single flickering lamp lighting the room. The King identifies the garland right as producing the illusion of a snake through its almost sinuous moments in the blowing breeze and in the half-light. The aesthetician Lollata (9th century), one of the earliest commentators on Bharata's *Natyasastra*, used exactly the idea of a rope being taken for and believed to be a serpent to denote the illusion created by drama and poetry, although the serpent and the rope semblance also became a great *topos* of Vedantic discourse. This 'secret impression' (to use Maurice Morgann's phrase regarding Shakespeare) made on the spectator of the problem of illusion provides a lead-in to the story-telling episode in which the jester starts with what bids fair to be a 'true story', the history of Udayana's relationship with Vasava. The king would have none of the story, since he is already too full of the thought of his lost beloved Vasava and the jester attempts to tell an imagined story but confuses the names of person and place and confuses himself so badly that the King is lulled into sleep. Left asleep by the jester, the King in bed is taken to be Padmavati by Vasava who arrives then. Another play of illusion. Indeed, this is preceded by a reference to yet another illusive experience in Udayana's adjuration to the jester that the story he starts narrating about himself and Vasava should be stopped and changed into another. Udayana is reminded all the more of how he misses Vasava who during the music sessions he had with her found her engrossed alike in playing on her lute and fixedly looking at him at the same time. As a result, she often failed to note that the bow had slipped from her hands and she kept on moving her fingers and hands as though playing on the air instead of on the instrument.

Yet, amidst such indications of illusiveness, the dream illusion of the sleeping Udayana of an encounter with his beloved Vasava, turns out to be a flesh-and-blood reality. Vasava, happening precisely to be at the moment his bed fellow, she has to go through a shock of surprise and acute embarrassment which for all the pleasure and happiness it might bring her, turns out to be a challenging situation when the king calls out her name in dream but also for real at the same time. In the preceding Act IV, the 'overhearing scene', both Vasava and Padmavati had listened in on the King's expression of his deep-felt pangs of nostalgic love and affection for the 'dead' Vasava expressed by the King. Now in the bedroom scene, Vasava takes the situation on hand, and carries on a conversation, and the effect turns out to be a subtle coalescence or at least a merger of the illusion of dream and the real-life actuality. A crystallisation of such a merging is the two successive stage moments of the king stretching out his hands while in dream to clasp Vasava and of Vasava touching the dangling hand of the King to put it in place on the bed. A reunion not without suggestions of reconciliation also takes place, fleeting and evanescent as it may be. No wonder that Udayana is unable to decide whether it is a waking experience or vision or a dream.

> If at all this was a dream, then it were a blessing
> not to have awakened from it, or if it be an
> illusion, let me be under the illusion for a long time.
> (Act V, Sloka 9)

This might suggest Caliban's celebration of his sensuous dreams (*The Tempest*, III.ii.137–8) and his account of how waking from his sleep he would be made to 'sleep again' and dream such dreams that

> When I wak'd
> I cried to dream again.

The experience of Udayana is more like what Keats said of Adam's dream.

> The imagination may be compared to Adam's dream—he awoke and found it truth.[9]

It is the truth of the imagination that grants the validity and truth of an illusion provided it is imaginative enough. The parallel with the situation of Madeleine in Keats's *The Eve of St. Agnes* is striking. Madeleine's St. Agnes Eve's vision of her lover Porphyro materialises in the actual presence of Porphyro in her bedroom, and it leads to their union and happy match. When towards the close of *Svapnavasavadatta* (Act VI), the reunion of the King with Vasavadatta, and also with his minister Yougandarayana takes place, King Udayana contemplates:

> Is it a reality or dream, that she is again seen by me?
> For though seen by her, I was then the deceived.
> (Act VI, Sloka 17)

The lines prompt the thought of the indistinguishability of illusion and reality. Rather, it is the illusion of reality or the reality of illusion which is at issue.

Both Shakespeare and Bhasa, as playwrights, may be said to engage their dramatic energies and power in rendering the extistential force and sway, and the feel of reality, or of illusion. In the process

---

9. John Keats, Letter to Benjamin Bailey, 22 November 1817. Cited from *The Oxford Anthology of English Literature: Major Authors Edition*, Volume 11, p. 597.

they would seem to make available, in imaginative terms, the ground of intermingling of illusion and reality. They are, to that extent, less concerned to mark the quotidian black-and-white demarcation between the two, if only because they could take for granted the basic univocal contrast. Equally interestingly, the playwrights between the two of them, in the variations they make on the dream motif and the dream device, implicitly, vindicate dramatic illusion and the 'certainty' of drama for all the element of an 'insubstantial pageant' it carries. More, the two dramatists would seem all but to make an intuitive anticipation of the later theorists' likening of drama to 'a waking dream'.

21

Effects of *Trompe L'oeil*: Some Shakespeare, Bhasa and Kalidasa Instances

One of the forms in which the play with illusion which is a *raison d'etre* of drama evidences itself in Shakespeare and the Elizabethans as well as in the classic Sanskrit masters of drama such as Bhasa and Kalidasa is by way of an intricate interplay of illusion and reality. Such a handling of dramatic illusion by the playwright generates possibilities of effects at once of multiple layers of illusion and of the interpenetration of these into levels of reality apprehended in and through illusion; indeed, it is an open invitation to the spectator to savour the suggestions. These effects of a juxtaposition, or of approximation, and frequently of an interweaving of illusion and reality, may for convenience be characterised as examples of *trompe l'oeil* using the term in an extended, generalised signification of the breaking in into each other of art and actuality.

Shakespeare, Bhasa and Kalidasa, writing as they did, in a theatrical tradition based on conventionalism which is often called 'non-illusionism' by critics like J.L. Styan, could naturally explore and exploit the poetic–dramatic and stage-and-theatre possibilities of the 'multiconsciousness' (in S.L. Bethell's memorable term) inherent in the tradition. These playwrights belonging to vastly different eras of time and to two different climes bring forward instances of the telescopic complex of illusion–reality to varying degrees, purposes and effects. Yet, differences notwithstanding, there are striking similarities of concept, practice and outcome in these playwrights' deployment of the technique of a dramatic merger of make-believe and the reality of the world of the play. A consideration of some comparable examples of such a technique of *trompe l'oeil* in the two traditions will provide cross-illumination into the workings of the device and highlight the common ground in cultural sensibility between the traditions in which the dramatists wrote, while also alerting us to the differences.

A set of examples relates to a particular kind of anticipatory, and often uncannily, polyvalently suggestive, use of garments or items of costume. Another group of instances consists of stage moments when the pictorial or statuesque representation of a character or characters would seem to materialise *in propria persona* in a *frisson* of surprise. A third category would include various examples of a certain manifestation of the playwright's art of dramatic juxtaposition in which the timing of the entry or of the offstage or onstage utterance of a character produces the effect of a crystallisation of some key dramatic point or significance. The core common feature of the three categories is the evocation of a sense of a curious intercommunication between levels of illusion and reality.

As representative of the category of the prefigurative or proleptic use of costume may be chosen the scene at times called the *valkala* (bark-garment) episode in Bhasa's second Ramayana play *Pratimanatakam*; the opening of the scene of the sheep-shearing feast in *The Winter's Tale* and the scene of Prince Hal's putting on of the regal crown of his father King Henry IV's by his bedside (IV.v); and the decoration of Sakuntala in *Abignanasakuntalam* (Act IV) with the queenly bride's garments miraculously yielded by trees.

Bhasa conceives and renders the scene of the aborted coronation of young Rama with an innovativeness in ideation and stagecraft alike. In an original departure from Valmiki, Bhasa not only extenuates Kaikeyi but presents her in a relatively favourable light. He invents the *valkala* episode, brings it centre-stage and exploits it as a master-stroke of dramatic power in its future-directed suggestiveness while also making it serve the purpose of absolving Kaikeyi of the signal blame she carries in Valmiki of presenting Rama, Sita and Lakshmana with bark garments after getting them banished to the forest. The bark-garment in question is indeed a theatre costume; it is, precisely, a costume from the wardrobe of the palace-theatre in the stage world of the play. Appropriated for fun by a maid of Sita's, it attracts Sita's attention when she is in the process of dressing herself for Rama's coronation. Taking a fancy for it, Sita puts it on, blissfully unaware that Rama was at the very moment to be sent into fourteen years of exile into the forest at Kaikeyi's behest and that she would follow in his footsteps. At that moment, Rama, returning from the interrupted coronation, enters and Sita tries to conceal the bark-wear under the ceremonial costumes she is in the process of donning, but he detects the bark-garment and, to crown the irony, expresses a desire to try it on himself and proceeds to do so. It adds up to a stage situation of uncanny irony, anticipation and prolepsis, for, immediately after, the cancellation of the coronation and the banishment of Rama to the forest for a fourteen-year period are announced. It is in the self-same bark-garments, all from the wardrobe of the palace theatre which had been commissioned to put up a play as part of the coronation celebrations, that all three, Rama, Sita and Lakshmana, depart for the forest. The inlaying of the three or more strata of illusion within illusion and also the multiple layers of reality—the 'myth' of the Ramayana, its Valmiki version, the stage world of Bhasa's version, the stage rendering of it, and the palace theatre within the circumambient Bhasa theatre, and the actors' attires carried out in Bhasa in a subdued and minimally suggested 'multiconsciousness' about levels of reality, whereas corresponding and qualitatively different instances in Shakespeare would seem to exhibit a more active 'multiconsciousness' in this regard in different degrees in the different examples.

Prince Henry's wearing of the regal crown of his father Bolingbroke in *King Henry IV, Pt. II* (IV.v.) under the false impression that the king has breathed his last is a premature, anticipatory, albeit momentary, crowning of the prince whose coronation takes place towards the close of the play. It also links with Falstaff wearing the tavern seat cushion as his crown in his improvisation of the King's role in his tavern charade with the prince (*King Henry IV, Pt. I*, II.iv), and with Prince Hal in his turn assuming in that charade the role of King Henry IV.

> Lo! here it sits,
> Which heavens shall guard; and put the world's strength

Into one giant arm, it shall not force
This lineal honour for me.

(*Henry IV, Pt. II*, IV.v.42–5)

When the sleeping king on waking discovers that the prince had left with the crown and concludes that his heir-apparent had been too unceremoniously hasty to assume kingship, Warwick assures him that the prince who took the crown genuinely mistaking the king's stillness in his sleep to be his death has been seen by him to be the very picture of filial grief. In the encounter with the king that follows, the prince vindicates his loyalty and responsibility of king-like concern, and the king discourses with feeling on how 'uneasy lies the head that wears the crown'. The crown, with both its legacy and the inheritance of it, is the text of the sermon, and it is the point of reference not only in these speeches, not only in this play but is carried over as one into *Henry V* (iv.i. 312–25). The crown is both object and subject of discourse in the scene in question.

King Henry God knows, my son,
By what by-paths and indirect crook'd ways
I met this crown; and I myself know well
How troublesome it sat upon my head
. . . . All these bold fears
Thou seest with peril I have answered;
For all my reign hath been but as a scene
Acting that argument; and now my death
Changes the mode: for what in me was purchase'd?
Falls upon thee in a more fairer sort;
So thou the garment wear'st successively.[1]

(*Henry IV*, Pt. II., IV.v.182–200)

In response the prince reaffirms his resolve to hold the crown, reaffirming and reechoing his earlier assertion.

1. The Shakespeare references in this paper are keyed to the old Oxford Shakespeare, ed. W.J. Craig (London: Oxford University Press, 1974). So also A. C. Woolmer and L. Sarup, ed. *Thirteen Plays of Bhasa* (Delhi: Motilal Banarsidas, 1985) and C.R. Devadhar, ed. *Works of Kalidasa, Vol. 1: Dramas* (Delhi: Motilal Banarsidas, 1966) have been used for the plays of Kalidasa and Bhasa.

Prince My gracious liege,
You won it, wore it, kept it, gave it me;
The plain and right must my possession be:
Which I with more than with a common pain
'Gainst all the world will rightfully maintain.
(IV.v.219–23)

The theatrical references employed in the king's speech and the centre-stage prominence given to the stage property of the crown make for a rousing of a sense of multiple layers of illusion and reality, especially in the context of the reference the *Henriad* of Shakespeare has to the Hal myth and to the popular play, *The Famous Victories*. The crown serves at once as a strong symbol of royalty, kingly care and cares. (Wilson Knight emphasised the force of the crown as a symbol, though it is another matter that he used the idea and the history plays for wartime propaganda of a somewhat jingoistic slant.) The 'multiconsciousness' evoked is part of the general dramatic tradition of the Elizabethan period.

However, the use of a corresponding garment motif in a play of late Shakespeare like *The Winter's Tale* is in terms of a more pronounced self-conscious theatricality characteristic of the Jacobean theatre. When Perdita appears decked in the attire of the Queen of the Sheep-shearing Feast (IV.iii.), the costume becomes an object of attention both by Perdita and by Florizel. Florizel's assumed rustic guise also comes in for comment. Florizel stresses the auspicious purpose of the 'transformation' the pair have undergone as the feast is also to be transformed into their nuptials, though in the event interrupted nuptials. The polyvalent significance radiated by the discussion on the art–nature antithesis between Polixenes and Perdita, which follows soon after, is given an added dimension by the fact of Perdita's essential royalty, existential commonalty and the state of queen and goddess assumed by her through her costume. Supervening on all this is the stage fact of the player of Perdita being a 'boy-actress'. The ensemble thus turns out to be a piquant and probing, although tacit and implicit, unravelling of an intertwined strand of theatrical illusion and play-world reality all of which goes to make the 'subtle knot' of complex theatrical communication.

A different, less intricate theatrical self-reflexivity marks the change or assumption of costume as it occurs in Shakespeare's *The*

Tempest. Besides attention being specifically called to the almost miraculously well-preserved state of the ceremonial wedding wear of King Alonso and party by Gonzalo (II.i.65—8), Prospero's assumption or divesting himself of his magical robes on several occasions in the play's course, and especially his appearance towards the close in his ducal robes ('How fine my master is' is the comment of Caliban, V.i.261), are signals of 'transformation' of his roles or status. In some ways similar use of the garment/ornaments motif is made by Kalidasa in his *Sakuntalam*. In the only highly ceremonial scene of Act IV when Sakuntala, already quick with child by King Dushyanta, is elaborately prepared to be taken to her husband's palace in Hastinapura, after the holy bath and sacramental aspersions she receives, she is decked in queenly and bridal garments and priceless ornaments which are brought to her as items materialising from a tree, a *Kalpataru* 'with a difference' which has yielded these at the merest wish of saga Kasyapa. The effect is one of a graded yet fairly swift transformation of Sakuntala from her forest hermitage dress into a lady in the splendour of queenly and bridal attire. This is the first and practically the only time in the play when Sakuntala is a stage-presence of such splendour of attire, for when she is presented to King Dushyanta in Act V only to be rejected by him thanks to the amnesia caused on account of Sage Durvasa's curse on Sakuntala for her innocent lapse, she remains veiled for the most part, the veil being taken off by Gautami only towards the close of the fateful interview. The irony is that the bridal attire leads only to a kind of broken nuptials and Sakuntala also becomes the despised queen though taken charge of by the apsara world and finally restored to her Dushyanta with their son Sarvadamana-Bharata.

Instances abound especially in the Sanskrit drama of Kalidasa and Bhasa, and occur occasionally in Shakespeare, of the *trompe l'oeil* of absent or presumed-to-be-dead characters-in-pictures or-in-statues making their appearance, with a certain effect of dramatic surprise, as flesh-and-blood figures on the stage. The classic example in Sanksrit drama is to be found in Bhasa's *Swapnavasavadatta*. It pertains to Vasavadatta living *incognito* in the court of Padmavati's father as she is believed to have perished in a fire by her husband King Udayana who weds Padmavati. Though a favourite and confidante of Padmavati almost always by her side, serving in the fashion of Shakespearian heroines like Viola and Julia as a consultant in the love of Padmavati for her own husband, and also making the wedding garland of Padmavati, Vasavadatta remains unseen by Udayana till the very last but for a fleeting glimpse in his state between sleep and waking. She sees him and listens to, by overhearing (among other things), Udayana's expression of loyalty and love towards her after her presumed death, though. Towards the close of the play, the wedding portrait of Vasavadatta and Udayana, with which the runaway match of the two was solemnised by Vasavadatta's parents, is exhibited to King Udayana whose mind has been full of the thought of Vasavadatta all the while. Padmavati, now queen of Udayana, recognises the close resemblance of the 'former' queen in the picture to her maid Avantika (assumed name of Vasavadatta). It results in Vasavadatta being led to reveal herself, and also Udayana's minister Yaugandarayana arriving back in the guise of a Brahmin in which he had earlier come and left Vasavadatta as Avantika in deposit with Padmavati. Multiple recognitions and reunions ensue. The wedding portrait is actually a carry-over from the close of the preceding Bhasa play *Pratijnana Yaugandarayanam* on the Udayana–Vasavadatta legend. The much-missed and pined-for Vasavadatta appears in picture form, and soon after presents herself in reality to be reunited with her husband who has also recovered the lost part of his kingdom, thanks to Yaugandarayana's plans.

Yet this presentation of herself by Vasavadatta and her reunion with Udayana find a prefiguration of greater effect than the event itself in the play in the dream-scene in Act V, a masterpiece of imaginative conception and theatrical art. The king lies asleep dreaming, as ever, about Vasavadatta and a reunion with her when Vasavadatta actually lies awake by his side mistaking the sleeping figure to be Padmavati. An all-too-brief conversation ensues, Vasavadatta speaking in her waking state, with Udayana still in his dream conversation with his dream girl, a fine example of a *trompe l'oeil*-like intercourse between dream-illusion and reality. Vasavadatta soon has to withdraw herself by rushing out of the chamber to avoid detection, and Udayana wakes up just in time to catch a much-too-evanescent glimpse of the lady. So much so that when the final reunion does take place Udayana is still made to wonder:

> Is it a reality or a dream that she is
> seen again by me? For once seen by me,
> I was duped by her.
>
> (Act VI, Sloka 17)

which in its own way suggests the uncertainties and also at the same time the 'certainty' of both dramatic and other illusion and reality.

The motif of the person-in-the-picture in dramatic correlation to the person-of-the-play operates almost throughout Kalidasa's first play *Malavikagnimitra*. King Agnimitra falls in love with Malavika (ostensibly a maid of the queens) at first sight when he sees her in the painted group picture. At her first appearance on the dance contest stage (Act II), the king feels:

> I beheld her picture, I thought she
> would belie the loveliness of it, but
> now I think that the painter who
> limned her likeness had not secured
> full concentration
>
> Act II, Sloka[2]

Similarly, Malavika in her lovelorn state, thanks to the impediments brought by the queens Dharani and Iravati who are rivals in love to her, contemplates the reproduction of Agnimitra in the same painted group picture with the queens and herself figuring in it, and expresses her feelings in this regard. Lo and behold! Agnimitra has been listening in and watching, even as Malavika bemoans that even in a dream she cannot achieve union with Agnimitra. He presents himself in person before Malavika for a central love union with her in the play. So also queen Iravati communicates with the King's semblance in the picture asking for his forgiveness and reconciliation with him, just a little before encountering the King and catching him red-handed with Malavika.

By the same token, in Kalidasa's *Vikramorvasiam* the Vidushaka advises King Vikrama to find union with Urvasi in a dream or to

---

2. R. Devadhar, ed. *Malavikagnimitra: Works of Kalidasa's Dramas,* Vol. 1 (Delhi: Motilal Banarsidas, 1966), p. 39.

paint her likeness and gaze upon it, and thus quench his desire (Act II). Moments later, Urvasi the apsara, hovering about the spot in invisible form, presents herself to him making herself visible. In Act IV after a long frantic quest in the *apsara* land by him, Vikrama's accidental embrace of a creeper in his mad love melancholy results in the creeper turning precisely into Urvasi at his touch which cures the curse that wrought the earlier metamorphosis.

The picture–person correlation by way of dramatic juxtaposition or of shading off of picture into person is employed by Kalidasa in all three plays of his. In *Sakuntalam* it occurs at a crucial turning point after the providential restoration of the memorial ring to King Dushyanta when he paints a detailed picture of Sakuntala in her hermitage and contemplates it giving it touches of improvement, now that she has come back to his memory causing him great remorse for rejecting her. Soon after this pictorial appearance of Sakuntala, Dushyanta undertakes the rescue operation on behalf of Indra and after his success has his meeting with his son Bharata and his reunion with Sakuntala.

Cognate theatre moments of pictorial or other representation in a fashion translating itself into reality are relatively infrequent in Shakespeare. An example is Hamlet's agonised display in Gertrude's chamber of his father's picture in contrastive conjunction with that of his uncle Claudius:

> Look here, upon this picture, and on this
>
> (III.iv.53)

whether the pictures were Elizabethan miniatures, one worn by Hamlet and the other by Gertrude, or they were two hanging wall pictures as in the illustration in Rowe's edition of Shakespeare. Very soon after this, the Ghost of the elder Hamlet ('My father, in his habit as he liv'd,' III.iv.134) makes its appearance, its last in the play. But the most remarkable instance is that of Hermione's statue coming alive at the end of *The Winter's Tale*, marking the 'resurrection' of Hermione. The intricate, Chinese-box-like inlaying of all but bewilderingly multiple levels of illusion and reality in the episode makes it a most complex and intensely effective invoking of the principle and technique of *trompe l'oeil*. For one thing, contrary to his customary practice, Shakespeare in *The Winter's Tale* (compare Hero's 'death' or Helena's) holds back from the spectator till the last the secret of Hermione's preservation. For another, the encounter with the statue is so rendered that the enactment of the statue by the 'boy-actress' playing Hermione, its presentation to the whole set of onstage viewers, and their response, especially the key reaction of Leontes, are ordered by the playwright in exactly such terms, hints and suggestions that it brings a nice balance, almost a perilous one, between engagement and disengagement, between theatrical self-consciousness and the sense of verisimilitude evoked. The statue 'comes alive' in a gradation of subtle intimations in and through the references to the 'life as lively mock'd as ever,' wrinkles and all, Perdita's offer to kiss the hand of the statue and Leontes's to kiss its lips, and Paulina's warning about wet paint, and Leontes's statements about its signs of life and his offer to take the statue by the hand, and, above all, Paulina's proffered gesture of white magic by which she would make the statue move endowing it with life.

A few examples should suffice of the stage phenomenon of an utterance apparently unrelated to a character or the utterance of his or her name or references to him or to her leading to a sudden, unexpected appearance of the character on the stage. Such invoking in which a verbal reference concretises itself in the entry of a character may be regarded as another variation of the motif of *trompe l'oeil*. In *Sakuntalam* (Act I), Dushyanta sets eyes on Sakuntala while in hiding and keeps tracking her as she moves in the company of her associates. When she is bothered by a bee chasing her, they tell her to call upon Dushyanta since he as king is protector of the holy groves, and, ironically, Sakuntala looking about, complains:

> How even here he follows me!

The reference is, if anything, more appropriate to Dushyanta who unknown to Sakuntala and her friends, has been tracking her. It is at this moment that Dushyanta reveals himself to them offering help. There are the successive appearances of Urvasi before Vikrama in *Vikramorvasiam*. On several occasions Urvasi, with her gift of invisible aerial movement, comes to stand before King Vikrama when he keeps pining for her company and discoursing about her absence to his Vidhushaka in his pleasure garden.

This technique of telling synchronisation of utterance and appearance, which produces a kind of anamorphic *trompe l'oeil* effect is exemplified strikingly by Bhasa in his *Abhiskekanatakam* (Act V). The scene is one of Ravana's meeting with Sita in the *asokavana*, after Rama had entered Lanka with his army. Ravana, as a ploy to force Sita to submit to him, produces his two severed heads closely resembling Rama and Lakshmana created by Vidyujjihva through magic, and presenting them to Sita, tries to pin her down asking:

> By whom do you hope to be saved now?

Sita faints, and right then a messenger enters with his offstage announcement, 'By Rama, by Rama,' to convey the news to Ravana that his dear warrior-son Indrajit has been killed by Rama and Lakshmana. Ravana who cannot believe it, spends his ire on the messenger but soon realises the truth and it is he who goes into a faint now, after Sita has revived at the news.

A sample Shakespeare instance of the playwright's art of synchronisation and juxtaposition would reveal the characteristic irony of vision with which Shakespeare sets characters and their actions and situations often in polysemous light. Jaques's references at the end of his 'seven ages of man' aria to old age:

> Last scene of all,
> That ends this strange eventful history,
> Is second childishness and mere oblivion,
> Sans teeth, sans eyes, sans taste, sans everything.
> (*As You Like It*, II.vii.163–6)

is almost accompanied by the entry at a door of the stage of old Adam carried by Orlando on his back, and the lines cover the approach of the two to the banquet spot on the long and large platform stage of the Globe. The Duke welcomes them with

> Welcome. Set down your venerable burden
> And let him feed.
> (II.vii.167)

Jaques's invoking of old age and its helplessness finds a crystallisation in the helpless figure of Adam and provides a kind of endorsement. At the same time, the stage image of Orlando carrying the old man on his back recalls the emblematic picture of Aeneas carrying his parents on his back in filial piety, thereby giving the lie direct to the cynically dismissive attitude to old age behind

Jaques's utterance. Age is not always unregarded or in old corners thrown, nor is it all that 'unnecessary'. Moreover, the Duke's words of concern and warm reception further reinforce the later impression; the synchronisation thus works with multidirectional force.

The several kinds of effect wrought on the principle of *trompe l'oeil* by the three different playwrights, sometimes differently in their own plays in the ultimate analysis, serve to exemplify how an intermingling of strata of illusion and reality has more or less constantly been an essential part of playmaking. The suggestion of a spiral interweaving of theatrical illusion and reality has remained a constituent of dramatic experience, thanks to the 'multiconsciousness' inherent in the dramatico-cultural traditions to which the playwrights and the plays in question belong. However, the different kinds and degrees of exploitation that Shakespeare, Kalidasa and Bhasa make of the possibilities of a criss-cross of illusion and reality are worth noting. The metadramatic perceptions vary from playwright to playwright and from play to play. It might be an oversimplification to assume that Shakespeare's was a commercial theatre and that the classical Sanskrit playwright's was a theatre of courtly patronage. Shakespeare's theatre was a commercial one no doubt, but it was none the less a theatre of popular cultural tradition which did not sever itself from the learned, and also of its own courtly affiliations, for all its being a commercial theatre. Similarly, Bhasa and Kalidasa, courtly patronage as they had, wrote for a wide range of audience without losing contact with popular cultural traditions. Yet the Sanskrit dramatists show a subdued and evanescent sense of dramatic self-consciouness while Shakespeare's and the Jacobean playwrights' sense of the theatricality as well as of the world-as-theatre *topos*, is more active, deliberate and pronounced. Though both the theatres were basically 'non-illusionistic' and conventionalistic, the extent of the use of conventions or the use of stage properties must have varied between the two. On the Sanskrit stage, actresses played women's roles. Hence the com- plications of the Shakespearian play with the convention of the boy-actress were not for the Sanskrit playwrights. At best we have occasions as especially in Kalidasa's *Malavikagnimitra* of inbuilt compliments of elaborate detail to the skill of the actress of Malavika in the verses spoken by King

Agnimitra in the scene of the inset dance performance in competition in Act II and in Act IV (sloka 9) when the King, watching from his hiding place, comments on Malavika's reactions in her viewing of the picture of the king in the court group portrait. The cases which have been considered represent an actually effected or intimated shift or intermixture of modes of make-believe and of actuality, and thus contain an element which may be identified as that which is more than what meets the eye. At any rate, the final impression conveyed through such *trompe l'oeil*-like double play with illusion and reality in both the dramatic traditions as we have considered makes possible, an apprehension of a profound sense of the illusion of reality and of the reality of illusion.

Index